THE
SPIRIT–PARACLETE
IN THE
GOSPEL OF JOHN

GEORGE JOHNSTON

CAMBRIDGE
AT THE UNIVERSITY PRESS
1970

Published by the Syndics of the Cambridge University Press
Bentley House, 200 Euston Road, London N.W.1
American Branch: 32 East 57th Street, New York, N.Y.10022

© Cambridge University Press 1970

Library of Congress Catalogue Card Number: 72–98697

Standard Book Number: 521 07761 3

Printed in Great Britain
at the University Printing House, Cambridge
(Brooke Crutchley, University Printer)

The next thousand years may be expected...to concentrate on the third article [of the Creed], namely to wrestle with the task of revealing God in society. The double concern of this epoch will be the revivification of all dead branches of the single human race, and the re-inspiration of all mechanized portions of the single human life. Since the successive stages of an individual's biography and the shifting demands of industrialized society both involve us in a repeated change of roles, the breath of life must be allowed to take hold of us again and again with original renewing power, lest whole drab stretches of life and of mankind remain uninspired. The history of the Church and the history of the world will have to be matched by a history of all mankind. And who is man? The being which can be inspired.

Eugen Rosenstock-Huessy, *The Christian Future or The Modern Mind Outrun*. New York (1946), page 116.

CONTENTS

PREFACE

In the course of writing this book I have received help and encouragement from many people.

I am indebted first to McGill University and the Governors of United Theological College, Montreal, who granted me a sabbatical leave for the second half of session 1966–7. Dr John C. Kirby undertook the work of the New Testament department during my absence, and Dr J. Arthur Boorman acted as Principal of United Theological College.

The Faculty Fellowships Commission of the American Association of Theological Schools awarded me a stipend to enable me to study and write in Jerusalem and Rome, and this was much appreciated.

In Jerusalem I had helpful discussions with several scholars, and I wish to mention in particular Professor David Flusser of the Hebrew University. He welcomed me to his seminar and made many stimulating suggestions on the subject of the spirit and the paraclete in the Gospel of John.

During our stay in Rome, where the first draft of the book was completed, I was warmly welcomed to the Waldensian Theological Faculty by Dean Vinay and his staff. The Faculty librarians, Professor Alberto Soggin and Signora Soggin, met all my requests most graciously. Of others who made our stay in Rome enjoyable and fruitful I must mention the Reverend and Mrs Alexander MacLean of the Church of Scotland, for their hospitality was boundless.

I have also to acknowledge considerable and always ready assistance from Miss Norma Johnston and her colleagues in Divinity Hall library, McGill University. Much of the typing required has been done by Mrs R. de la Ronde and my secretary, Mrs Harold Kennedy.

For useful criticisms and suggestions I have specially to thank Professor C. F. D. Moule, Dr Robin Wilson, and Professor Matthew Black, the General Editor of the New Testament Monograph series.

ix

It is a particular pleasure for me that the book is published by the Cambridge University Press, and I wish to express to all its staff my appreciation of their careful work and very generous assistance.

In every place and in every way my chief gratitude must be to my wife, to whom this volume is affectionately dedicated.

GEORGE JOHNSTON

Montreal, Canada
August 1968

ABBREVIATIONS

A.J.S.L.	*American Journal of Semitic Languages and Literatures.*
C. K. Barrett, *H.S.G.T.*	*The Holy Spirit and the Gospel Tradition.*
R. Bultmann, *Komm.*	*Das Evangelium des Johannes.*
C.I.S.	*Corpus Inscriptionum Semiticarum.*
E.T.	English Translation.
H.D.B.	Hastings' *Dictionary of the Bible.*
H.D.C.G.	Hastings' *Dictionary of Christ and the Gospels.*
I.B.	*The Interpreter's Bible,* 1952–7.
I.C.C.	*The International Critical Commentary.*
I.N.T.	*Introduction to the New Testament.*
J.J.S.	*Journal of Jewish Studies.*
J.Q.R.	*Jewish Quarterly Review.*
J.S.S.	*Journal of Semitic Studies.*
J.T.S.	*Journal of Theological Studies.*
LXX	*Septuaginta,* ed. A. Rahlfs, 1935.
N.F.	Neue Folge.
N.T.S.	*New Testament Studies.*
R.B.	*Revue Biblique.*
R.G.G.	*Die Religion in Geschichte und Gegenwart*[3].
R.Q.	*Revue de Qumran.*
R.S.R.	*Recherches de science religieuse.*
Strack–Billerbeck, *K.T.M.*	H. L. Strack and P. Billerbeck, *Kommentar zum Neuen Testament aus Talmud und Midrasch.*
T.W.N.T.	G. Kittel and G. Friedrich, *Theologisches Wörterbuch zum Neuen Testament,* Stuttgart, 1933–.
Z.N.T.W.	*Zeitschrift für die neutestamentliche Wissenschaft und die Kunde der älteren Kirche.*

SIGLA: Greek Text   As in Nestle–Aland or the new Bible Societies' text, ed. Aland, Black, Metzger and Wikgren, 1966.

xi

Qumrân Scrolls   As in D. Barthélemy and J. T.
Milik, *Discoveries in the Judaean Desert I*:
Qumran Cave I, 1955.

Abbreviations for the books of the Old Testament, New Testament, Apocrypha and Pseudepigrapha, rabbinic and early Christian literature, Philo and Josephus, follow the standard practice.

PART I
'SPIRIT' IN THE FOURTH GOSPEL: A GENERAL SURVEY

CHAPTER I

THE MEANINGS OF 'SPIRIT'

In the Gospel of John the Greek word πνεῦμα is used variously for *wind, breath, oneself,* or divine *power,* but also in specific ways as related to *God* or *Christ.* The phrase '*holy spirit*' appears in the narratives of Jesus' baptism and of the commission given to the apostles by their risen Lord. To some extent this usage can be explained from the occurrences of πνεῦμα in Greek literature of many periods up to the middle of the first century A.D. The primary source for understanding it, however, is in the LXX and in the Hebrew meanings of רוּחַ (*ruaḥ*).[1]

The original sense of רוּחַ may have been *air in motion,* and so it denotes *wind,*[2] either gentle or violent, then by an easy transition *breath,*[3] that is, the air by which men and women live, the principle of life.

---

[1] Of special importance are David Hill, *Greek Words and Hebrew Meanings,* pp. 202–300, though he fails to show the historical development in OT passages; and the articles under πνεῦμα in *T.W.N.T.* VI, 357–443—the Jewish material mainly by F. Baumgärtel, W. Bieder and E. Sjöberg, the NT material by E. Schweizer. παράκλητος is dealt with in *T.W.N.T.* V, 798–812, by J. Behm, and VI, 441–3, by E. Schweizer. See also 'Spirit' in *A Theological Word Book of the Bible,* ed. Alan Richardson (1950); and the valuable listings in D. S. Russell, *The Method and Message of Jewish Apocalyptic,* pp. 402–5, and J. E. Yates, *The Spirit and the Kingdom,* pp. 238–51.

[2] E.g. Amos 4: 13; 1 Kings 18: 45; Gen. 3: 8; Exod. 14: 21; Hos. 4: 19; Isa. 7: 2; Jer. 2: 24; 4: 11 f.; 14: 6; Ezek. 1: 4; 5: 10, 12; Isa. 41: 16, 29; 64: 6. Cf. 1QH 7: 23 (this seems to be a rare usage in the Qumrân scrolls). In the LXX, Wisd. Sol. 5: 11, 23; 13: 2; 17: 18; Sir. 39: 28; 43: 17, etc. See too W. A. L. Elmslie, *How Came our Faith* (Cambridge, 1948), pp. 123 f., and E. A. Speiser on Gen. 1: 2 (Anchor Bible), citing H. M. Orlinsky, *J.Q.R.* XLVII (1957), 174–82. There is an older view which denies that *ruaḥ* in Gen. 1: 2 means 'a wind sent from God', for מְרַחֶפֶת does not suit this rendering (G. J. Spurrell, *Notes on the Text of the Book of Genesis* (1896), p. 4).

[3] E.g. 2 Sam. 22: 16; Pss. 18: 15; 135: 17; Isa. 25: 4; 30: 28; 42: 5; Hab. 2: 19; Jer. 10: 14 (51: 17); Lam. 4: 20; Ezek. 37: 5–14 (a passage full of *double entendre*); Gen. 6: 17; 7: 15, 22; Eccles. 3: 19. 'Breath' is a possible meaning in 1QH 1: 27–9. On 1QM 6: 11 f., horses 'sound of wind', i.e. of breath, see Y. Yadin's edition of the War Scroll, p. 287 (E.T.). In the LXX, Wisd. Sol. 2: 3; 15: 11, 16; 16: 14; Sir. 38: 23; Tobit 3: 6, etc.

Behind man himself and behind all natural phenomena the ancients divined mysterious powers that could be either kind or malevolent. God stands as it were at the apex of these spiritual beings. At one stage he may be simply the mightiest One among many deities, at another (in monotheism) he is the all-powerful One who alone creates and grants vitality. The forces of Nature are almost always regarded as the instruments of the divine. It is God that orders the stars in their courses, sends the wholesome rains, and influences seers, prophets and the leaders in every walk of life. God controls the rise and fall of nations; and as Yahweh he covenants only with Israel, the seed of Abraham. It is God the Creator who endows bird and beast with life and blows the vital breath into the man made in his image (Gen. 1: 1 ff.; Isa. 40: 26, 28; Matt. 5: 45; 6: 26; Luke 12: 6 f.).[1] Man's own years, said a psalmist, 'come to an end like a sigh' (Ps. 90: 9), but to the existence of God there is no end.

'Spirit' in the Old Testament primarily means the active agent of divine work in nature, history, and chosen servants like the prophets. It is the *energy* or *power of God*.[2]

In his very significant volume on the Old Testament teaching about *ruah* Daniel Lys shows that, as the centuries advanced, the Jews concentrated this word less on natural processes and less even on so-called supernatural or Godlike realities. More and more it described the *moods* and *dispositions of man*, his very self.[3] They did not, of course, cease to believe that man is the creature of God in whose will is peace, from whom alone will come lasting blessings in the freedom of national life.

The humanist emphasis continued in the apocalyptic

---

[1] In *The Hunter and the Whale* (1967), p. 76, Laurens van der Post refers to prayer in the ancient Amangtakwena way: 'They greet the day by breathing into the palm of the right hand until it becomes damp and warm, holding it up to the dawn till the morning air has fanned it cool and dry, taking that as a sign that the breath of their lesser life has been made one with the breath of a greater.'

[2] Judges 6: 34 (on Gideon); 13: 25; 14: 6 (on Samson); 1 Kings 10: 6, 10; 11: 6 (on Saul); 16: 13 (on David); 18: 12 (on Elijah); Isa. 31: 3; 44: 3; 63: 7–14; Ezek. 11: 4 f.; 39: 29; Hag. 2: 5; Zech. 7: 12; Joel 2: 28; Job 12: 9 ff. Cf. Pss. 62: 11; 66: 5 ff.; 78: 104–7 on the *magnalia Dei*.

[3] E.g. Ps. 51: 10, 12, 17; 142: 3; Ezek. 3: 14; 36: 26; Isa. 57: 15; 65: 14; 66: 2; Zech. 12: 1; Job 7: 11; 17: 1; 27: 3; Dan. 2: 1; 5: 12, 14; 7: 15. D. Lys, «RÛACH». *Le Souffle dans l'Ancien Testament* (1962).

writings and it is noteworthy in several of the Dead Sea Scrolls. *Spirit* is man's vital power or capacity; sometimes it may be translated by our word 'person'.[1] Frequently the reference is to the emotional tone of one's inner being.[2]

Occasionally *spirit* refers to the ongoing life of a human being after death, e.g. in relation to a 'resurrection body' (Jub. 23: 31; 1 Enoch 67: 8 f., and more than a score other examples) or to 'translation' beyond this world (1 Enoch 71: 1, 5 f., 11). In view of Qumrânian and later Christian use it is of some interest that the phrase 'holy spirit' seems to be applied to man in Jub. 1: 21, 23. Several investigators agree that it is hard to distinguish in the intertestamental literature references to human spirit, divine spirit, or the invisible 'spirits' of the air both good and wicked.[3]

This is particularly true of the material in the Dead Sea Scrolls, especially the *Manual of Discipline*, the *Thanksgiving Hymns*, and the *War of the Sons of Light against the Sons of Darkness*, which provide information that is fascinating to the New Testament student and essential for understanding the background of the Gospels and St Paul. A. A. Anderson writes:

One of the most frequent uses of Ruaḥ is to denote the spirit of man either as a 'constituent part' of man and often practically equivalent to 'self', or as expressing the varied behaviour of men, their different characteristics and moods...The spirit of man may be destined for the days of eternity and it may share in the lot of God's angels, but in itself it is neither eternal nor indestructible.[4]

[1] E.g. Dan. 5: 12; Jub. 1: 21; 12: 3; 20: 8; 1 Enoch 56: 5; 60: 4; 71: 11; 98: 7; Pss. of Sol. 17: 42.

[2] Russell, *loc. cit.* quotes from Dan., Jub., 2 Esdras and Tests. XII Pat. to illustrate man as affrighted, distressed, faint, grieved, groaning, hardened, hasty, inflamed, longing, patient, perturbed, refreshed, reviving, small, sorrowful, troubled, vexed, weak, wearied.

[3] Interesting information on the 'spirits' in modern Africa is collected by F. Kaigh, *Witchcraft and Magic of Africa* (London, 1947), e.g. pp. 80–90. This casts light on ancient ideas.

[4] 'The Use of "Ruaḥ" in 1QS, 1QH and 1QM', *J.S.S.* VII (1962), 294. Cf. J. Coppens, 'Le Don de l'Esprit d'après les textes de Qumrân et le Quatrième Évangile', *Recherches Bibliques*, III (1958), 209–23; J. Licht, 'An Analysis of the Treatise of the Two Spirits in DSD', *Scripta Hierosolymitana*, IV (1958), 88–100; George Johnston, '"Spirit" and "Holy Spirit" in the Qumran Literature', in *New Testament Sidelights*, ed. H. K. McArthur (1960), pp. 27–42; W. Foerster, 'Der Heilige Geist im Spätjudentum',

The poet speaks of himself as 'a perverted spirit', and even as 'a spirit of flesh' (1QH 3: 21; 13: 13). Some passages in the *Manual of Discipline* suggest that a man's spirit may have been understood as the *measure* or perhaps the *quality* of his entire being as one who is advancing in godliness and angelic communion because he is an elect 'son of the Light', or as one who becomes increasingly the slave of Belial, Prince of Darkness, a man ungodly and unwholesome like the *gollum* and other vicious servants of 'the Enemy' in J. R. R. Tolkien's *The Lord of the Rings*. For the enlightened the end will be joy in the divine realm, but for the darkened it will be wrath and the awful desolation of death. Unfortunately it is extremely difficult to perceive how the struggle within a man is shaped and how far anyone can grow in grace and in knowledge of the truth; whether indeed each man is fated to belong for ever to the Light or to the Darkness.

Inevitably attention has been focused in recent research on the 'essay' contained within the *Manual of Discipline* (1QS 3: 13–4: 26).

There it is said that men are divided by divine decree (for the God of their Old Testament tradition always remains in ultimate control of everything in earth and heaven) into two classes or 'lots' governed respectively by a *spirit of truth* and a *spirit of error*, 'walking in their ways' to produce the fruits of their obedience in marked traits of character: the parallel to Gal. 5: 19–23 was soon remarked. It is not yet agreed by scholars, however, how *spirit* in the essay is to be interpreted. There is much to be said for the view that it refers generally to the human person as endowed with a given portion of good and evil elements.[1] On the other hand, *spirit* sometimes alludes to an *influence* or *power* exercised from without man by the Prince or

N.T.S. VIII (1961–2), 117–34; F. Nötscher, 'Geist und Geister in den Texten von Qumran', in *Vom Alten zum Neuen Testament: Gesammelte Aufsätze* (1962), pp. 175–87; J. Schreiner, 'Geistbegabung in der Gemeinde von Qumran', *Bibl. Zeit.* (N.F. 1965, Heft 2), pp. 161–80.

[1] On this see now J. M. Allegro, 'An Astrological Cryptic Document from Qumran', *J.S.S.* IX (1964), 291–4, esp. Col. II, lines 7 f., 'He has six (parts) spirit in the House of Light, and three in the Pit of Darkness', and Col. III, lines 5 f., 'He has [ei]ght (parts) spirit in the House of [Darkness] and one (part) from the House of Light'. Does man consist of nine spiritual elements?

Angel of Light in one case and by Belial, the Angel of Darkness, in another. The 'spirit of error' seems to be identified with 'angel of darkness', but it is not so clear that 'spirit of truth' should always refer to an angel; if it does not, then 'spirit of error' too may be ambiguous. A third interpretation is possible: that *spirit* in the essay should be taken primarily as referring to one of the angelic chieftains himself. For it is abundantly evident that the two Princes are engaged in a deadly and relentless struggle for the allegiance of those who are predestined (!) to adhere to either the party of the Light or the party of the Darkness.[1]

One may point to two rather distinctive features in the usage of *spirit* in the intertestamental literature as a whole, including the Qumrân scrolls:

First, the concentration of interest on man's spiritual nature did not mean that the spirituality of God himself was lost sight of, even at a time when divine transcendence seems to have removed him from intimate communion with the saints. There are numerous references to the spirit of God as *creative* power; as that which *inspires* certain persons, for example the anointed priest or prophet or king, thus the source of wisdom and strength; as a way of speaking about the *presence* in time and space of the almighty One, the 'Lord of spirits', Israel's everlasting Hope.[2] As such, this spirit is 'holy'.

Debate continues on the question of the sources for what is undoubtedly a dualistic theology. Some allowance must surely be made for Iranian influence, as Kuhn and others argue. But it may well be that the chief influences are rather to be found in a piety nourished on Ps. 51: 11; Isa. 63: 11 and the teaching of 'second Isaiah' as a whole; and especially on Ezekiel (e.g. 11: 19 f.; 18: 31; and 36: 25 ff.).[3]

---

[1] This problem will engage us later in this volume (see below, pp. 103–5). Wernberg-Møller tends to the psychological interpretation of *spirit* except where it obviously refers to God or to an angel (see his Commentary on 1Q S and also his 'A Reconsideration of the two Spirits in the Rule of the Community (1Q Serek III, 13–IV, 26)', *R.Q.* 3 (1961–2), 413–41).

[2] E.g. Pss. of Sol. 8: 15; 17: 42; 18: 8; 2 Baruch 21: 4; 23: 5; 2 Esdras 6: 39; 1 Enoch 68: 2; 106: 17; Tests. of Jud. 24: 2 f.; Levi 18: 7, 11; 1QS 3: 6; 4: 21; 8: 16 (revelation to prophets, as in CD); 1QH 7: 6 f.; 9: 32; 12: 12.

[3] In the article cited earlier I examined the use of 'holy spirit' as applied to God in QL. Menahem Mansoor's edition of 1QH and Y. Yadin's

7

Second, *spirit* very frequently refers to angelic beings. There are good spirits that serve the high and holy God as messengers and warriors. There are also wicked demons that seek to pervert the inclination even of the righteous and are allowed by God to wage war against the saints. Much of this too may indeed reflect Iranian and other Eastern sources.

But here also we must reckon with a native tradition in the long development of post-exilic ideas among both the Samaritans and the Jews. Note in particular: Job 1: 6; Ezek. 40: 3 ff., where the man-like guide is also a revealer of the divine truth; Zech. 1: 9 ff.; 2: 3 ff.; 3: 3 ff.; 4: 1 ff.; Dan. 8: 15 ff., referring to Gabriel the interpreter; 10: 13, 21; 12: 1, referring to Michael the guardian angel of Israel, who must do battle against the guardian angels of Persia and Greece as the ally of Gabriel. The examples of *spirit* for angel or demon in 1 Enoch, Jubilees and the Testaments of the Twelve Patriarchs are too numerous for citation here. In the Scrolls we may note 1QS 3: 24; 1QSa 2: 8 f.; CD 12: 2; 1QH 3: 18, 22; 8: 12; 11: 13; 13: 8; 1QM 10: 12; 12: 9; 13: 2, 4 f., 10, 12; 14: 10; 15: 14. The good angels are *spirits of truth*, or *spirits of knowledge*, or *holy spirits*.[1]

The great wealth and range of these meanings for *spirit* must have been accessible to John the Baptist, to Jesus of Nazareth, and to the early apostolic Church, though in what degree one cannot guess. *Spirit* in its Hebrew, Aramaic or Greek form was available for any who chose to speak about the mystery of the God who made heaven and earth, who elected and disciplined Israel, who made his mysterious presence and will felt amid the clash of empires, who raised up defenders of the ancient faith first known to Abraham and the patriarchal age and then to Moses, to Samuel and David and the first prophets, who inspired the hopes for a new age with fresh messiahs.

The Fourth Evangelist, if we may provisionally set his *floruit* about A.D. 50–90, must also have fallen heir to traditional

edition of 1QM should also be consulted. Cf. A. Jaubert, *La notion d'alliance* (1963), pp. 239 ff.; Millar Burrows, *More Light on the Dead Sea Scrolls* (New York, 1958), p. 291; Sir G. R. Driver, *The Judaean Scrolls* (Oxford, 1965); M.-A. Chevallier, *Esprit de Dieu, paroles d'homme*, p. 87; the Two Spirits are discussed in an unpublished dissertation by my former student, Miss Phyllis N. Smyth (St Mary's College, University of St Andrews).

[1] See M. Mansoor, *The Thanksgiving Hymns* (1961), pp. 77 ff.

Hebrew and Christian ways of thinking about divine and human 'spirituality' and about angelic or demonic activity. For we know from the Acts of the Apostles and the Pauline letters that John lived in an age when vast redemptive and sanctifying energies of the spirit were at work in the congregations of Jesus' disciples; when, as leading rabbis at Jamnia would have claimed, the synagogues of Judaism too were seeking and finding new modes of survival and divine service, to sustain life and to face the future with hope in the face of Christian schism and all the disasters of a Roman war.

Here, then, we may turn to the evidence of the Gospel of John.

First, to conclude this chapter, we examine the few examples that employ πνεῦμα in the meanings of *wind, breath*, and *self.*

There is one verse where *spirit* is clearly related to *wind*:

3: 8: τὸ πνεῦμα ὅπου θέλει πνεῖ, καὶ τὴν φωνὴν αὐτοῦ ἀκούεις, ἀλλ' οὐκ οἶδας πόθεν ἔρχεται καὶ ποῦ ὑπάγει· οὕτως ἐστὶν πᾶς ὁ γεγεννημένος ἐκ τοῦ πνεύματος.

The saying belongs to the speech which mystified Nicodemus, 'Israel's teacher' (3: 10). Its formula about 'coming and going' will appear again to describe the otherworldly element in Jesus' mission (7: 27; 8: 14, 23 echoing the 'from above' of 3: 3; 13: 33; 14: 4; 16: 5). Here the mystery applies to all others who experience the second birth, the begetting 'from above', that is from God (cf. 1: 13).

Spirit had been employed already at 3: 6 in opposition to 'flesh', the merely mortal and creaturely in man. Hence in 3: 8 we are faced with a typical Johannine *double entendre*. 'The spirit blows' means:

(*a*) *The wind blows.* We are meant to think of the strange freedom (as it was understood in that early time) of east wind or west wind, in its invisible impulsion above the land, over the deep wadis, on the face of the lake. For this is parabolic of the free and mysterious action of God himself in the re-creation of his people who will see and enter his new order ('kingdom') if only they come to understand what is afoot in the ministry of Jesus.

(*b*) *The divine spirit is blowing.* It is active in the world at that very moment of Nicodemus's interview, and in John's own community; and it never ceases to blow so long as God's purpose here is incomplete.

9

'Born of spirit' (3: 8) corresponds to ἐκ θεοῦ ἐγεννήθησαν of 1: 13 and γεννηθῇ ἄνωθεν of 3: 3, and ἐξ ὕδατος καὶ πνεύματος of 3: 5. All this is in sharp contrast to normal human generation, ἐκ τῆς σαρκός (3: 6), ἐκ θελήματος σαρκός (1: 13). The article with σάρξ and πνεῦμα is not to be pressed. Spirit in these passages, except the wind example, refers to the divine will and power, the act beyond human control and comprehension that renews human life through discipleship to Jesus, the incarnate Logos. In such a paragraph, therefore, pneuma may also be translated as the breath of God. H. B. Swete may be quoted:

That the wind is at work we know by the familiar sounds of breeze or gale, but its origin and its destination are hidden from us. Such ᵗthe manner of the Spirit's working...there is the same mystery surrounding it, the same ignorance on man's part of the laws by which it is governed, the same certainty that its existence and its presence are matters of fact, since its effects fall within the range of observation, even within the cognizance of the senses; the Spirit's voice is heard in human utterances and the Spirit's power felt in human actions, though the Spirit itself is inaudible and invisible.[1]

There are two or three places in John where pneuma probably denotes breath (apart from the possible example in 3: 8; cf. Ezek. 37: 1 ff.).

1: 33: οὗτός ἐστιν ὁ βαπτίζων ἐν πνεύματι ἁγίῳ.

It is true that 3: 22 describes a baptizing ministry of Jesus that parallels John the Baptist's, and presumably then it was also a baptism with water, rather than 'baptism in, or with, holy pneuma'. Hence, this can hardly be the fulfilment of the oracle reported at 1: 33.[2] For that surely comes at 20: 22: καὶ τοῦτο εἰπὼν ἐνεφύσησεν καὶ λέγει αὐτοῖς· λάβετε πνεῦμα ἅγιον. The peculiar form of 'baptizing' prophesied by John the Baptist must be similar to what is intended in 4: 14 by the promise to give men and women who become disciples 'a spring of water that gushes up to life eternal'.[3] The tenses implied are all future, as we see from 4: 14; 6: 51 and 7: 38. Consequently at 1: 33 the

---

[1] The Holy Spirit in the New Testament, p. 134 (my italics).
[2] I take 4: 2 to be an editorial addition by someone who did not accept this as genuine Johannine or historical tradition.
[3] Cf. R. E. Brown, The Gospel according to John (I–XII), pp. 178–80.

present participle should be translated of action about to happen: 'This is he who is going to baptize with holy spirit.' Since this agent is, for the Evangelist and his Church, in fact the Logos-god (1: 1), such a 'baptism' will be a gift of his own divine 'breath' (20: 22).

Now John 1: 1 is quickly followed by the statement that 'everything was created through him and apart from him was nothing made. What came into existence in him was life' (1: 3 f.). John is narrating a new genesis which is to be understood only in the light of the incarnation of the Logos-Christ and his death on the cross. The old Genesis of scripture had spoken of *ruaḥ*, 'spirit', as active in the divine creation of the universe and man (Gen. 1: 2; cf. Pss. 33: 6; 104: 29 f.): the new speaks rather of the divine Logos or 'word', as in Ps. 33: 6. It is manifest from the literature of the intertestamental period that *spirit, word* or *wisdom* could be used in descriptions of God's dynamic work as the Creator. See especially Ps. 104: 24; Prov. 8: 22–31; Wisd. Sol. 9: 7 ff.

So at the dramatic close of his Gospel John shows us this Logos-Christ, incarnate in Jesus and now 'raised' to fresh glory as the Victor over death and over the Devil, making this new genesis an effective reality. He 'breathed into' the disciples, as God had 'breathed into' the nostrils of man the 'breath of life' (Gen. 2: 7, LXX: ὁ θεὸς ... ἐνεφύσησεν εἰς τὸ πρόσωπον αὐτοῦ πνοὴν ʒωῆς). It was, naturally, a 'word' of creative power that Jesus uttered: 'receive holy spirit', i.e. receive the breath of God.[1]

At 19: 30 also *spirit* means breath: καὶ κλίνας τὴν κεφαλὴν παρέδωκεν τὸ πνεῦμα. Matthew and Mark in the parallel passages here speak simply of Jesus' death. Luke adds a citation of Ps. 31: 5 (LXX 31: 6), 'Father, into thy hands I commit my spirit', quite possibly an authentic cry of Jesus from the cross. 'My spirit' also means 'me', myself. In the Johannine text, however, there is the unusual verb, παρέδωκεν. This too, it has sometimes been thought, is a case of *double entendre*:

---

[1] The text is not λάβετε τὸ πνεῦμα τὸ ἅγιον, 'receive the Holy Spirit', as if *pneuma* were intended to denote the Third Person of the Holy Trinity. 'Spirit' means the *vital power* that springs from God. In this book it will be printed 'spirit' in lower case in order to keep this primary sense in the foreground.

(a) he handed over his soul or spirit, that is, to God (with this cf. Eccles. 12: 7);

(b) he handed down his spirit, that is, he bequeathed to his disciples the legacy of his own spiritual power. C. H. Dodd noted this possibility but did not 'feel able to decide' between the two translations.[1]

There would be a formal contradiction to 20: 22 if we were to adopt the second proposal; yet this would not constitute any insuperable difficulty in the case of so profound a writer as John the Evangelist. There are many attractions in the idea of a legacy and it is well suited to spiritual and homiletical application. It must however be rejected. For the Christ of the Fourth Gospel lives and dies in communion with his Father (cf. 17: 5). His spirit was not to be released until he had returned to the Father (7: 39). John, like the other Evangelists, means to emphasize that Jesus, incarnate Word though he was, really and truly died on the cross. Because he was a man, he died with a man's last cry fading away into the air.

Pneuma means *self* in 11: 33 and 13: 21. In the parallel text 12: 27 ψυχή is used instead of πνεῦμα.[2]

---

[1] *The Interpretation of the Fourth Gospel*, p. 428.
[2] On 11: 33 see C. K. Barrett, *The Gospel according to St John*, pp. 332–3.

CHAPTER 2

SPIRIT OF GOD, SPIRIT OF CHRIST

Pneuma in most of the Johannine examples has important theological meaning, chiefly as relating to God, Jesus the Christ, 'the spirit of truth', and the disciples of Jesus who probably represent the catholic Church.

I. SPIRIT OF GOD

(1) ὃν γὰρ ἀπέστειλεν ὁ θεὸς τὰ ῥήματα τοῦ θεοῦ λαλεῖ· οὐ γὰρ ἐκ μέτρου δίδωσιν τὸ πνεῦμα (3: 34).

After δίδωσιν the later ecclesiastical text, supported by Bezae (D), Koridethi (Θ) and certain versions, adds ὁ θεός—an easier reading, but not to be accepted. The omission has the backing of good early Eastern as well as Alexandrian authorities.

τὸ πνεῦμα is omitted by Vaticanus (B) and the Sinaitic Syriac, so it may be an interpretative gloss on the phrase 'he does not give by measure'.

The paragraph (3: 31–6) within which this text appears is sometimes regarded as one that has been editorially displaced. J. G. Gourbillon puts it after 3: 13;[1] Bernard, Bultmann and Moffatt, after 3: 21;[2] R. E. Brown, the latest editor, considers that 3: 11–21; 3: 31–6 and 12: 44–50 are all variants of the same speech.[3] He accepts the view of Dodd[4] that the present position was intended to serve as a summary and a comment on the scenes in which the Baptist and Nicodemus have appeared.

At this point we have to say that every theory of displacements is open to grave doubt. Rearrangements are as varied as the subjective judgments of scholars. Brown, for example, has produced a highly complex and therefore thoroughly suspect thesis of many stages and versions:

[1] 'La parabole du serpent d'airain', *R.B.* LI (1942), 213–26.
[2] See *I.C.C. ad loc.*; Bultmann's *Komm.* p. 116; and Moffatt's translation of the NT.　　[3] *John I–XII* (Anchor Bible), p. 160.
[4] *Interpretation*, pp. 308–11.

We posit five stages in the composition of the Gospel. These, we believe, are the *minimal* [my italics] steps, for we suspect that the full details of the Gospel's prehistory are far too complicated [!] to reconstruct...We should probably think of a close-knit school of thought and expression. In this school the principal preacher was the one responsible for the main body of Gospel material. Perhaps, too, in such a school we may find the answer to the problem of other Johannine works, like the Epistles and Revelation...If the historical tradition underlying the Gospel goes back to 40–60, and the first edition of the Gospel is dated somewhere between 70 and 85 (a dating which is very much a guess), then the five stages we have posited...would cover over forty years of preaching and writing.[1]

A theory that multiplies the hypotheses like this should be rejected in favour of the simplest reasonable explanation. The evidence, in our judgment, warrants only that the book was left unfinished and has been edited by persons unknown; its author may well be also the writer of 1 John at a later period in his life, perhaps in the closing decade of the first century A.D.

There are in fact several indications that 3: 31–6 belongs precisely where we find it: e.g., the contrast between Jesus and the Baptist refers back to 1: 6–8, 15, 27, 30 and 3: 28. There are echoes of verses 27, 28 and 29 in the actual wording of 31–6; and verse 36 sums up important assertions of the Nicodemus discourse. Hence the idea of 'giving the spirit' fits admirably. God who sent the Logos-son commissions him with spirit, power. And he does this perfectly.

For ἐκ μέτρου is a Semitic piece of Greek that picks up the salient fact in the claim that the spirit descended and rested on the Messiah (1: 32). Rabbinic passages like *Sheb.* 8: 3 and *Lev. R.* 15: 2 teach that prophets received only a limited portion of the spirit. Qumrân, as we noted earlier, seems to have held that each man receives by divine allocation a certain 'measure' of good and evil spirit (J. M. Allegro has noted the parallel). The Messiah himself was to possess and to distribute spirit (Pss. of Sol. 17: 22, 36 f., etc.), and since he is eternal Logos he must be perfectly *spiritual*, like God.

Accordingly, we learn from 3: 31–6 that spirit was given to Jesus as *power for his Messianic mission.*[2] This came from God 'on high', from 'above', to use the natural mythology, and it

---

[1] *John I–XII*, pp. xxxiv, xxxv, lxxxvi.
[2] This point will be elaborated in ch. 5.

14

enabled the Messiah to fulfil the prophecies about an age of the spirit (cf. Ezek. 34: 15 f., 23; 36: 26 f.; *Exod. R.* 48).

(2) From 3: 34 we pass easily to 4: 24, where Jesus tells the Samaritan woman πνεῦμα ὁ θεός κτλ.

Formally the sentence is similar to ὁ θεὸς φῶς ἐστίν (1 John 1: 5) and ὁ θεὸς ἀγάπη ἐστίν (1 John 4: 8). Note that none of these statements is a palindrome, because *pneuma is not God*. We have already seen how wide a range of meaning the word *pneuma* has, especially as a rendering of *ruah*. It may refer to a prophet speaking in ecstasy or under the influence of wine; it may also denote an angel or a demon.

On the other hand, God is 'the Lord of spirits' according to 1 Enoch (cf. 1QH 10: 8; Test. of Abr. 13). It is by his permission that the prince of darkness and his agents seek to work their opposition to his purposes, and that human rulers vex his anointed. Thus Pilate holds his authority, ἐξουσίαν, not merely from the overlord in Rome but from the Overlord in heaven, i.e. 'from above' (ἄνωθεν, 19: 11). The Evangelist offers us no theodicy, however.

It is worth-while to spend some time on the meaning of this concept that '*God is spirit*'.

In the first place, it affirms that *power belongs to the Lord* (Ps. 62: 11). This Lord is the Holy One, just, kind and merciful, as Israel's scriptures had defined these terms. He is also the Father revealed in the Logos who has provided for men the true exegesis (John 1: 18): and this Father is not only the Lover of mankind (3: 16), he is the One, True God, the Holy Father and Judge of all men and everything in the world (5: 29; 6: 65; 8: 21; 9: 41; 15: 10; 17: 3, 11).

In the second place, it directs attention to the mystery of divine *invisibility* (cf. 1: 18; 5: 37 f.).

This too was basic to the theology of the traditions now contained in the OT and the intertestamental literature. For Israel had found in historical events 'signs' that manifested God at work for eyes that could see, and these were recalled in religious education and in the cult (Deut. 6: 20 ff.; 11: 18–21; Pss. 105–7). Allusions to this theology should be heard in John's references to Abraham (8: 34 ff.), Moses (1: 17; 3: 14; 5: 45–7; 6: 31 ff.) and Isaiah (12: 38–41). It is no surprise that the

Evangelist introduces a narrative of 'signs' about the divine power present in Jesus the Messiah.[1]

It is of course a difficulty that the Jesus who is said to be the revealer and interpreter of an unseen Father is now himself invisible (20: 29). All the more significant, then, is the Gospel message of the continuing activity of Jesus' spirit because Jesus is the living Lord (16: 6 ff.; 20: 1 ff.). One may assert that this activity, which is itself God's own, becomes visible in a very real way in those 'representatives' or '*paracletes*' who are the Christian prophets, remembrancers, teachers and martyrs of the Johannine Church and the Church in all ages since John, as we hope to demonstrate in Part II of this book.

The beginning of the new age comes with the donation of 'holy spirit' to the first disciples (20: 22). This is Christ's gift, but it is also the Father's, for in all things the Logos is the Father's servant. It may be this same gift that is intended by the promises of 14: 17, 26 and 15: 26: God will give you...'*the spirit of truth*'; 'I shall send to you from the Father... "the spirit of truth".' Since the truth is in Jesus (14: 6), this spirit must have some connexion with him. But the phrase may mean nothing more than '*the true spirit*'; or it could signify a *power* that issues from the one true God (17: 3). On the other hand, the well-known passage 1 John 4: 1–6 introduces us to a spirit of truth as opposed to a spirit of error, in a context of crisis and the appearance of many 'antichrists'. The world lies in the power of the Devil (1 John 5: 19). We are reminded of the Test. of Jud. 20: 1 ff., 'Know, therefore, my children, that two spirits wait upon man, the spirit of truth and the spirit of error'; and of the two spirits in 1QS 3: 13–4: 26. In the light of this we must take seriously the possibility that 'the spirit of truth' in the Fourth Gospel, perhaps identical with 'holy spirit', means an *angel*, comparable to the guardian angel of Israel, the nation that claimed to be the people of God.

These matters must await fuller discussion at a later stage, but in the meantime they pave the way for the next section in which we look at *pneuma* in John as it is related to Jesus Christ.

[1] John may have used a 'signs' source, as Bultmann thinks. Cf. D. M. Smith, 'The Sources of the Gospel of John: an Assessment of the Present State of the Problem', *N.T.S.* x, No. 3 (April 1964), 336 ff. See also R. T. Fortna, *The Gospel of Signs*, Society for New Testament Studies Monograph Series, No. 11 (Cambridge, 1970).

II. SPIRIT OF JESUS CHRIST

(1)   1: 31–4, especially verse 32: τεθέαμαι τὸ πνεῦμα καταβαῖνον ὡς περιστερὰν ἐξ οὐρανοῦ καὶ ἔμεινεν ἐπ' αὐτόν.

(a) In this Gospel John the Baptist is shown as a great witness
to Jesus Christ (1: 6–8, 15; 5: 33 f.). 'He was a burning and
shining lamp, and you were willing to rejoice for a while in his
light', says Jesus to the Jews (5: 35). As prophet and as herald
Forerunner, John must have been commissioned with his own
gift of spirit, yet the Gospel declines to make any explicit
statement to this effect, probably for polemical reasons. The
same explanation holds for the allusiveness of the references in
the Baptist's words to Jesus' baptism at his hands: (i) the phrase
'coming after me' which is a *double entendre* (1: 15, 27, 30;
cf. Mark 8: 34); and (ii) the words 'heaven opened' (1: 51)
which remind the Christian reader of Mark 1: 10.

Baptism made Jesus in some significant sense a disciple of
John, but he had gone his own way to a greater destiny. John
is however a recognized Figure: a martyr (3: 24, if this is not
a gloss) and like Jesus himself a witness to the truth (5: 33;
18: 37). It is clear that the Fourth Gospel was written by one
who knew the traditions now embodied in the Synoptics.
Nevertheless the evidence that he was acquainted with any of
the written Synoptic Gospels is ambiguous, and we accept the
view that John was independent of them all.

It is surprising to find a reference to a descent of the spirit on
Jesus after the amazing assertions of the Prologue. Since the
Logos is called 'god' he must also be 'spirit'. John makes no
attempt to resolve the contradiction, for the tradition of an
unusual spiritual experience at baptism was too strong. The
beginning of the Christian Gospel was the ministry of the
Baptist.[1]

Moreover, this is the Gospel that insists over and over again
that the Logos was made man, a Jew. Jesus had disdained
neither the material water nor the inferior witness of John the
Baptist. He had not appeared miraculously out of nowhere
(cf. 1: 45). The divine Logos as spirit had not fallen upon him in
mystic union at the river Jordan, because Jesus from the very

[1] 1: 19 ff. should be read before 1: 1–18, for the Prologue is less an
historical preface than a confession of faith.

beginning of his life was the incarnate Logos, Son of God. And yet it was sheer matter of historical fact that the baptism was the occasion for a spiritual impulsion that could not be denied. The Evangelist offers no explanation, but leaves us to contemplate a mystery.

(b) No special weight attaches to the verb τεθέαμαι in 1: 32. It is a synonym of ὁράω (1: 33 f.) and θεωρέω (14: 17). There is a similar cluster of synonyms at 20: 1–8. An analysis of Johannine usage shows that all the verbs of seeing are employed both for *ordinary looking* at earthly things like boats, stones, cloths, people, and looking at the outward appearance of reality; and also for *vision* or spiritual perception into divine mysteries. βλέπειν tends to be used for the former (e.g. 9: 7, 15 ff.), but note 5: 19, 'seeing the Father'. There is a tendency for θεωρεῖν to denote vision, yet the other meaning is found at 6: 40; 9: 8; 12: 45[1] and 20: 6 (6: 19 is ambiguous). ὁρᾶν is the verb used most frequently: approximately twelve times for ordinary sight, seventeen for vision, with several examples doubtful.[2]

There is therefore no necessity to think that John the Baptist really saw a dove come down from the sky nor spirit fall out of heaven from God. The mythological language points to an unusual religious experience: an ecstatic state or some vision. Part of our problem is that the Baptist is simply a mouthpiece here for the Christian evangelist and he is made to recite a tremendous catholic confession, 'Behold! The Lamb of God that takes away the sin of the world' (1: 29). If we apply to the narrative the insight of Louis Martyn,[3] we may say that in this literary account John the Baptist plays two rôles: his own as an historic Figure, and also that of some Christian minister at a baptism in the Johannine Church.

(c) What precisely, then, does the witness of the Baptist positively affirm? It is surely this: *Jesus had received his Messianic endowment at his baptism.*

We seek now to understand why the dove is introduced and what lies behind the symbolism of the story. Few scholars would be ready to claim that everything in the narrative has already

---

[1] In 6: 40 and 12: 45 there are two levels of sight, since John's Jesus is no longer visible. Seeing is also believing.
[2] Cf. R. E. Brown, *John I–XII*, p. 503; F. Mussner, *The Historical Jesus in the Gospel of St John* (1967).   [3] *History and Theology in the Fourth Gospel*.

been explained. The clue, we suggest, will be found in Jewish Messianic ideas and in certain scriptures as read in the Septuagint.

The verb καταβαίνω is used in the LXX for יָרַד, and it may refer to the coming of the Lord's spirit to guide Israel (Isa. 63: 14; cf. John 16: 13); and also to other supernatural phenomena, i.e. what may be associated with God's 'dwelling place' or what seems to come down 'from heaven': examples are *dust* (Deut. 28: 24) and *fire* (4 Kingd. 1: 10).

The preposition ἐπί appears in the LXX of Exod. 24: 16, καὶ κατέβη ἡ δόξα τοῦ θεοῦ ἐπί κτλ., for the Hebrew וַיִּשְׁכֹּן כְּבוֹד יהוה עַל־. It is used also in Deut. 28: 24; and again significantly, of the spirit, at Isa. 61: 1, πνεῦμα κυρίου ἐπ' ἐμέ.

Hence we find nothing strange about the wording of John 1: 32. If it seem peculiar that John should write, ἔμεινεν ἐπ' αὐτόν, it may be noted that this is a dynamic use of Greek and it is justified by the nearness of καταβαῖνον. It is characteristic of John to use μένειν (see e.g. 3: 36; 5: 38), and this may explain his preference for it over a verb with Messianic associations, namely ἀναπαύομαι as in Isa. 11: 2, καὶ ἀναπαύσεται ἐπ' αὐτὸν πνεῦμα,[1] or a similar verb, ἐπαναπαύομαι, which is found in the story of Eldad and Moded (Num. 11: 26–9) and in the narrative of *Elijah's spirit resting* on Elisha in 4 Kingd. 2: 15, ἐπαναπέπαυται τὸ πνεῦμα Ηλιου ἐπὶ Ελισαιε.

If we assume that μένειν is a Johannine equivalent for Isaiah's ἀναπαύεσθαι, we may now indicate a remarkable connexion of ideas by which *rest* (ἀνάπαυσις) calls up *dove* (περιστερά). The LXX of Gen. 8: 8 f. reads:

καὶ ἀπέστειλεν τὴν περιστερὰν ὀπίσω αὐτοῦ ἰδεῖν εἰ κεκόπακεν τὸ ὕδωρ ἀπὸ προσώπου τῆς γῆς· καὶ οὐχ εὑροῦσα ἡ περιστερὰ ἀνάπαυσιν τοῖς ποσὶν αὐτῆς ὑπέστρεψεν κτλ.

Various proposals have been made in order to explain the dove symbolism of the baptismal narratives,[2] but none is really satisfactory: in Gen. 1: 2 *spirit* and *water* are associated, and the

---

[1] M.-A. Chevallier shows how important this text was for Messianic concepts (*L'Esprit et le Messie*, pp. 4 ff.). Cf. C. K. Barrett, *H.S.G.T.* p. 41. ἀναπαύομαι is found in the NT at 1 Pet. 4: 14.

[2] See H. Greeven, περιστερά, *T.W.N.T.* vi, 63–72; C. K. Barrett, *H.S.G.T.* pp. 35–50. J. E. Yates quotes a fanciful play on words suggested by H. Sahlin, 'as a dove', i.e. 'under the wings of the Shekinah' (*The Spirit and the Kingdom*, p. 184).

spirit seems to hover over the water like a dove: καὶ πνεῦμα θεοῦ ἐπεφέρετο ἐπάνω τοῦ ὕδατος. Or, attention may be directed to the inclusion of turtle doves in the detailed regulations of Lev. 5: 7 for the sin-offering (cf. Lev. 12: 6, 8; Num. 6: 10). Or the *moaning of the dove* mentioned in such passages as Isa. 38: 14; Nah. 2: 7; and Ezek. 7: 16, since the rabbis interpreted a voice from heaven, a *bath qol*, as a moaning. Or, finally, an attempt is sometimes made to link dove, Israel, Bride of God, and Jesus as the new Israel on the basis of Cant. 2: 10–14; 5: 2, 12; 6: 9. This is far-fetched!

Noah associations with Christian baptism are attested, on the other hand, in early Church art and in 1 Pet. 3: 18–21 (the NT passage may of course be the immediate source for the artistic scenes). At any rate, Gen. 8: 8 f. and Isa. 11: 2; 63: 14 sufficiently connect *Messiah, water*, a *heavenly descent*, and a *dove resting*, to let us proceed to explain the symbolism of the dove in the baptismal narrative. As the dove found its resting place in the midst of the flood waters, so the spirit of God found a resting place in Israel (or, among men) in the Man who stood in the midst of water. The Man was about to fulfil a ministry of atonement for the sins of the world, at the cost of his own life (1: 29, 36, etc.).[1] Light is shed now on John 14: 16 f. where the spirit–paraclete (it is promised) will find a resting place in the life of Jesus' disciples.

Another way of solving the dove problem was suggested early in this century by E. A. Abbott in his book, *From Letter to Spirit* (1903), pp. 106–35. The theory was revived in 1955 by Max-Alain Chevallier.[2]

The theory is that the dove reference goes back to a variant text of Isa. 11: 1 f.: 'Then a shoot (or, a rod) will come forth from the stump of Jesse... (like) a dove the Spirit of the Lord (will rest) upon him.' The grounds for such a reading are found in (i) *Protev. of James* ix, 1, where Num. 17: 1 ff. are rewritten to include the sentence, 'A dove came forth of the rod and flew upon the head of Joseph';[3] (ii) confusion between יונה, a dove,

---

[1] C. K. Barrett, *H.S.G.T.* pp. 35 ff.; A. Feuillet in *R.S.R.* XLVI (1958), 524–44.

[2] *L'Esprit et le Messie*, pp. 60–2. (This important book should be made available in English.)

[3] E.T. as in M. R. James, *The Apocryphal New Testament* (Oxford, 1924), p. 42. Cf. Joseph Gaer, *The Lore of the New Testament* (1952), pp. 31 f.

the MT וְנָחָה, 'it will remain' or 'it will rest', and a possible verb with the same meaning, ינוח.

Unfortunately the evidence for this reading in Isa. 11: 1 f. is far too thin to bear the weight even of a dove, and we are compelled to reject it and the solution of Abbott. Our conclusion is that Gen. 8: 8 f. in combination with Isa. 11: 1 f. (LXX text) has provided the essential background for Christian imagination as it described the Messiah's baptism in Jordan.

(d) A final comment may be added here on the nature of that 'spirit' with which Jesus was equipped for his mission.

It was not gentle, whatever the dove may be. His message did not sound timid like the cooing of the dove, however kind and compassionate he could be. The spirit that was in him was, in the Johannine picture, a power fit to raise the dead (5: 28; 11: 1 ff.), to convert Samaritans, no less! (4: 4 ff.), and to give immortal life to believers (6: 57–63). The emphasis must therefore be placed on the Christian conviction that this spiritual power was in solemn and glorious truth 'from heaven' and that it remained permanently in the man Jesus Christ.[1]

(2) 3: 34 need not detain us further. The Son possesses power 'not by measure', in no limited fashion, because God his Father chose to furnish it. Here is an aspect of the Johannine Christology that in elevating Jesus the Messiah underlines his servanthood. Jesus always acts as the plenipotentiary of the Father.

(3) Although there is no use of *pneuma* in 4: 10–14, it must be mentioned here. For the living water offered to the woman by Jesus is certainly an allusion to his gift of the spirit of life. As Kingsley Barrett comments:

Life-giving water appears in several important passages in John: 3.5; 4.10–15; 7.38; 19.34...The 'water' is pre-eminently the Holy Spirit, which alone gives life (cf. 6.63). It proceeds from the side of the crucified Jesus; it is the agent of the generation of Christians; and it forms the fountain of life which for ever springs within Christians, maintaining their divine life. John uses the expression no doubt partly because it aptly conveys what he wishes to say, partly

[1] In this connexion one may recommend a reading of George Adam Smith, *The Book of Isaiah* (1903), pp. 183–8.

because of its twofold, Jewish and Greek, background, and partly because its double meaning conformed to his ironical style...[1]

I should prefer to substitute either 'holy spirit' or simply 'spirit' for Barrett's 'the Holy Spirit', since this will be read inevitably by many as a reference to the Third Hypostasis of the Holy Trinity of later orthodoxy; and in John even 'holy spirit' rather means the power flowing from a holy God, or from the divine Son.

With many scholars I leave unsolved the question whether the sayings here may go back to original words of Jesus. There is no reason to doubt that he was perfectly capable of employing the water allusion.

(4) We pass to 6: 63, a most important text.

τὸ πνεῦμά ἐστιν τὸ ζωοποιοῦν, ἡ σὰρξ οὐκ ὠφελεῖ οὐδέν · τὰ ῥήματα ἃ ἐγὼ λελάληκα ὑμῖν πνεῦμά ἐστιν καὶ ζωή ἐστιν.

The contrast between πνεῦμα and σάρξ is familiar, for σάρξ like Hebrew בּשׂר means the creaturely as opposed to the divine (cf. Isa. 31: 3).[2] The immediate reference in John is to 3: 1–10 where σάρξ is primarily man in the natural order (cf. 1: 13) and πνεῦμα is a heavenly seed of life (see 1 John 3: 9). Since the driving motive of John is to promote belief in Jesus as Messiah, the Son of God (20: 31), it is to be expected that believing should be stressed at 3: 12–15 and 6: 60–4.

We observe that in both these last passages the Son of Man who descends and ascends is a revealer of secrets and the teacher who mediates life to the elect (1: 12; 5: 24; 8: 47; 10: 29; 11: 25–7; 15: 16; 17: 6, 14 should be consulted also). These associations of Son of Man, second birth into life, the words of the Logos, and the action of spirit are remarkable. They make it tempting to read 6: 62–3 in a fresh way: 'Suppose then you were to see the Son of Man ascending...? His spirit it is that is life-giver; his flesh is of no value.'

These texts have created difficulties for exegetes. In a book that insists on the enfleshment of the Logos, how can it be asserted that flesh has no value? Was the Evangelist at this point quoting the claims of gnostic spiritualists and consenting

[1] *The Gospel according to St John*, pp. 195 f.
[2] On this see C. H. Dodd, *Interpretation*, p. 224.

with them that flesh as such, the outward and the material, is not the redemptive medium, because only spirit, the invisible, the potent, the divine can redeem? Or was the object of attack some materialist exposition of the bread and wine offered in the Christian Eucharist?

The new translation proposed has the merit of focusing interest on what is absolutely central to the entire discourse of ch. 6, namely Jesus Christ as the Son of Man who causes schism among men and women. Can it be sustained by the rest of the Son of Man teaching in this Gospel? The answer is Yes.

There are two basic affirmations:

(i) The Son of Man descended from the realm of divine glory and he will depart thither again, once he has found his greater glory on the cross.

For this point, see *inter alia* 1: 51, the allusion to a new Bethel and a new Jacob (Israel). It is in and through Jesus of Nazareth that men receive revelation, meet their destiny, and become members of the new Israel, the Vine of the Lord.[1] For Jesus is more than 'Jacob', he is the rightful King of Israel (1: 49; 12: 13). His glory is symbolized by the brazen serpent (3: 13–15; Num. 21: 9), and his exaltation will be noted again at 8: 28 (cf. 8: 23); 12: 23, 34; and 13: 31. With all this evidence 6: 62 agrees: 'Suppose you were to see the Son of Man ascending where he was before?' It is he that is the Heavenly Man, he that dispenses the divine gifts (living water, spirit and life) and performs everything that the Father commits to his charge.[2]

(ii) The second primary predicate of the Son of Man is life-giver, precisely as in 6: 27, 53.

Hawk-eyed readers of the Gospel might have recalled the text of Num. 21: 9 in the LXX, ἐπέβλεψεν ἐπὶ τὸν ὄφιν καὶ ἔζη. The final words announce the claim that Israel will live because of the serpent and Moses the servant of God. In John the enjoyment of life eternal comes from belief in Jesus the Messiah,

---

[1] This may have a polemical reference. Even the angels must be subordinated to the Son of Man. Nothing escapes his rule: all things, all people, all angels are subject to him (1: 3; 3: 35; 5: 22 f.). So Michael too is servant, not co-ruler.

[2] There is yet another polemical reference here: John refutes the exaltation of Moses, 'the first Redeemer', in the Jewish synagogues. Cf. Louis Martyn, *History and Theology in the Fourth Gospel*, p. 125, n. 178.

greater than Moses (20: 31), but also from *eating and drinking* Christ's flesh and blood (6: 53). Once, they could handle him and eat with him, now in the Church he is a Presence whose Gospel message is *heard and read*. The glory of Jesus is demonstrated (amongst other media) in a written drama of his ministry like the book of our Fourth Evangelist (cf. 21: 24 f.). 'Blessed are they who have not seen and yet believe' (20: 29). When this act of faith does take place, for a Nathanael or a Thomas or a reader of John's book in the late first century or for a student of John in our own day, then, to use the out-of-date jargon of mythology, heaven is opened and angels are seen to ascend and descend upon Jesus, the Son of Man (1: 51). We may re-mint the claim by saying that the mind of the believer suddenly sees the meaning of life, the purpose of God. His life is re-oriented and this historic Man becomes the centre of his hope for all time and for eternity, and the genuine inspiration for new ambitions and a distinctive kind of loving service.

So the Son of Man who replaces Moses and any other claimant to unique revelation and salvation is identified with Jesus of Nazareth. He is the mediator between the true God and mankind, he is the communicator of spiritual power to those who welcome him and love him.[1]

We must be careful not to leave the impression that John was unaware of other elements in the tradition and of darker features within the Church. Even in his time men were wondering when hope would be fulfilled, when new life would be granted to the dead (cf. 11: 25 f.). Members of his congregrations died. Some Christians were martyred. Roman power held sway in his world, perhaps power in the hands of the blasphemer Domitian. It may well be the Evangelist's voice we hear in 1 John 2: 18, 28; 3: 2, 14: 'It is the last hour...When the Lord appears, we shall see him and be like him...Christians have migrated from death to life!'

The principles of exegesis in John include no doubt the kind of double reference Martyn suggests, to the times of Jesus and

---

[1] E. Käsemann goes farther, since the Son of Man is the Logos-god: 'Der Menschensohn ist eben nicht ein Mensch unter anderen und auch nicht die Repräsentation des Gottesvolkes oder der idealen Menschheit, sondern Gott, in die menschliche Sphäre hinabsteigend und dort epiphan werdend', *Jesu letzter Wille nach Johannes 17*, p. 29 (E.T. *The Testament of Jesus* by G. Kroder, 1968).

to the times of the Johannine Church; and also the idea that surface meanings give way to deeper truths, that is, to the anagogical message of the spirit (to use the language of Origen). Johannine 'irony' serves this latter purpose.

It is surely not matter of pedestrian fact that the Logos was made flesh! How can that be the case if the Logos was (eternally) god? The Son of the Father as Logos is *pneuma*; how can he be *sarx*? Pressed to its apparent logical end, this might easily lead to docetic heresy: 'Spirit is too pure to live in human flesh. God cannot be embodied in a man.' Yet it is John who insists on the element of *sarx*, and indeed, in ch. 6, on the *flesh and blood* of Jesus.[1]

The question is whether listeners and readers will see the divine presence in the historical event. Is it true that Jesus is 'God with us...Emmanuel'? (Matt. 1: 23; cf. John 3: 2). Within the narrative of the Gospel the Jewish opponents taunt Jesus with being a false prophet, a 'Samaritan' heretic, a blasphemer (5: 18; 8: 48; 10: 31–9). Perhaps he was also a madman (7: 20; 8: 49). A few marvelled at his words of gracious truth (1: 17) and at his healings (4: 46 ff.; 5: 2 ff.; 9: 1 ff.; 11: 1 ff.).[2] Only these few discovered his secret.

Of course it was after the death and departure of Jesus that Christians had the task of insisting on the flesh of Jesus. He was ἄνθρωπος, a man like ourselves (7: 46). This they could affirm because their eyes had been opened and their faith remained (cf. 9: 1–7, 35–8). Nevertheless John, like Paul (2 Cor. 5: 16), had to insist that even the fleshliness of the Son of Man is not enough. In so far as it is taken as mere flesh, it will not release men from the grip of evil and sin.

It should further be noted that for John life means more than spiritual communion with the Father and the Son. There is also to be resurrection at the last day, whether that come late or soon; whether he means (as Kingsley Barrett once suggested) the believer's own last day, or the end of the whole world-order. The temporal aspect of eschatology probably did not mean much to John (see 15: 1–11; 17: 21, 23).

[1] Against Käsemann, *op. cit.* p. 51, n. 41, 'Der heute fast durchgängig behauptete Antidoketismus des Evangeliums ist ein reines Postulat'.

[2] According to Louis Martyn's thesis, such charges were also levelled at Christian leaders in John's own area.

It would therefore be consonant with his dramatic irony if 6: 63 were intended to say that 'his spirit is the life-giver; his flesh does not profit at all'. Those who are spiritually blind will still protest, 'Is this not Jesus, the son of Joseph? don't we know his father and mother?' and so he can't be anyone special! (6: 42; cf. 1: 45 f.; 7: 25–8). Those who can really see say rather, 'Rabbi', for even to the Jewish synagogues Jesus may be presented as the right teacher of the divine will; 'Son of God, (true) King of Israel', for by both Jews and Samaritans he is to be recognized as the One who was to come (1: 49). And in him all men may see the Father, the God of all flesh (cf. 12: 32; 14: 9 f.).

We turn now to the second half of 6: 63, 'the words that I have spoken to you are spirit and life'.

C. H. Dodd, followed by R. E. Brown, conjoins 'spirit and life' as a hendiadys.[1] But a careful examination of John 1: 14; 3: 5; 4: 24; 11: 25 (the longer reading); 1 John 2: 24 and 2 John 3 indicates that the nouns are coordinate; neither should be swallowed up by the other. Against Dodd it may also be noted how the words of Jesus are related on one side to the Father, heaven or spirit;[2] and to everything that makes for the enjoyment of life, health, sight and the conquest of death, on the other side.[3] It is remarkable how seldom in fact spirit is related to life, for 20: 22 is ambiguous and 6: 63a is exceptional. If Jesus says, 'I am (the) life', he does not claim, 'I am the spirit'.

How then should we interpret 6: 63b?

(a) *His words are spirit.* What Jesus has to teach about real manna or anything else that bears on divine–human fellowship is God-inspired. His words are therefore *revelatory* (7: 16; 8: 40), and their truthfulness brings genuine *emancipation* (8: 39–47; cf. 17: 17). Those who truly hear the word of God in and through Jesus become the children of the Father (1: 12; 8: 35 f.). From the victorious Jesus in a direct word (with appropriate action?), 'Receive holy spirit (vital power)', his disciples are

---

[1] C. H. Dodd, *Interpretation*, p. 342; R. E. Brown, *John I–XII*, pp. 297, 300.
[2] See 1: 14; 3: 12, 34; 4: 26, 39–42; 8: 47; 12: 49; 14: 10, 24, 26; 16: 13; 17: 8.
[3] See 4: 14, 50; 5: 24, 26, 40; 11: 43.

graced with new status and new functions. Not that the words are identical with the power; rather, he who speaks is himself filled to the brim with divine powers for the accomplishment of his work (3: 34).

(b) *His words are life.* Because he is the incarnate Logos, Jesus possesses creative power (1: 1–4). Through his speech rightly heard and obeyed men make contact with their Creator (cf. 10: 10). The life that is thus received is abundant, *inexhaustible* (10: 10), *immortal* (11: 26; cf. 5: 21, 24–6), since it is life in communion with the Father in his kingdom (3: 3–15; 14: 23). The legacy of Jesus' words outranks the biblical traditions derived from Abraham, Moses, Isaiah or any of the prophets; yet even the Old Testament scripture ought to be read as witnessing to Jesus as the true Messiah and Saviour (5: 39).

It may be assumed that by the time John wrote, Christian literature existed in some form, and certainly the words of Jesus had been collected and employed in proclamation, argument with Jew and Gentile, and domestic teaching within the Church. How far any of it was technically 'scripture' is doubtful; but nothing can obscure the dignity of Jesus' words as revelation and final truth for the disciples: even unwritten, they still took precedence over the existing Bible.

Yet at this point questions of interpretation must have arisen, to judge by the activity of Christian teachers in the application of Jesus' words. If Paul could argue in the case of the written Torah of Moses that Christ brought spiritual freedom (2 Cor. 3: 12–18; cf. 1 Tim. 4: 13–16; 2 Pet. 3: 15 f.), did the same liberty hold in the use to be made of Christ's written word? It is precisely at this point that the hermeneutic function of the spirit–paraclete (14: 26; 16: 14 f.) becomes exceedingly interesting and intelligible.[1]

One final word about 6: 63 and its context:

This verse is part of a private communication to the disciples. It is unnecessary, in my view, to connect 60–5 directly with

[1] The Fourth Gospel follows the making of the first Christian books (cf. Luke 1: 1–4; Acts 1: 1 f.; John 20: 31; 21: 25). I assume that 6: 63 refers to Jesus' words in the oral tradition and at the same time in their book form.

35–50, as Bornkamm proposes; and it is certainly unwise to follow Brown in regarding 51–8 as eucharistic material that was removed from its proper place in a narrative of the Last Supper and rewritten to fit a midrash on the Bread of Life. The repetitive style is typically Johannine, and verses 51–8 are most suitable for the writer's anti-docetic purpose. Professor Brown offers no plausible reasons for leaving a glaring gap (as now exists in John 13: 1 ff.) in the story of the Supper. In his view the eucharistic elements are in any case already implicit in ch. 6 without the intruded paragraph.[1] The whole procedure is extremely odd.

I take verses 51–8 to be a Johannine development on the Bread of Life theme, making a fresh point about understanding Jesus as the true and living bread from heaven. This is the Jesus who is to give his life as an atonement for the world. Fellowship with him becomes fellowship with the Father: 'I live because of the Father, (and) he who eats me will live because of me' (6: 57). With this compare 14: 10, 23; and 17: 24. Their life is eternal and everlasting.

Verses 60–71 of ch. 6 go on to say that *the Christ in his words is the life-giver.* He is the ascended Son of Man, who sends the spirit–paraclete to remind the Church of his words, to interpret their truth, and to reveal new things (note 15: 3, 7, 20 and the theme of obedience to the words as commandments, as well as 14: 26; 16: 13–15).

Accordingly, 'flesh' in 6: 63 is not a reference to the sacramental species. It is to be understood christologically in relation to the Son of Man, greater than Moses.

---

[1] *John I–XII*, pp. 287–90. The multiplication of analyses proposed for John 6, listed by Brown on pp. 293 f., suggests that the Gospel material does not naturally yield any analysis at all! It is astonishingly integrated, so that literary dissection is itself a grave disservice to exegesis.

CHAPTER 3

THE SPIRIT–PARACLETE

In this chapter we shall examine the texts that have special interest for this investigation, but only in a preliminary fashion. Their setting in the Gospel as a whole, the very question of their right to be accepted as integral to the work of the original Evangelist, and the full range of their message fall to be considered as the major portion of this monograph. It is however necessary to underline here that these texts belong with a general survey of the Johannine use of 'spirit'. Put in another way: we were led through the various stages of our research not to focus merely on the so-called paraclete problem, but rather and initially on the whole question of John's teaching about the spirit. It will be clear from this that our conclusions about the authenticity of the paraclete pericopes decided their inclusion in a wider study of the spirit of God, the spirit of Jesus the Christ, and spiritual phenomena within the Christian Church.

(1) 14: 16–17: κἀγὼ ἐρωτήσω τὸν πατέρα καὶ ἄλλον παρά-κλητον δώσει ὑμῖν, ἵνα ᾖ μεθ' ὑμῶν εἰς τὸν αἰῶνα, τὸ πνεῦμα τῆς ἀληθείας, ὃ ὁ κόσμος οὐ δύναται λαβεῖν, ὅτι οὐ θεωρεῖ αὐτὸ οὐδὲ γινώσκει· ὑμεῖς γινώσκετε αὐτό, ὅτι παρ' ὑμῖν μενεῖ καὶ ἐν ὑμῖν ἔσται. Two textual matters fall to be considered first:

(i) Against the run of all major witnesses, codex Bezae (D) has μεθ' ὑμῶν at the end of the ἵνα clause. Vaticanus (B), Sinaiticus (S), and the Old Latin place this phrase immediately after ἵνα; whereas Curetonian Syriac, 33 and 3 have it after the verb ᾖ.

The position of ᾖ itself also varies: after ἵνα, D, 33, e, Syr.cur.; between μεθ' ὑμῶν and εἰς τὸν αἰῶνα, S, Old Latin, accepted by Tischendorf; at the end of the clause and before τὸ πνεῦμα, B, accepted by Westcott and Hort, followed by the editors of the 1966 Bible Societies' text.

We accept the reading ἵνα ᾖ μεθ' ὑμῶν εἰς τὸν αἰῶνα because it helps to explain the weak ecclesiastical text of the Latin

29

Vulgate and the Byzantines, namely, ἵνα μένῃ μεθ' ὑμῶν εἰς τὸν αἰῶνα which is the text of Alexandrinus (A), supported by the Syriac Peshitto and the Armenian and Ethiopic versions.

μένῃ may be due to misreading ΗΙΜΕΘ; or else it has been influenced by the following ΜΕΝΕΙ.

(ii) In verse 17 it is not always clear how the best uncials intended ΜΕΝΕΙ to be understood. Accented μένει, it is a present tense; accented μενεῖ, it is a future. Some help is provided by the next verb.

Two future verbs are read by Nonnus and by some versions, and this appears to be logical. For the next four pericopes about the spirit–paraclete use the future, and in John the holy spirit of Jesus is breathed into the apostles at an Easter appearance. Nevertheless, futures are not well attested in 14: 17.

Undoubtedly the best supported reading is μένει...ἔσται as in 𝔓⁶⁶, 𝔓⁷⁵, S, A, Θ, Fam. 13, the two Cyrils, and others. Yet there is a problem: if prayer for the spirit–paraclete is to be made in the future, how can it be said that it rests among the disciples already in the present? and why include a future ἔσται after a present μένει? The prepositions παρά and ἐν provide no help, since there is no detectable difference in meaning. The strongest argument in favour of a present tense followed by a future is precisely that this is the most difficult reading.

Vaticanus apparently takes both verbs as present, and with this agree the Old Latin, most of the Old Syriac witnesses, Fam. 1, D and W. To this text the 1966 edition of the Bible Societies' *Greek Testament* assigns merely a D rate of probability.

Perhaps two present tenses should be accepted and understood as referring to an impending future. Perhaps verse 17 b is a gloss that has darkened counsel. We accept two futures, however, as the best of a perplexing set of variants.

In verse 17 we encounter the phrase 'the spirit of truth' and we should be reminded here that *spirit* may mean power, or breath, or angel. Is this the '*true spirit*' that God sends to men? Is it *a spirit that mediates the truth*, either as the 'ultimate reality' or as 'final doctrine'? Or is there reference in the words to God's '*true angel*', perhaps Gabriel, the wise interpreter and revealer of divine secrets (Dan. 8: 16, etc.), perhaps some other angelic figure like Michael, the guardian Prince of Israel (Dan. 10: 13,

21; 12: 1) and the Commander of the heavenly hosts (Rev. 12: 7)?

We need not stop to enquire yet how such a spirit can be described also as 'another paraclete'.

It is evident, however, that this spirit is meant only for the disciples of Jesus and not for the cosmos. In the Gospel of John the cosmos is the object of divine love and saving grace; at the same time it is the realm of darkness and untruth. Cosmos also denotes the congregation of those who bitterly and malevolently oppose the true God; it is therefore sometimes identifiable with actual groups of people like the Jewish Synagogue.[1]

(2) 14: 26: ὁ δὲ παράκλητος, τὸ πνεῦμα ὃ πέμψει ὁ πατὴρ ἐν τῷ ὀνόματί μου, ἐκεῖνος ὑμᾶς διδάξει πάντα καὶ ὑπομνήσει ὑμᾶς πάντα ἃ εἶπον ὑμῖν [ἐγώ].

In this verse the words τὸ ἅγιον after τὸ πνεῦμα are to be omitted, following the Sinaitic Syriac, because this reading best accounts for the variants. Nowhere else in John do we encounter the full phrase τὸ πνεῦμα τὸ ἅγιον, so that one rightly suspects that its appearance here is due to later orthodox theology. The insertion of τὸ ἅγιον may have been done innocently by a scribe in order to bring the text into harmony with other NT passages and with the creeds (for a somewhat similar emendation, the addition of τὸ πνεῦμα, see 3: 34).

At the end of the verse the word ἐγώ is unnecessary. It is oddly situated. We bracket it as dubious, in spite of the support given by Vaticanus (B).

It will be observed that the Father gives (14: 16) or sends (14: 26) the spirit–paraclete; but in 15: 26 it proceeds from him (ἐκπορεύεται). John also says that Jesus Christ after his departure sends this spirit, which as paraclete and spirit of truth unfolds whatever belongs to Christ (16: 13–15). In 16: 7, 13 the verb is comes. This is at first sight a very confusing pattern (cf. with it 7: 39), and it is complicated by the use of 'holy spirit' at 1: 33 and 20: 22.

The figurative speech in all these passages should be noted: spirit like water is a cleansing agent (1: 33); spirit like breath is a vital element (20: 22); spirit as teaching, guiding, defending,

---

[1] I have discussed cosmos in 'Οἰκουμένη and κόσμος in the New Testament', N.T.S. x, No. 3 (April 1964), 352–60.

is a divine power (chs. 14–16). Unifying them all is surely the concept of a *Christlike power* that is finally in the control of God, the heavenly Father. Readers who are accustomed by the liturgy, the creeds, and the general usage of catholic Churches to concepts (however vaguely defined) of 'the Holy Spirit', must learn to examine John without such presuppositions. The Gospel material is more readily aligned with ideas of supernatural powers than with the Christian doctrine of the Third Person of the Blessed Trinity.

(3)   15: 26 f.: ὅταν ἔλθῃ ὁ παράκλητος ὃν ἐγὼ πέμψω ὑμῖν παρὰ τοῦ πατρός, τὸ πνεῦμα τῆς ἀληθείας, ὃ παρὰ τοῦ πατρὸς ἐκπορεύεται, ἐκεῖνος μαρτυρήσει περὶ ἐμοῦ· καὶ ὑμεῖς δὲ μαρτυρεῖτε, ὅτι ἀπ' ἀρχῆς μετ' ἐμοῦ ἐστε.

This text gives evidence of several typically Johannine usages, and they are worth spelling out:

Resumptive ἐκεῖνος is very Semitic Greek. For John's use, see 1: 6 f., 18, 33; 7: 18; 9: 37; 10: 1.

Repetition is also a very common feature of John's style, as can be tested at 1: 1–3; 3: 16–21; 5: 19–29; 6: 35–51; 8: 12–20; 10: 7–15; 12: 27–36, 44–50; 15: 12–17; 16: 25–8; and 17: 1–19. The result is a certain monotonous tone to Johannine writing.

The *witness theme* almost dominates the Gospel:[1]

(a) *John the Baptist* testifies: 1: 7f., 19ff.; 3: 25–30; 5: 33–6.

(b) The *works* that Jesus performs point to his heavenly origin and commission: 5: 36; 10: 25, 32–8; 14: 10f.; 15: 24; and 17: 4.

(c) *God the Father* testifies to Jesus in many ways—(i) through Moses in scripture, 5: 39–47; (ii) through Isaiah in prophecy, 12: 38–41; (iii) by words of heavenly import and truth, as uttered by the incarnate Word, 3: 12; 5: 24; 7: 16; 8: 42–7; 12: 47–50; 14: 10; 15: 22; and 17: 8, 14; (iv) by a voice from heaven (*bath qol*), 12: 28.

(d) *The Son witnesses to himself*, to the chagrin of his Jewish opponents. For he knows whence he has come and whither he is going. No divine secrets are hidden from his eyes. But it seems to be assumed that this witness of the Son is *self-authenticating to the Elect of God*: 6: 44; 8: 47; 10: 26; 15: 19; and 17: 6, 11.

Perhaps we may be allowed to develop further the issues that are raised by this connexion between *witness and election*.

---

[1] There is a tendency in recent scholarship to over-emphasize the forensic character of this witness.

Election is the divine side of man's believing, which in John is never defined by the noun 'faith' (1: 12). It is nowhere said that anyone is prevented from acting in a believing manner, yet John like most early Christians shared the dilemma of the prophet Isaiah, namely, the mystery of revelation and disbelief (Isa. 6: 10; John 12: 40). The disbelief must be seen not as something 'pagan', for it is a phenomenon within the community of God's chosen People. The issue is dramatically presented in John 9. The parents of the blind man who was healed apparently do not become believers in Jesus, since they took seriously the threat of excommunication; and yet they could not deny the fact of the cure (9: 18–23). The Pharisees cannot see how Jesus can do what Moses had forbidden (he broke the law of the Sabbath, 9: 14), and still be regarded as a true servant of God. They 'see' at one level, but fail to perceive God's *new* word and act in Jesus (9: 41). The man with sight for the first time (he had been blind '*from birth*', 9: 1) does see and does perceive, for his inner eyes too had been opened, he had come to that new birth 'from above' that Nicodemus had wondered at (3: 4; 9: 35–8).[1]

John fails to illuminate the situation, because he does not show *how* the blind man could do what the educated Pharisees could not do. He was simply 'there', so that God's working in Jesus of Nazareth should be manifested in the daylight of Jerusalem (9: 3). He was elected to be the recipient of grace.

We may, however, find further light on this from three other texts:

(i) 5: 42: Jesus said to the Jews, 'But I know that you do not possess love for God in you'.

Their failure to recognize God at work in Jesus was due, not to laziness or impiety or intellectual obtuseness, but to the lack of a genuine godly love. Because it is godly, such love cohabits with humility, self-criticism and a sense for the fitness of things. When God seeks to reveal himself and his work to one with the rudiments of these virtues in him, he is made welcome and can bring grace to fruition (cf. elsewhere, Matt. 5: 43–7; Mark 10: 21; 12: 28–34; Luke 6: 46; 7: 36–50, one of the most daring statements of the truth; 11: 42). This love for God belongs in

[1] On the drama of ch. 9 see J. Louis Martyn, *History and Theology in the Fourth Gospel*, pp. 1–39.

John with grace and truth, and especially with the 'new commandment' (1: 17; 13: 34 f.; 15: 9–17).

(ii) 7: 17 f.: Jesus answered:

If any man intends to do God's will, he will come to know whether my teaching is from God or whether I speak on my own. One who speaks on his own is seeking his own glory. But he who seeks the glory of him that sent him (that is, an apostle or a prophet) is genuine and there cannot be falseness in him.

Even Jesus is a man under authority, who speaks *ad maiorem Dei gloriam* (cf. Mark 11: 27–33). The appeal he makes is to men who already frequent the Temple, God's house, and study his will in the synagogue and school. They assume that God is not dead, they proclaim his power to create and his right to judge. So to them the invitation is, 'Come and see for yourselves, but expect little unless you are sincere in your profession as servants of the divine will'. Intellectual dogmatism is discouraged; the essential duty of obedience to the will of God is emphasized. The same invitation is extended through the book of the Gospel to all other 'believers'.

(iii) 8: 28: 'So Jesus said, "When you have exalted the Son of Man (i.e. on the cross), then you will realize that I am he; that I do nothing merely on my own, but speak exactly as my Father instructed me"' (cf. 12: 49 f.).

Viewed within the *Sitz im Leben* of the Church, this text suggests that it is first the event, and then the message of the Crucified One that prompts men to confess that 'Jesus is Lord' or to say like Thomas, 'My Lord and my God' (20: 16–18, 28; cf. 1 John 2: 22f.; 5: 20; 1 Cor. 12: 3). This is the basic theme of the preaching by Christian witnesses (15: 20, 27; 17: 20), and John, it must be noted again and again, writes from a situation in which the message produced the converts. Jesus was exalted in the spoken and written story of the cross. This too must be related to the witnessing by the spirit–paraclete (15: 26; cf. Rom. 10: 8, 15, 17).

(4) 16: 7–11: ἀλλ' ἐγὼ τὴν ἀλήθειαν λέγω ὑμῖν, συμφέρει ὑμῖν ἵνα ἐγὼ ἀπέλθω. ἐὰν γὰρ μὴ ἀπέλθω, ὁ παράκλητος οὐ μὴ ἔλθῃ πρὸς ὑμᾶς· ἐὰν δὲ πορευθῶ, πέμψω αὐτὸν πρὸς ὑμᾶς. καὶ ἐλθὼν ἐκεῖνος ἐλέγξει τὸν κόσμον περὶ ἁμαρτίας καὶ περὶ

δικαιοσύνης καὶ περὶ κρίσεως· περὶ ἁμαρτίας μέν, ὅτι οὐ πισ-
τεύουσιν εἰς ἐμέ. περὶ δικαιοσύνης δέ, ὅτι πρὸς τὸν πατέρα
ὑπάγω καὶ οὐκέτι θεωρεῖτέ με· περὶ δὲ κρίσεως, ὅτι ὁ ἄρχων
τοῦ κόσμου τούτου κέκριται.

In these verses *spirit* and *spirit of truth* do not appear, but it is
obvious from the context that the *paraclete* here is the same spirit
as in 16: 13 and elsewhere; should we take 7–15 as a single
pericope? The unusual 'personal' verbs in the passage are so
impressive that many exegetes and theologians insist that the
spirit–paraclete should never be predicated with 'it' or with
anything that is 'impersonal'. This is true, for we are bound to
interpret it as the spirit of Jesus or God; but John probably did
not hypostatize the spirit.

Verse 8, *the world*: see 16: 20, it will have its moment of
unholy glee, and 16: 33, in the last analysis it is a defeated power.
Cf. also 14: 27–30.

Verse 9, *they do not believe*: contrast 16: 27, 31.

Verse 10, *I go to the Father*: this picks up verse 5 and points
forward to verses 17 and 28. But see also 13: 33; 14: 4, 28; and
17: 11.

you will see me no more. This reminds us of 14:
19 and it will be repeated in verse 16. At first sight the statement has no particular connexion with the *cosmos* and its condemnation.

Verse 11: *the ruler of this world*. Cf. 14: 30; 17: 15 (the Evil
One). War between the disciples and the world dominates the
picture in chs. 14–17 (esp. 14: 22, 27; 15: 18–25; 17: 6–19).
The *world* of John's day included the Synagogue, but also the
unbelieving society of the Graeco-Roman empire. Hence the
power of the evil spirit might be made visible to the faithful in
the leaders of rabbinic Judaism and also in the Roman Emperor
or one of his representatives.

The focus of this pericope is quite different from that of the
others: now the business of the spirit–paraclete is to convict the
cosmos as at some Great Assize. Elsewhere it was to be companion, teacher, remembrancer and witness. There is a
remarkable parallel to 16: 7–11 in Acts 24: 25, where Paul the
prisoner is acting as his own defence counsel before Felix. He
defines the Christian message that he preaches ('the faith in
Christ Jesus') and sums it up under three heads: righteousness,

self-control, and future judgment (περὶ δικαιοσύνης καὶ ἐγκρατείας καὶ τοῦ κρίματος τοῦ μέλλοντος). In Johannine terms, Paul functions here as a *paraclete*. One cannot fail to recall the Synoptic promises of Mark 13: 9–11, 'you will stand before governors and kings for my sake...do not be anxious in advance...for it is not you who are going to speak, but the holy spirit'; Luke 12: 12, '...for the holy spirit will teach you'; and Matt. 10: 20, '...but the spirit of your Father speaking through you.' In some form this must be an authentic promise on the lips of Jesus, who saw the spiritual and political situation of his time with clear eyes, and whose word kept coming alive for the Church in its own difficulties.

(5)   16: 12–15: ἔτι πολλὰ ἔχω ὑμῖν λέγειν, ἀλλ' οὐ δύνασθε βαστάζειν ἄρτι· ὅταν δὲ ἔλθῃ ἐκεῖνος, τὸ πνεῦμα τῆς ἀληθείας, ὁδηγήσει ὑμᾶς εἰς τὴν ἀλήθειαν πᾶσαν· οὐ γὰρ λαλήσει ἀφ' ἑαυτοῦ, ἀλλ' ὅσα ἀκούει λαλήσει, καὶ τὰ ἐρχόμενα ἀναγγελεῖ ὑμῖν. ἐκεῖνος ἐμὲ δοξάσει, ὅτι ἐκ τοῦ ἐμοῦ λήμψεται καὶ ἀναγγελεῖ ὑμῖν. πάντα ὅσα ἔχει ὁ πατὴρ ἐμά ἐστιν. διὰ τοῦτο εἶπον· ὅτι ἐκ τοῦ ἐμοῦ λαμβάνει καὶ ἀναγγελεῖ ὑμῖν.

Verse 13. Instead of ὁδηγήσει some Old Latin witnesses, supported by the Latin Vulgate and (in part) Eusebius and Cyril of Jerusalem, read διηγήσεται (cf. ἐκεῖνος ἐξηγήσατο, 1: 18). The use of ὁδηγεῖν with πνεῦμα is attested by the LXX of Isa. 63: 14, κατέβη πνεῦμα παρὰ κυρίου καὶ ὡδήγησεν αὐτούς, and there is little reason not to accept it here. Cf. also Ps. 25 (24): 5, and Ps. 143 (142): 10, τὸ πνεῦμά σου τὸ ἀγαθὸν ὁδηγήσει με ἐν γῇ εὐθείᾳ.

εἰς τὴν ἀλήθειαν πᾶσαν is the text of B, A, Didymus, and some readings in Origen. It is read also by the important Old Latin e. For all that, however, it may be an Alexandrian revision of the rather more unexpected ἐν τῇ ἀληθείᾳ πάσῃ which has the backing of ancient Eastern versions (Sinaitic and Palestinian Syriac), b, c, ff² of the Old Latin; D; and in addition the Alexandrians S and 33. It is the text of Nonnus, Cyril of Alexandria, and sometimes of Augustine. On the other hand, the reading in B and A is to some extent strengthened by εἰς πᾶσαν τὴν ἀλήθειαν in Western authorities, Tertullian and some of the Old Latin, and in the Eastern Fathers, Basil and Chrysostom.

The evidence is finely balanced, but on the whole we prefer ὁδηγήσει ὑμᾶς εἰς τὴν ἀλήθειαν πᾶσαν because it most easily explains the variants.

C. K. Barrett prefers ἐν τῇ ἀληθείᾳ, and his reason should be noted: εἰς τὴν ἀλήθειαν 'suggests that, under the Spirit's guidance, the disciples will come to know all truth…'; whereas ἐν τῇ ἀληθείᾳ 'suggests guidance in the whole sphere of truth; they will be kept in the truth of God…which is guaranteed by the mission of Jesus'.[1] This does not seem to cohere with the context. Guidance is surely to lead the disciples forward towards fuller comprehension as well as into new insights (cf. Ps. 25 (24): 5). Things to come are to be revealed, no doubt on the basis of the revelation already given in Jesus Christ.

ἀκούει, the reading of S and 33, is 'more difficult' than a simple future ἀκούσει as in B, D, and the Latin Vulgate, or a future with ἄν as in D^c and Θ, or an aorist subjunctive ἀκούσῃ as in A and the later ecclesiastical text. The present of indefinite action in the future has been accommodated to the other future tenses which are appropriate in the context.[2]

None of the other textual variants requires discussion.

This final pericope concerning the coming of '*the spirit of truth*' heavily underlines its christological dependence; and one can scarcely emphasize too strongly how significant this is for John's meaning.

Thus it is Jesus, the Logos incarnate, who has more to say; and it is therefore into his truth that the interpreter spirit is to guide disciples. Accordingly, 'all the truth' may be paraphrased by 'all the truth there is to know about me' or 'all the truth I have to reveal'. Readers have been well prepared for this amazing assertion by texts like 1: 17; 3: 2, 34 f.; 5: 22; 6: 63; 7: 18; and 8: 26, 31 f. We may note especially 8: 38, 'I speak of what I have seen with my Father', which should be compared with 16: 13, 'whatever the spirit of truth *hears* it will declare, for it will *not* speak *on its own*'. And again, 8: 45, 'I tell the truth'; 5: 30, 'as I *hear*, I judge'; 8: 40, 'a man who has spoken to you the truth which I *heard* from God'; 14: 28, 'the Father is greater than I'. As the Logos-son is the servant of the

---

[1] *The Gospel according to St John*, pp. 407 f.
[2] Cf. R. Bultmann, *Komm.* p. 443, n. 1.

Father and his spokesman, so the spirit of truth, the spirit–paraclete, is the servant of the Christ and his spokesman.

The time of the Logos incarnate is past (for John and for us); the time of the spirit–paraclete is the age of the Church. In and for the Church some men are chosen witnesses, with authority and therefore spiritual power for their task (15: 27; 17: 20; 20: 22 f.). *John locates the activity of the spirit within the Church*, and is apparently not at all concerned to enquire if the spirit of God operates outside the Church. For him, apostles and Christians in general are *the visibility of the unseen spirit*. Of course, they are not to be identified with the spirit, any more than the words of Jesus are the spirit in 6: 63. Rather, this divine, Christ-like power makes them its instruments.

Precisely to what did the Church witness? To the message that in Jesus of Nazareth, the son of Joseph, men and women could 'see' the I AM of the Mosaic covenant, the Eternal One who inaugurated the 'age to come' by the incarnation of his Son.

Testimonia for this theology, quite apart from specific words of Jesus, were found in the Old Testament, e.g. in the following passages in second Isaiah:

43: 10: 'You are my witnesses', says the Lord, 'and my servant whom I have chosen (Jacob or Israel), that you may know and believe me, and understand that I am he...' (Cf. Isa. 44: 8; John 8: 24.)[1]

45: 19: I the Lord speak the truth, I declare what is right.

49: 3: The Lord said to me, 'You are my servant, Israel, in whom I will be glorified.' (Cf. John 8: 54; 12: 41; 17: 1, 5.)

49: 6: I will give you as a light to the nations. (Cf. John 8: 12; 12: 35 f.)

Such prophecies could be applied first to Jesus and then to his Church as the successor to Israel (cf. John 4: 22). How could the Church fulfil its 'Israelite' rôle and destiny unless God were to bless it with spiritual powers as the scriptures of Isa. 44: 3; Jer. 31: 31–4; and Ezek. 11: 19 f.; 34: 11–24; 36: 24–8 predicted? The Qumrân Community probably took the same sort of tack.

John's Gospel as a whole makes sense in a situation of multiple conflict, where the catholic claims for Jesus as the

---

[1] See Barrett's helpful note, *John*, p. 283.

Christ and for the *Ecclesia* as the Community·of God were being challenged. On one side may be seen the adherents of Moses and the Old Synagogue; or the disciples of John the Baptist, a kind of Old Pretender from the point of view of some Christians. On the other side may be seen the heretics later known as Ebionites and Docetists. Were there also sectarians who were denying the sufficiency as well as the uniqueness of Jesus and therefore had introduced angel mediators? Were there sectarians in John's area who had an organization with its own grades of initiates (if this is how 1 John 2: 12–14 should be understood)?[1]

There is also a new theme in John 16: 12–15, namely that 'the spirit of truth' will announce what is to come. It will make predictions about the future.

Prediction is part and parcel of prophecy (see Deut. 13: 1–5; Amos 7: 10 ff.). It belongs with divine revelation, for it is Yahweh, the Lord, who clarifies the future and his are the purposes that will come to their goal (Isa. 41: 22 f.; 42: 9; 44: 7; 48: 5 f.). The Lord acts in the freedom of his own being, by his own wisdom and knowledge, *by his own spirit* (Isa. 40: 13; Joel 2: 26–9; Zech. 4: 6). For its elucidation, therefore, the Johannine teaching requires us to examine the place of prophecy within the Church.

To conclude: 16: 15 is a comment on the claim of Jesus that 'all truth' will be revealed in the future by 'the spirit of truth'. If the Father really committed the *all* to the jurisdiction and ministry of the Son, then nothing of what this spirit may say or do can possibly be alien to Jesus Christ. The Father is to send it in the Name of Jesus (14: 26) and that means, stamped with Jesus' power, wisdom, grace and love. The spirit will testify to Jesus as he was and is (15: 26). In fact, says Jesus with sovereign simplicity, 'I myself will send the spirit–paraclete' (16: 7).[2]

---

[1] This idea was suggested to me by Prof. G. W. Buchanan, Wesley Seminary, Washington, D.C.

[2] An important and suggestive discussion of the spirit–paraclete sayings, their language and Johannine character, is to be found in F. Mussner, 'Die Johanneischen Parakletsprüche und die apostolische Tradition', *Biblische Zeitschrift*, N.F. 5, Heft 1 (Jan. 1961), 56–70.

CHAPTER 4

THE SPIRIT IN
THE CHURCH OF DISCIPLES

It is no far cry from the texts just reviewed to those that apply specifically to Jesus' disciples.

(1) 3: 5–6: ἐὰν μή τις γεννηθῇ ἐξ ὕδατος καὶ πνεύματος, οὐ δύναται εἰσελθεῖν εἰς τὴν βασιλείαν τοῦ θεοῦ. τὸ γεγεννημένον ἐκ τῆς σαρκὸς σάρξ ἐστιν, καὶ τὸ γεγεννημένον ἐκ τοῦ πνεύματος πνεῦμά ἐστιν.

(*a*) H. H. Wendt in his important *The Teaching of Jesus* held that the words ἐξ ὕδατος were added to an original saying of Jesus 'with direct reference to the Christian baptism of water',[1] and he was followed by Kirsopp Lake in his inaugural lecture at Leiden in 1904.[2] But the textual authority for retaining them is overwhelming. Their omission would be arbitrary, and would constitute a genuine failure to appreciate the Johannine mind.

(*b*) The use of 'kingdom of God' is remarkable in John, who normally refers to life or eternal life. Such life is a joyful communion with God the Father and it is made possible through the ministry of his Son (1: 12). It is here and now life in the Church, an aspect that has peculiar significance for John's theology.[3] It is also life beyond death in 'the Father's house' (6: 27, 39 ff.; 14: 2; 17: 24). Hence the kingdom in John 3: 3, 5 refers primarily to blessings mediated now and hereafter by Jesus the Messiah, the saviour of the world.[4]

At the same time this is not to be divorced arbitrarily from another meaning of the kingdom of God, one that is more prominent in the Synoptics, namely, 'God acting in royal, redemptive power for the sake of his people, Israel, in the hour

---

[1] *The Teaching of Jesus*, II, 91 f. Wendt realized that this is only a conjecture. Cf. F. C. Burkitt, *Evangelion da Mepharreshe* (Cambridge, 1904), II, 309 f.
[2] See H. B. Swete, *The Holy Spirit in the New Testament*, p. 132.
[3] Note 5: 24; 10: 27; 11: 52; 17: 2.
[4] N. Perrin, *Rediscovering the Teaching of Jesus*, p. 60.

of their supreme need'. For in the Gospel of John Jesus is the kingdom in this sense. God has equipped Jesus with the powers of the spirit for just this purpose. And do not the Synoptics themselves predict through the Baptist that there will be a new baptism with spirit?

We must therefore be careful not to exaggerate the differences between John and the Synoptics.[1] One may conclude indeed that it was the historical Jesus himself who alternated between 'eternal life' and 'kingdom of God' as blessings of salvation. For in his synoptic teaching disciples 'enter the kingdom' or 'precede' others into it (Mark 9: 43–7; 10: 15, 17–31; Luke 16: 16;[2] Matt. 21: 31). Does Jesus mean that now, in the time of the Baptist's preaching and Jesus' own ministry, the believing penitents actually enjoy the blessings of the new age when God redeems? If so, we have here the essence of what has been called 'realized eschatology' or 'inaugurated eschatology'. Or does Jesus simply mean that present belief and turning again towards God fix a man's destiny at the coming Day of God's decisive intervention? The latter would give us a more consistent and simpler picture, but for many reasons it is not acceptable.

(c) Birth and re-birth are terms that suit the concept of new life, and they agree with the message of Jesus elsewhere that one can receive the kingdom only by becoming as a little child (Mark 10: 15).[3] The children of God are those 'who were born, not of blood nor of the will of the flesh nor of the will of man, but of God' (1: 13). The mediatorial function of Jesus as the life-giver is emphasized frequently (5: 22–4; 6: 68; 10: 10, 28; 12: 24 f.), and this is associated with water in 4: 10–15 and 7: 37–9, perhaps also in 13: 5–11.

(d) Water played a special part in the life and piety of the Jewish people, as we learn from Ezek. 36: 25; Judith 12: 7;

---

[1] See now an important and suggestive essay by C. H. Dodd, 'The Portrait of Jesus in John and in the Synoptics', in the *Festschrift* for John Knox, *Christian History and Interpretation*, eds. W. R. Farmer, C. F. D. Moule and R. R. Niebuhr, pp. 183–98.

[2] N. Perrin, *Rediscovering the Teaching of Jesus*, pp. 74–7, argues for the authenticity of the parallel Matt. 11: 12, 'From the days of John the Baptist until now, the kingdom of heaven has suffered violence, and men of violence plunder it'. In this case too the kingdom is a present force.

[3] Perrin, *op. cit.* p. 146, quoting C. G. Montefiore.

1QS 4: 19–21; Mark 7: 1 ff. and other places.[1] Washing in water could represent and effect spiritual washing, though we cannot be certain of how the material or 'fleshly' was considered to bring about the 'spiritual' result. John, it is clear from our present text (3: 5–6), saw a substantial difference between the flesh and the spirit. Yet somehow the heavenly power, the re-creative energy of God, inhered in the use of water. Birth 'of water and spirit' is one event, just as 'Logos become flesh' results in one Man, Jesus.

Other concepts are related to this wonderful new creation. Thus, cleansing, which is akin to repentance, comes about via the 'word' spoken by Jesus (15: 3). This word corresponds to 'spirit', for the words of the Logos incarnate are drenched in spiritual power (3: 34; 6: 63b). Again, Jesus prays that his disciples may be consecrated 'in the truth. Thy word is truth' (17: 17); for they belong to the Father who entrusted them to his Son. This consecration is realized at the resurrection by the insufflation of the Lord's breath, not by water (20: 21 f.). This may be due to the fact that the disciples were baptized in water at an earlier stage (1: 35 ff.; 3: 22; though this evidence is somewhat obscure).

Water, word, spirit: the Johannine ambivalence in the use of these terms not surprisingly has split the exegetes into those who detect a sacramentalism that some of them dismiss as unspiritual, and those who seek to understand the insistence on both water and spirit for the new life.[2] It appears to me that the principle of incarnation enables us to perceive why water remains as an instrument of the divine presence and power; and yet it is foolish to find a sacramental reference every time the word water appears in the Gospel. It is thus quite unnecessary to excise in John 3: 5 the phrase 'of water' in order to focus on the more important reality in the reference to spirit.

Nicodemus is 'teacher of Israel' (3: 10) and so 'a son of the kingdom' (Matt. 8: 12). He admits that Jesus is a true rabbi

---

[1] Joseph Thomas, *Le Mouvement baptiste en Palestine et Syrie* (1935), pp. 341–56, should be consulted.

[2] See R. E. Brown, *John I–XII*, p. 140; R. Bultmann, *Komm.*, *ad loc.*; K. Lake, inaugural lecture, Leiden, 1904, and *Beginnings of Christianity*, eds. Foakes-Jackson and Lake (3 vols., London, 1920–6), Part I, v, 105, 110; J. E. Yates, *The Spirit and the Kingdom*, p. 187.

come from God, words that could apply to Jesus' time and also to the time of the Johannine Church (3: 2; cf. 4: 31; 6: 69; 20: 16). But neither Jesus nor the later Church can accept this as an adequate title and confession. The kingdom of God is the realm of life eternal that can be reached and enjoyed, not by the study and service of Moses (3: 14), but by accepting the revelation of the Son of Man (3: 12; note 'heavenly things') and responding rightly to the death of this Son of Man (3: 15–17). The light of God shines in this Jesus and most manifestly in his redemptive death (3: 20 f.; cf. 5: 21; 6: 51; 8: 12). So 'believing' is bound up with 'being born from above' (3: 3), 'born of water and spirit' (3: 5) in Christian baptism (cf. 8: 24; 20: 23, since baptism always included the assurance of the forgiveness of sins). The evidence of chs. 14–16 will show how essential to the life of the Church is the gift of spirit, both for its own communion in God and for its task of witnessing to Jesus and seeking to convert the world.

(2) 4: 23 f.: ἀλλὰ ἔρχεται ὥρα καὶ νῦν ἐστιν, ὅτε οἱ ἀληθινοὶ προσκυνηταὶ προσκυνήσουσιν τῷ πατρὶ ἐν πνεύματι καὶ ἀληθείᾳ...πνεῦμα ὁ θεός, καὶ τοὺς προσκυνοῦντας αὐτὸν ἐν πνεύματι καὶ ἀληθείᾳ δεῖ προσκυνεῖν.

The temptation to dwell on the large issues raised by this chapter must be resisted: it is not possible to say how far the Fourth Evangelist has been influenced by the existence of a Samaritan Church (cf. Acts 8: 5–25), or by certain parties within the wider Christian community that were interested to an unusual degree by the relation of Jesus to the Prophet that was to come (Deut. 18: 15, 18; John 6: 14; Acts 3: 22 f.) or to the *Ta'eb* of Samaritan expectation who may have been identified with the Moses *redivivus*.[1] The willingness of Jesus to stay in a Samaritan city (4: 5, 39 f.) as well as to converse with the Samaritan woman may well point to a special Johannine regard for Samaria.[2]

[1] Cf. J. Bowman, 'Early Samaritan Eschatology', *J.J.S.* vi (1955), 63–72; M. Black, *The Scrolls and Christian Origins*, pp. 157–70.

[2] A case for 'The Samaritan Origin of the Gospel of John' is argued by G. W. Buchanan in the E. R. Goodenough memorial volume, *Religions in Antiquity*, ed. Jacob Neusner, Supps. to *Numen*, xiv (1967). 'King of Israel', John 1: 41, 49, need not have a northern reference: in Pss. of Sol. 17: 42 this is the title of the Jewish Messiah.

If Jesus is here to be seen as the true Successor to Moses, who fulfils all the hopes of Galileans, Samaritans and Judaeans, then it is only to be expected that his dispositions will include some regulation or instruction about the Cult. For the powers of the first Moses covered matters cultic and political and theological.[1] In the Gospel we may cite the evidence for Jesus in the triple rôle of *true worshipper, prophet,* and *expositor of divine truth*:

(a) *worshipper*: 2: 16; 4: 34; 10: 18; 14: 28; 15: 10; 17: 1, 4, 15, 20, 24.
(b) *prophet*: 3: 12; 4: 44; 5: 43; 7: 52, etc.
(c) *expositor*: 6: 25ff.; 7: 16; 8: 47; 10: 34–7.

The Temple associations of Mount Gerizim near Sychar make it natural for John to present Jesus in a discussion about true worship. He is the expected Messiah (4: 26), who can declare everything that needs to be known about God's name and will (6: 14, 68 f.; cf. 2: 13–22 for another Temple theme).[2] But the Messiah thus made known is far more than a teacher of liturgy. In his own person he is the one that takes away the sin of the world (1: 29). In him therefore the aim of all ritual sin-sacrifices, wherever offered, is fulfilled. He was sent to save, so that, when they accept his word for themselves (4: 41), the Samaritans properly acclaim him by the extraordinary title, 'the saviour of the world' (4: 42).

It is thus inevitable that worship 'in spirit and truth' be comprehended only in relation to this Christ. What does it mean?

'Worship in spirit' could refer to the ecstatic forms of divine service, as in Rev. 1: 10, dreams, trances and rapture of a Dionysian type. There is abundant NT evidence for marvels of this sort in the life of the early Church;[3] and Paul himself grants considerable opportunity to visions, ecstasy and glossolalia.[4] He asserts that Christians are 'the true circumcision, who worship God in spirit' (Phil. 3: 3; a variant text reads, 'who worship by the spirit of God'). But Paul most emphatically

---

[1] See now Wayne A. Meeks, *The Prophet-King*, pp. 21–5, 250–4.
[2] The parallel between what is said of the Messiah in 4: 25 f., 'when he comes, he will declare everything to us', and of the spirit of truth in 16: 13, 'when (it) comes...it will declare to you what is to come', is especially notable.　　　[3] E.g. Acts 2: 3 f., 43; 4: 29–31; Heb. 2: 4.
[4] 2 Cor. 12: 1 ff.; 1 Cor. 12: 10; 14: 39b.

makes decisive for right worship in a Christian assembly the use of man's intelligence, the higher gifts (love being the greatest of all), and what he calls 'prophesying'.[1]

So in the Fourth Gospel we might consider that Jesus' seven signs are intended to remind readers of contemporary wonders, like healing the sick, and that these would be highly regarded in connexion with Christian worship. Yet in John 4: 48 there seems to be a contemptuous reference to a credulous acceptance of 'signs and wonders', without which a man might not come to believe in Jesus. The fact is that John is not interested in a Dionysian type of worship.

The context in John is a polemical one, for there is a clear contrast between worship made possible by Jesus and that of the Samaritan or Jewish rites, both as to time and place: 'not on a mountain...the hour is coming, and now is (here)'. As true Messiah, Jesus liberates men for the service of his Father (8: 36; 12: 20–6). Prayer in his name is prevailing prayer (14: 13 f.; cf. Matt. 7: 7–11 ‖ Luke 11: 9–13). The outlook and mentality of John strongly indicate that we are to interpret 'worship in spirit' as inward worship, the offering of the heart, done out of love and not within a legal system like that of the Synagogue (cf. Rom. 2: 28 f.; 8: 16 f.; 12: 1; 15: 16). The supreme reward of such worship is that the Father and the Son come 'to make a home' in the life of the worshippers (14: 23).

Again, the words 'in truth' mean that the Church is in the grip of divine truth, and is blessed by the presence within it of the divine reality. It is a communion of the Children of God who confront (in the fact of the rabbinic Synagogue and in the terrible power of the Roman Empire) the Children of the Devil (1: 11; 5: 40; 8: 44–7; 9: 34, 41; 15: 19; 18: 19–24; 19: 10 f.; cf. 1 John 2: 15–17).

Correspondent to *truth* (as knowledge as well as reality) are *grace* or loving-kindness (1: 14–17), *love* (13: 34), and *unity* (17: 11, 21). John leaves it to his interpreters to develop these magnificent themes in relation to the Christian worship of God; but this is not the place to consider (for example) how *grace* might affect the examination of candidates for baptism, confirmation or absolution; how *love* should give tone to the eucharistic assembly and to songs of praise; or how *unity* must be

---

[1] 1 Cor. 12: 4–11 ('for the common good', vs. 7); 14: 1–5, 13–19.

made real within the Christian family, else it can never 'become flesh' anywhere. These, and not the minutiae of archaeological liturgics, are the primary matters that need to be in the forefront of any church that would worship 'in spirit and truth'.

John's setting is also domestic, that is, he faced a contemporary struggle to survive in the face of deadly menaces of persecution and excommunication (15: 18–16: 11).

If the disciples' Church was to be equipped for its life in the world, if finally indeed the whole world was to be drawn to Jesus, if loving fellowship should mark the community of 'Jesus' friends', then there would have to be *sacrifice* (12: 24 f.), *consecration* (17: 17), and wholehearted *obedience* to the Master and Lord *who set the example* (10: 18; 13: 15; 17: 19).[1] The need of the Church could be summarized in one phrase: 'the energy of Jesus' or 'the spirit of Jesus'; so they had to be *baptized with holy spirit!* (1: 33; 20: 22).

The 'place where' of the Samaritan woman's talk has no corresponding Christian location; though we know that the disciples met in the homes of certain members (Jesus must have stayed in a Samaritan house or hostel, 4: 40), sometimes in a synagogue, sometimes in a rented hall (Acts 19: 8 f.). Yet for almost two centuries they showed no signs of acquiring their own real estate.

If, however, we apply with some imagination John's principle of incarnation, we must surely consider that the Evangelist was never unmindful of actual assemblies (1 Cor. 11: 17 ff.), of neophytes at baptism (Tit. 3: 5; 1 Pet. 3: 21) and others at ceremonial washings (Heb. 10: 22); nor of the daily problems that affected the faithful: marriage, divorce, hospitality, the relief of prisoners, the care of widows, orphans and the poor, the demands of the tax collectors (Rom. 12: 1–15: 6; Heb. 13: 2–5, 15 f.; Jas. 1: 27). Brotherly love had to become alive 'in deed, not in word only' (1 John *passim*). None of these indications should be neglected if we seek to do justice to John's concern for his own public (20: 31).[2]

[1] In view of these texts, the denial in some later dogmatics that Jesus is the spiritual and moral example to his followers is an absurd aberration (cf. 14: 12).

[2] See also Käsemann, *Jesu letzter Wille nach Johannes 17*, pp. 61–3: 'Gottesdienst und Sakramente spielen in unserm Evangelium keine beherrschende Rolle.'

Does not the story of the Samaritan woman tell the same message?

She comes solitary, in the heat of the day, and so for reasons that are to her discredit. She cohabits sinfully with a man not her husband, and she has already gone through five husbands. She is woman, alien to a man in the conditions of her society. She is Samaritan, alien then as now to a Jew. She is shifty and without much spiritual perception. Who can she be but the world in Samaritan dress? And it is to her that day that the Son of God said, 'God is spirit, and those who worship him must worship in spirit and truth'.

Given all that, such worship cannot be sectarian, world-denying, individualist and 'pietistic'. Even for worship in spirit there had to be provided words and shape and organization.

It may be noted finally that the woman and her fellow-citizens represent 'the lost sheep of the house of Israel', now found by the Good Shepherd. Christ still has other sheep, neither of the Judaean fold nor the Samaritan (10: 16). The hour has not yet come when worship can be offered to One God in joy that the darkness has been overcome and that the entire world of men has been attracted to Jesus.

(3) 7: 37–9: ἐν δὲ τῇ ἐσχάτῃ ἡμέρᾳ τῇ μεγάλῃ τῆς ἑορτῆς εἱστήκει ὁ Ἰησοῦς καὶ ἔκραξεν λέγων· ἐάν τις διψᾷ, ἐρχέσθω πρός με καὶ πινέτω ὁ πιστεύων εἰς ἐμέ· καθὼς εἶπεν ἡ γραφή, ποταμοὶ ἐκ τῆς κοιλίας αὐτοῦ ῥεύσουσιν ὕδατος ζῶντος.

τοῦτο δὲ εἶπεν περὶ τοῦ πνεύματος οὗ ἔμελλον λαμβάνειν οἱ πιστεύσαντες εἰς αὐτόν· οὔπω γὰρ ἦν πνεῦμα, ὅτι Ἰησοῦς οὐδέπω ἐδοξάσθη.

Verse 37. ἔκραζεν is read by S, D, and Θ, but the aorist is supported by other passages like 7: 28 and 12: 44.

πρός με is omitted by 𝔓66, S, D and some Old Latin authorities like b, e, and Cyprian, as well as two Syriac Fathers, Aphraates and Ephraem. Boismard has noted a parallel between 'come and drink' and 'come and see' (1: 39, 46; 11: 34); also 'come, see' (4: 29) and 'come and eat' (21: 12). In spite of the early attestation and Semitic flavour of the Bodmer text, however, we should retain πρός με in view of the phrase ὁ ἐρχόμενος πρὸς ἐμέ in 6: 35.

Verse 39. οὗ is defensible, though ὅ as in B is possible. ἦν πνεῦμα, S, Θ, and some others, is a difficult reading that explains the text of Vaticanus, 'holy spirit was not yet given'. οὐδέπω has been corrected by the Alexandrians, with support in D and Θ.

On the last day, the great day of the feast, Jesus stood and shouted: 'If any one thirst, let him come to me, and let him drink who believes in me. As the scripture said, "Rivers of living water will flow out of his belly".'

Now he said this concerning the spirit, which those who came to believe in him would receive; for spirit was not yet, seeing that Jesus had not yet been glorified.

This passage bristles with difficulties, and a lucid statement may be found conveniently in R. E. Brown's recent Commentary in the *Anchor Bible*, pp. 320–9. The translation offered above will indicate our view of certain of the questions.

A close scrutiny of verses 38 and 39 demonstrates to our satisfaction that they are thoroughly Johannine and not editorial intrusions.[1]

An excellent case can be made for interpreting the biblical quotation of Jesus himself, and a large number of scholars do so; but the opposite view seems to us far simpler, requiring less allegorizing, and answering to Johannine subtlety and profundity. Disciples of Jesus will become a source of life! Within them water, that is the divine power of spirit, is to gush up inexhaustibly (4: 14), so that they can continue the mission of Jesus (4: 38; 14: 12; 15: 8, 14–16). In the background may lie Joel 3 (4): 18, 'A fountain shall come forth from the house of the Lord and water the valley of Shittim', and Zech. 14: 8, on the day of the Lord's victory (interpreted of Christ the Lord), 'living waters shall flow out from Jerusalem'.

Patristic interpretations that find in 7: 38 the antitype to the wilderness rock that provided water for Moses and Israel,[2]

---

[1] R. Bultmann thinks that vs. 38 is an intrusion. 'To receive the spirit' is not un-Johannine (cf. 14: 17; 20: 22; I John 2: 27; 'receive' occurs about fifty times). The phrase is common enough in Paul, and in Acts four out of five examples are due to a formula with 'laying on of hands'.

[2] See Hugo Rahner in *Biblica*, xxii (1941), 269–302, 367–403. To be supplemented by M.-E. Boismard's article in *R.B.* lxv, 4 (Oct. 1958), 523–46; and those of Pierre Grelot in *R.B.* lxvi (1959), 369–74, and lxvii (1960), 224 f., and lxx (1963), 43–51.

I find unacceptable; in spite of Ps. 105: 41, 'He opened the rock, and water gushed forth; it flowed through the desert like a river'. This is a significant verse because Ps. 105: 40 may be the nearest parallel to John 6: 31, and so the Evangelist may have had that psalm before him (cf. also Exod. 16: 4; Neh. 9: 15). Ps. 105: 41 concerns irrigation by a river of water, and not drinking lifegiving water.

Hence other texts may have to be noted as part of the background to John, namely Isa. 55: 1; Zech. 9: 9; 10: 1, 11; 13: 1; 14: 9a, 16, 21c. On this basis one might follow Grelot in finding Temple associations in John 7: 14, 28, and allusion to Ezek. 47: 11 f., 'because the water for them flows from the sanctuary'. Unfortunately the rabbinic interpretations cited by Grelot (*Tos. Succah* 3: 3–18; 4: 9 f.) are somewhat late; and John 7: 14 ff. contain no Temple ideas.

Boismard in the article cited in the footnote above (p. 48) makes an interesting proposal: the scripture referred to is either Ps. 78: 16 or an Aramaic targum of it, 'He led forth streams of water from the rock and brought down, as it were, rivers of flowing water'. In favour of this he argues that not Ps. 105: 40 but Ps. 78: 24 was the text for the midrashic homily at John 6: 31 ff. One difficulty here is the date of the targum; another is that Zech. 14: 8 provides a satisfactory allusion.

(4)   14: 16, 26; 15: 26f.; 16: 7, 13–15 should be listed at this point as texts in which *spirit* is related to disciples. They have already been noted and will receive detailed discussion later.

(5)   20: 22 f.[1] Here, as we have seen, *spirit* means breath or vital power. John does not enlarge on this metaphor of the new life for disciples in the age of spirit now beginning, but we may refer to 14: 17 (the spirit finds a resting place among them) and 15: 1 ff. (the communion of obedient disciples with Christ, the source of life).

If it is correct to link 20: 22 with 1: 33,[2] then the former text points to a permanent gift, like 14: 16. What was occasional and exceptional in the Old Israel is normal and permanent in the

---

[1] For another view of this passage, see E. Schweizer, *Neotestamentica*, pp. 265, 333–43.

[2] On this see J. E. Yates, *The Spirit and the Kingdom*, pp. 1–3, 7, 213–19.

New.[1] If the apostles are obedient, they will be fruitful and that involves the mediation of spirit, that is new life, to others (cf. 17: 20).

How then is such mediation related to *absolution* which is the primary topic of 20: 23?

For one thing, unbelief in John is a primary sin (8: 24; cf. 15: 22), so that its removal is essential to life in the service of God. The commissioners of Jesus are, like him, to pass on to others the Word of God, which is the word of truth. This leads them, if they are receptive, not only to knowledge but also to a communion: for 'truth' is the real state of affairs as established by the true God. So the disciples are teachers through whom knowledge of sin and forgiveness comes to their converts. The Samaritans knew that Jesus is Saviour because they had heard him (4: 42). Jesus tells the cured paralytic, 'Sin no more' (5: 14). Death is the penalty for sin (8: 24), but Jesus is a Liberator (8: 36). So the disciples deal with sin when they witness to Jesus in the power of the spirit–paraclete (16: 9).

When 20: 23, 'If you forgive the sins of any, they are forgiven; if you retain the sins of any, they are retained,' is read in the light of the whole Johannine message, it is seen to be not very different from the great Matthean texts, 16: 19 and 18: 18 about 'binding...and loosing'. For these can be taken to mean the interpretative function of a *teacher*.

It is not in the least likely that John conceives of the disciples as usurping the function of the incarnate Logos, the eternal God made man who is the Lamb that takes away the sin of the world (1: 29; cf. 1 John 1: 9; 2: 2; 3: 5; 4: 10). Such a Christology safeguards the unique work of Jesus Christ. It is the exalted Jesus the Righteous who is the heavenly *paraclete* of any who commit sin, provided they confess it (1 John 1: 9; 2: 1). Sins are pardoned not in the name of disciples but 'for his sake' (1 John 2: 12). This means 'because of Jesus' name, function and power'. There is nothing vague about it. So when the *spirit*-paraclete is said to deal with man's sin, it does so on the basis of belief and unbelief in Jesus (16: 9).

We hope to show later in more detail how this function of the

[1] Cf. 1 Cor. 12: 7. M.-A. Chevallier notes that early Judaism did not expect a gift of spirit to the whole people, *L'Esprit et le Messie*, pp. 1–50, 111–43.

spirit is fulfilled in and through the disciples, who are encouraged to pray in the name of Jesus (14: 13 f.; 15: 16; 16: 23 b).

Are these disciples to be reckoned as the apostolic plenipotentiaries of Christ? In some sense, Yes, as Mussner has ably argued.[1] But the Gospel evidence makes it extremely difficult to accept the position that John has in mind only the Apostles as they were remembered and honoured in the later Church. Would he not have referred to them more often as 'the Twelve'? The only three references seem pretty casual (6: 67, 71; 20: 24). If John had intended to allow them a high place, would he not have been anxious to give their names? We simply cannot tell which of those named belonged to this group: Andrew, Simon Peter, Philip, Nathanael, Judas Iscariot, Thomas, Judas ('not Iscariot'), Joseph of Arimathea, perhaps Nicodemus and Lazarus. The women named do not enter into consideration. All that remain are the mysterious Beloved Disciple, and, in the appended ch. 21: 2 only, 'the sons of Zebedee'. Nothing here demonstrates to my mind that John is speaking about a well-known 'Apostolic College'. Jesus made a fair number of disciples (4: 1); in the Upper Room it is 'disciples' that are assembled for supper and later for refuge from the Jews (13: 1, 5; 16: 17; 20: 19). So we consider the disciples to be representative of the entire faithful company, the apostolic Church.[2]

---

[1] 'Die Johanneischen Parakletsprüche und die apostolische Tradition', *Biblische Zeitschrift*, N.F. 5, Heft 1 (Jan. 1961), 56–70.

[2] Cf. among others, C. K. Barrett, *John*, p. 475; E. Käsemann, *Jesu letzter Wille nach Johannes 17*, pp. 56 f.

CHAPTER 5

'SPIRIT' AS POWER FOR A
MESSIANIC MINISTRY

In an earlier chapter it was said that John relates *spirit* to Jesus
as the Christ of God, whose mission was to bring the knowledge
of God, and for believers in this truth 'life abundant' even in a
dark and dangerous world (10: 10; 17: 2 f.). This has such
significance for the subject of this volume that it requires fuller
elaboration now.

I

Three trends in the Messianic Hope of intertestamental times
assume unusual interest in the light of John 1: 19–28.

It is shown there that the Baptist disavowed each of three
rôles, the Messiah's, Elijah's, and the Prophet's. We have to
deduce from this curious combination of two titles with one
personal name that Elijah conceals a title and a function. From
all that is presently known about the period concerned we can
say that this was the rôle of a Messianic priest, probably the
High Priest of the new age.[1] Personal names for the other
functions are easy to find: the Messiah or Christ is almost
certainly an equivalent here for 'King' and the King is David
(2 Sam. 7: 16; Pss. of Sol. 17; Luke 1: 69; cf. Rom. 1: 3, etc.).
The Prophet is Moses, on the basis of Deut. 18: 15–19;
4Q Testimonia; 11Q Melchizedek?; John 6: 14; Acts 3: 22 f.

Now, when we examine the Synoptic accounts (Matt. 4:
1–11 ‖ Luke 4: 1–13) of Jesus' desert temptations, the three
elements found in John's narrative can also be discovered:

(*a*) The Davidic or royal function is referred to in the offer of
the authority and glory of all the kingdoms of the world (Luke
4: 5 f.).

(*b*) The Elijah or priestly function must somehow lie behind
the enigmatic reference to the pinnacle of the Temple (Luke
4: 9), perhaps on the basis of Mal. 3: 1.

---

[1] Cf. Sir G. R. Driver, *The Judaean Scrolls*, pp. 276, 466 f., 481; L.
Ginzberg, *Eine unbekannte jüdische Sekte* (New York, 1922), p. 351.

(*c*) The Mosaic or prophetic function is in line with the temptation to 'command this stone to become bread' (Luke 4: 3).

In the light of this it can be no surprise that on the Mount of Transfiguration Jesus, the son of David (cf. Mark 10: 47), has for ghostly companions Moses and Elijah (Mark 9: 4). Every account of the Crucifixion agrees that Jesus went to death as one who claimed or was accused of claiming to be the royal Messiah. It is no part of our purpose to seek solutions to the vexed questions thus posed for any understanding of the person and work of Jesus. All that we seek to do is to show how *spirit* as divine power is associated with the Prince David, the Priest Elijah and the Prophet Moses.

David is a great warrior and judge; he is also to be wise, righteous, a peacemaker and a godly ruler. Important biblical passages are Isa. 4: 2; 11: 1 f.; and 61: 1, read alongside Jer. 23: 5 f.; 33: 14–16; and Zech. 3: 8; 6: 12 f.; and Ezek. 34: 23 f. read in the light of 11: 16–21; 34: 11–16; 36: 24–38; and 37: 1 ff. These prophecies, as well as 2 Sam. 7: 13–16 and Pss. 2: 2, 7; 72: 1, 12–14, fed the hopes we see in the Pharisaic Pss. of Sol., especially 17: 37 and 18: 7. It is generally held that the spirit of God would enable the Messianic ruler for his task.

New evidence has recently been found in 11Q Melchizedek, lines 18–21.[1] The combination here of prophetic, priestly and warrior concepts is reminiscent of the 'Hero Christology' of the letter to the Hebrews:

18. *And he that bringeth good tidings*: that is the anointed by the spirit ([מ]שיח הרו[ח]) as in Isa. 61: 1 (cf. CD 2: 12; Luke 4: 18).
20. to comfort...and instruct concerning all the times of wrath.
21. ...in (?) truth.

De Jonge and van der Woude have discussed possible parallels between Melchizedek and the warrior archangel Michael, both of whom may have been regarded as high-priestly figures.[2] The herald of good tidings in Isa. 52: 7 was identified sometimes with the royal Messiah, sometimes with Elijah. At any rate, an allusion to Isa. 61: 1 lay close at hand in each case. Both the

[1] M. de Jonge and A. S. van der Woude, '11Q Melchizedek and the New Testament', *N.T.S.* xii, No. 4 (July 1966), 301–26.
[2] For the former see Strack–Billerbeck, *K.T.M.* iv, 464; for the latter, *Ḥag.* 12*b*; *Zeb.* 62*a*; and *Men.* 110*a* in the Babylonian Talmud.

Prince and the Priest are 'anointed' with the spirit of God for an eschatological ministry.

The Priest Elijah, if this name was either current or implicit at the time, may be seen embodied in Joshua, the son of Jehozadak (Hag. 1: 12), who shared the work and the promises of the divine restoration (Hag. 2: 1–9): 'My spirit dwells among you. Fear not!' A levitical (priestly) Messiah seems to have been awaited by some groups in the pre-Christian era (Test. of Levi 18 and Test. of Judah 20, if we may still find pre-Christian ideas there).

It is not certain, however, that such priestly concepts were not also related to Moses, that great all-inclusive First Redeemer of Israel. He was a sovereign of a kind, and a supreme lawgiver, a servant of God in worship, and of course a prophet. So it is possible that 11Q Melchizedek may intend Moses rather than Elijah or an angel. If it is correct to find in l. 18 allusions to Isa. 52: 7; 61: 1, we may follow the editors in finding here too a reference to a Prophet (cf. CD 2: 12;[1] 6: 1; 1QS 9: 11; 1QM 11: 7). If so, this is probably the prophet like Moses.

Now, according to Exod. 2: 1; Num. 11: 17, 25, Moses was an *inspired* Levite, more than a prophet (Num. 12: 5–8). So it is said: 'There has not arisen a prophet since in Israel like Moses, whom the Lord knew face to face, none like him for all the *signs and wonders* which the Lord sent him to do...' (Deut. 34: 10 f.). He laid hands on Joshua so that to Joshua also was granted 'the spirit of wisdom' (Deut. 34: 9). Joshua maintained the tradition of astonishing miracles (Josh. 1–6).

The Successor to Moses in any of his God-given tasks must obviously be a man on whom the spirit of God rested.

Scholars have long realized that the Messianic hopes were far from being consistent or simple, and it is virtually impossible to define which expectation dominated the minds of the general public or the intelligentsia or the priestly establishment or the various obscure sects, during the Herodian period. The one common article of faith may have been, however, that *God would qualify his chosen agent by empowering him with spirit.*

The anointed personage would effect the liberation of God's people, but this almost always included their revival in godli-

---

[1] See the important note by P. Wernberg-Møller, *The Manual of Discipline* (Leiden, 1957), pp. 62–4.

ness and their purification, as predicted in such passages as
Ezek. 11: 17–20; 36: 22–38; 37: 1–14 ('I will put my spirit
within you, and you shall live'); and Zech. (or pseudo-Zech.)
13: 9; 14: 20 f. Occasionally this is put in terms of a renewed
Covenant as in Jer. 31; or of vicarious suffering as in second
Isaiah. The latter especially seems to have influenced the
Qumrân Community.[1] The poetry of the *Hodayot* (1QH)
contains profound ideas of divine grace made available for the
cleansing of sin and the strengthening of the pious.

So-called 'religious' functions were not the only duty of the
Messianic figure. Certainly the King or Prince was expected to
ensure peace and prosperity for the Jews, and even world
hegemony, in agreement with Isa. 11: 1 ff.; Ps. 72; Hag. 2: 9;
Zech. 2: 11; 8: 12; and Dan. 7, which were not wholly
'spiritualized'. One route to the achievement of these goals had
to be successful war, and the narrative of the Exodus battles
might provide plans and hopes for the needful campaigns
(cf. Num. 24: 17–19; Ps. 2: 8; Isa. 11: 4; Pss. of Sol. 17; and
the Qumrân War Scroll, 1QM).

The 'holy' nature of this war must not blind us to the harsh
realities implied, for citizens and commanders had need of
more than piety. They had to control the best martial arms and
be possessed of cunning, perseverance, courage, fortitude,
integrity, national unity, and what in modern parlance is called
'the spirit of sacrifice'.[2] The OT prototypes have shown already
that *spirit* applied to God's happy warrior as well as to servants
of the cult.[3]

II

What is the picture in the Fourth Gospel?

(1) John belonged to an age (we have said) that was dominated by the brute fact of Roman power, represented by Pilate
and his soldiers; yet the Evangelist paid no attention, apparently, to politics, economic policy, or diplomacy. But the

---

[1] 1QS 3: 6–12; 4: 6; 5: 6; 8: 6; 9: 4–6. See Wernberg-Møller, *op. cit.*
pp. 65, 79, 93, 125.
[2] Yadin reports such ideas from the so-called Temple Scroll acquired by
the Israelis after the June 1967 campaign.
[3] See above, p. 4, n. 2.

narrative of the King who was crucified was written on the assumption that both Rome and the nation-church of the Jews were held captive by the *cosmos* and the *cosmocrator*, Satan.[1] It was the Jewish nation through its leaders that delivered Jesus to the Romans. No Vatican II apology is made by John's Gospel for this crude recital of the facts! Jesus is a wicked fellow (18: 30), a royal Pretender (18: 33–9), and a claimant to divine status (19: 7). Treason is combined with blasphemy, and in each case the penalty was death (for the latter see *San.* 7: 5; *Ker.* 1: 1 f.). The prosecuting 'nation' of the Jews is represented by Annas, Caiaphas, the priests, the Levites, the Pharisees and the 'crowd'. But they are doomed (8: 24, etc.).

(2)   Paradoxically, the Gospel of John may be shown to have something to say about peace, prosperity and world leadership.

(*a*) Real peace is found in communion with the Father (14: 27; 20: 19, 21), for he is known in his Son.

(*b*) The Johannine use of 'water', 'bread' and 'light', like the references to a wedding, to blindness, paralysis and other facts of daily life, is not to be exhausted in pious interpretation (2: 1 ff.; 4: 10; 5: 3 ff.; 6: 34 f.; 8: 12; 9: 1). Nor is the 'wolf' of 10: 12 simply to be equated with demonic evil unrelated to the material world. Bread and water in an Oriental setting speak of genuine hunger and thirst, not only of religious longings.

(*c*) Jesus is no failure of a Pretender! He had marked successes among the people and the leaders of Galilee, Samaria and Judaea (1: 35 ff.; 3: 1 ff.; 4: 39–42; 4: 46–53; 6: 14 f.; 7: 50; 12: 42; 19: 38 f.). Greeks came seeking him (12: 20). No wonder the leaders of Jewry cried out, 'Look, the (whole) world has become his disciple!' (12: 19). The crowning touch is the imperialism of 12: 32, 'I will draw all men to myself'.

This is the Jesus on whom the spirit rested (1: 32).

(3)   It can be demonstrated in detail that Jesus is fully equipped with this divine power for his mission as the *Messianic teacher* (esp. 3: 34; 6: 63, 68; 10: 36); the *Royal man* whose kingship is 'not of this world' because it is from above, of the

---

[1] 14: 30; 16: 11; 1 John 5: 19. Satan may be the angel of death from whom men must be delivered.

spirit (18: 36). His servants do not fight to set him free, and yet he and they are engaged in a conflict (1: 5; 3: 20; 7: 7; 15: 23–5; 16: 2; 17: 6 ff.). Judas and Caiaphas, for example, are clearly men into whom Satan, the *spirit of darkness*, had entered (11: 51 refers to some kind of inspiration of the high priest; 13: 2, 27). But into Jesus and his followers it is the *spirit of God* that comes. Jesus is also, and most typically, the *Son of the Father*, united to the Father in love (10: 30; 14: 9, 23; 15: 9 f.; 16: 28). John could have written, ' *The Son of the Father is spirit*' or '*The Logos made flesh is spirit-filled*'.

What was true of the Master had to become true also for his servants: that is why the *spirit* is promised in chs. 14–16. They too were to be at war with evil powers, and they needed assurance that the *cosmocrator* had been condemned once and for all to defeat and annihilation. They were not looking for national freedom nor a Davidic empire nor a purified Cult. The Johannine Church rather anticipated that, when the Son of Man lifted up his voice in the final battle-cry, there would be resurrection. For evil-doers this would mean rising to face the Judgment. For the faithful it would mean eternal life and joy (5: 29). From this perspective we may interpret the absolution powers of 20: 22 f. as successful attack on the dominion of Satan (a theme that underlies the Synoptic stories of exorcisms). The disciples receive 'authority' (ἐξουσία) and this must be linked, not merely to humility and return to God ('repentance'), but to rebirth and 'baptism with holy spirit' (1: 33; 8: 23, 31 ff.; 11: 25; 20: 22).

It would be tedious to offer the demonstration of all this, or to show how similar results emerge from an examination of other titles like Son of Man, Lamb of God, Bridegroom, Bread of Life, the Lord, the True Vine, the Saviour, the First Paraclete (14: 16), the Way and the Resurrection. Always and everywhere Jesus is the healer, the conqueror, the creative Lord because he is possessed by the divine power of spirit.

III

We may imagine John like a greater Janus standing with his back to the historic ministry of the Messiah Jesus, the Son of God, and proclaiming in heraldic fashion over and over again how the creative and redemptive powers that were in Jesus continue to operate in this world through the disciples of Jesus. That is what 17: 17 and 20: 22 mean when viewed, as they should be, prospectively as well as retrospectively.

There was a vast array of Jews, Greeks, Syrians, Romans, Africans and others who had become Christian people between the year of the Crucifixion and the year when John's book was at last published (posthumously?). The sequence of that process by which they had entered into the life of God's true Vine was conversion and baptism;[1] and its fruits were joy, hope, divine communion, and peace amid the ambiguities, the frustrations, and the devilish warfare of the *cosmos*. This environment of hostility makes all the more precious the intercessions of the Master and Friend as expressed in 17: 9 ff. and the promises of chs. 14–16, 'I will come again...Ask, for I will do it...My Father and I will make our home with you...The spirit of truth will teach you...The other paraclete will never leave you.'

[1] Note the prospective meanings in 1: 12, 50 f.; 3: 6, 16; 5: 21–6; 6: 51 ff.; 15: 1 ff.

PART II

THE SPIRIT–PARACLETE,
THE SPIRIT OF TRUTH

CHAPTER 6

ARE THE SPIRIT–PARACLETE SAYINGS TRULY JOHANNINE?

I

It may be taken for granted that the spirit–paraclete sayings belonged to the Fourth Gospel at the time of its publication, but this does not of itself prove that they were composed and inserted by the Evangelist himself. Literary study shows that there are various strands in the Gospel and there are some obvious signs of editorial activity.

Thus 21: 24 f. seem to be intended to identify the author of the book with 'the disciple whom Jesus loved', one of the immediate witnesses of the historic ministry (cf. 21: 20–3). Other tell-tale indications may be seen at 4: 2 and 19: 35. We need not here attempt any full explanation of these facts. A convenient short treatment is available in Willi Marxsen's *Introduction to the New Testament*, pp. 254–8.[1] He holds that 'by means of "correctional" interpolations the "Church redaction" tried to make the original work fit' traditional Christian conceptions about eschatology, the Sacraments, and the leadership of St Peter. Within the last century it has also been thought that the spirit–paraclete texts had been interpolated: one of the more significant arguments for this view was that of H. Windisch in the *Festschrift für A. Jülicher* (1927).[2] More recently the distinguished French Catholic scholar, M.-E. Boismard, has identified the editor of the Fourth Gospel as Luke the Evangelist.[3] The Lucan insertions are as follows:

[1] E.T. 1968. See also W. F. Howard and C. K. Barrett, *The Fourth Gospel in Recent Criticism and Interpretation* (1955); and the classic commentary by R. Bultmann, soon to appear in English.

[2] There is a summary account in O. Betz, *Der Paraklet*, pp. 5–11. An E.T. by J. W. Cox was published in 1968 (Fortress Press: Philadelphia. Facet Books, Biblical Series, 20).

[3] 'Saint Luc et la Rédaction du Quatrième Évangile (Jean IV, 46–54)', *R.B.* LXIX, 2 (April 1962), 185–211.

1: 14, 17, 'grace and truth';

1: 17, the contrast between law and grace;

1: 18, the implicit contrast here with the epiphany of God at Sinai; and the use of ἐξηγέομαι;

1: 3, 14, 16, the concept of the creative *logos* and the use of πλήρωμα (mediated by Luke from Paul's usage in Col. 1: 16, 19; 2: 9f., 13);

4: 46–54, the official 'and his household' became believers, like the Philippians in Acts 16: 29–34;

13: 21–30, especially the words, 'then Satan entered into him' (cf. Luke 22: 3), and the reference to the 'beloved disciple';[1]

21: 1 ff., with which Luke 5: 1–11 may be compared.[2]

According to Boismard, Luke was an inveterate imitator. In the Third Gospel he imitated the style of the LXX; in the Acts his model was the style of his master Paul; while in the case of the Fourth Gospel he followed the Johannine style itself! Was it then Luke, Boismard asks, 'who regrouped the original Johannine traditions into a primitive Gospel which one could call Proto-John'? (There was still further editorial amendment of a sacramentalizing kind, but this we may ignore in the meantime.)

The spirit–paraclete sayings have been examined by Fr Boismard and his students in a seminar at the École Biblique, Jerusalem, but so far as I am aware the conclusions have not been published. I have reason to believe, however, that he regards them with suspicion and probably as interpolations by St Luke.[3]

It is imperative, therefore, that we should see for ourselves whether the sayings about the coming of the spirit of truth, the other paraclete, are really Johannine in language and style, in theology, and in their present setting.[4] The following investigation was done independently and later checked with some of the specialists in this subject.[5]

[1] *R.B.* LXXI, 1 (Jan. 1964), 5–24. All the references to the 'beloved disciple' are Lucan insertions (article cited in previous note).

[2] On John 21 see his article in *R.B.* LIV, 4 (Oct. 1947), 473–501.

[3] Through the kindness of Prof. Marilyn Schaub, a member of the seminar in 1966–7, I had the privilege of an interview with Fr Boismard on the subject of the spirit–paraclete.

[4] See Appendix 2 for a more detailed study of the literary structure.

[5] E. Schweizer, *Ego Eimi* (1939), pp. 88–90; P. H. Menoud, *L'Évangile de Jean après les recherches récentes* (1947), pp. 14–16; E. Ruckstuhl, *Die*

II

A 14: 16–17

(1) ἐρωτάω is frequent in John (almost thirty cases). It is not common in Matthew, Mark or Paul, but is found more than a score of times in Luke–Acts. The verb αἰτέω is employed more often in the Synoptics and Acts. It is also found in John (ten times) and 1 John (five). The use of synonyms in this way is typically Johannine.

(2) παράκλητος is of course Johannine: cf. 1 John 2: 1.

(3) τὸ πνεῦμα τῆς ἀληθείας, so far as the NT is concerned, is confined to the Fourth Gospel and 1 John 4: 6. ἀλήθεια is almost a technical term in John, and in the Lucans there is nothing comparable to it or to 'spirit of truth'.

(4) κόσμος too is virtually a technical term in John and 1 John.[1] It occurs four times in Luke–Acts.

(5) θεωρέω, never used in Paul and seldom elsewhere, is found about equally in John and Luke, but in the former (as we saw above, p. 18) it forms part of a cluster of verbs denoting sight and perception.

(6) γινώσκω is frequent in the Synoptics, Acts and Paul. It is however distinctive in the Johannine literature.

(7) μένω is a verb that is quite uncommon outside Luke, John and Paul in the NT. It is no more Lucan than Pauline, however, whereas in John it is technical. With 14: 16 f. compare 1 John 2: 14; 3: 9, 24.

The use of the preposition ἐν is also peculiarly Johannine.

From this evidence it might easily be concluded that the first spirit–paraclete pericope was composed *in the style of the First Epistle of John!* Nothing compels us to see the hand of Luke.

B 14: 25–6

(1) ὄνομα: references to the 'name' of Jesus occur in the Paulines, e.g. Rom. 10: 12 f.; 1 Cor. 1: 2; 12: 3. But this is far more characteristic of both John and Luke.

literarische Einheit des Johannesevangeliums (1951), pp. 190–205; F.-M. Braun, *Jean le Théologien* (1959, 1964): I, *Jean le Théologien et son Évangile dans l'Église ancienne*; II, *Les grandes traditions d'Israël*; R. E. Brown, *John I–XII* (Anchor Bible, 1966), pp. cxxxv–cxxxvii. I regret that I did not have access to M. Miguéns, *El Paráclito* (1963).

[1] See my article 'Οἰκουμένη and κόσμος in the New Testament', *N.T.S.* x, No. 3 (April 1964), 352–60.

(2) διδάσκω is used of the holy spirit in the Lucan parallel to Mark 13: 11: 'For the holy spirit will teach you in that hour what you ought to say' (12: 12). On the other hand, note 1 John 2: 27 where χρῖσμα may mean 'the gift of the spirit': 'As his anointing teaches you about everything, and is true, and is no lie, just as it has taught you, abide in him.'

(3) ὑπομνήσει is used here only in John. Cf. 3 John 10, ἐὰν ἔλθω, ὑπομνήσω αὐτοῦ τὰ ἔργα κτλ. There is nothing Lucan about this.

C   15: 26–7

(1) In verse 26 the significant wording seems at first sight to be altogether Johannine, e.g. 'the paraclete', sending (used of divine commissioning), 'the spirit of truth' and 'from the Father'.

(2) παρὰ τοῦ πατρός: see 1: 14 (anarthrous); 6: 45; 10: 18; 15: 15; 16: 28 (the reading of 𝔓²², S, and others). We may ignore Matt. 18: 19, but not Acts 2: 33, τῇ δεξιᾷ οὖν τοῦ θεοῦ ὑψωθεὶς τήν τε ἐπαγγελίαν τοῦ πνεύματος τοῦ ἁγίου λαβὼν παρὰ τοῦ πατρὸς ἐξέχεεν τοῦτο. This combination of 'received from the Father' and 'the promise of the holy spirit' is of some importance (cf. 1 John 2: 25). Standing alone, however, it proves nothing.

(3) ἐκπορεύεται: cf. 5: 29, some of the dead will 'proceed' to the resurrection of life, others to the resurrection of judgment. This verb is also used of words that 'proceed' out of the mouth: Deut. 8: 3, qu. at Matt. 4: 4 (not Luke 4: 4); cf. Luke 4: 22, of Jesus; in the LXX see also Ezek. 33: 30; 47: 1. There is no application of the verb in Luke to the spirit's procession from God.

(4) μαρτυρήσει: the 'witness' function of the spirit is clearly stated at 1 John 5: 6 (RSV 5: 7), in a passage that is full of parallels to John (see verses 1–6, 9, 11 and 13). Before we decide that this is a primary source for the Fourth Evangelist, we have to note other NT texts like 1 Thess. 2: 10; Rev. 1: 5; 2: 13; 3: 14; and in particular Luke 24: 48, 'You are witnesses of these things'; and Acts 1: 8; 5: 32; 10: 39, 41; 13: 31; 22: 15, 20; 26: 16.

This is an impressive array, and one notes a Johannine ring in such a passage as Acts 5: 32, 'And we are witnesses to these things, and so is the holy spirit that God gave to those who obey him.' On the other hand, John does not use the noun 'witness' nor the full title 'the holy spirit'. If we look at Luke 24: 48 f. and Acts 1: 4, 8, we find a Lucan verb ἐξαπο-στέλλω, the noun δύναμις, and ἐνδύω, which never appear in John. Lucan influence is uncertain.

(5) ἀπ' ἀρχῆς: this phrase is by no means Lucan (see Luke 1: 2; Acts 26: 4). There are three examples in Matthew, two in Mark, one in Paul (variant reading in 2 Thess. 2: 13), one in 2 Peter. Besides John 8: 44; 2 John 5, 6, see 1 John 1: 1; 2: 7, 13 f., 24; 3: 8, 11.

Once again the linguistic usage makes it a safer conclusion that the hand of the Johannine letter writer is to be noted in the Fourth Gospel; coincidence with Lucan material may be accidental, due to harmonization, or may point to some common traditions.

D 16: 7–11

(1) Quite apart from words already known as Johannine, e.g. ἀλήθεια, παράκλητος, κόσμος, it is to be observed that the three περί phrases have a special sense here:

(a) ἁμαρτία in John, as we have seen, is associated with 'unbelief' in Jesus as the Son of God: 3: 18; 8: 24, 46 f.; 9: 41; 15: 22.

(b) δικαιοσύνη probably does not mean in this verse 'justice' or divine 'vindication' or God's own 'righteousness' as a system of order in the universe, nor 'the goodness of Jesus'.[1] I suggest that, as shown by 16: 10, 'because I go to the Father', it defines the unique status of Jesus, the incarnate Logos, and should be translated by 'my proper place' or 'my just due'.[2]

(c) κρίσις is common in John. Indeed the thought of Judgment dominates large sections of the Gospel, for the coming of the Logos inevitably divides the children of light from the children of darkness (3: 19; 5: 22–30, etc.; cf. 1 John 4: 17). We noted above a remarkable parallel in Acts 24: 25, but

---

[1] Barrett, *John*, pp. 406–7, accepts this last meaning.

[2] 1 John 2: 1 is in keeping with this translation. The title 'the Just One', applied to Jesus as the rightful Servant of the Lord, is not likely to have been typical only of one party within the primitive churches.

'righteousness' there is used in its regular Pauline sense, so that the resemblance is not very close.

(2) Other clearly Johannine expressions are ὁ ἄρχων τοῦ κόσμου τούτου (cf. 14: 30), ὑπάγω and θεωρῶ (cf. 14: 28; 16: 16 ff.).

(3) ἐλέγχω cannot be cited as distinctive of John. It is employed with 'spirit' in Wisd. Sol. 1: 3–8 (ἅγιον γὰρ πνεῦμα ἐλεγχθήσεται ἐπελθούσης ἀδικίας). There is an interesting example at Tit. 2: 15, where ἐλέγχω is combined with παρα-καλῶ to describe the work of a Christian presbyter-teacher and ruler. Nevertheless, there have occurred already two important examples of ἐλέγχω in John 3: 20; 8: 46. It is unnecessary therefore to see an intrusive hand in 16: 8.

E   16: 12–15

(1) ἀφ' ἑαυτοῦ, 'on his own authority' or 'by his own volition', with its parallel ἀπ' ἐμαυτοῦ, refer in John to the Son as the agent of the Father: thus with ποιεῖν (5: 19, 30; 8: 28); with ἔρχεσθαι (7: 28; 8: 42); and with λέγειν (11: 51; 18: 34, the reading of W, Θ, 33, and others). We may compare 2 Cor. 3: 5, 'sufficient of ourselves'; Luke 12: 57, 'judge for yourselves', and 21: 30, 'see for yourselves', for this use of ἀπό. But John uses the verb λαλεῖν with ἀπό four times (7: 17 f.; 12: 49; 14: 10). There is one other case of this in the NT, namely 2 Pet. 1: 21, where ἀπό should be read, with Vaticanus, instead of ἅγιοι. It may be inferred from this evidence that λαλεῖν ἀπό is Johannine.

(2) τὰ ἐρχόμενα. The only other example in the NT is John 18: 4 (cf. 13: 1, 3 for Jesus' foreknowledge).

(3) λαμβάνειν with ἐκ: cf. 1: 16. This too is a Johannine usage.

(4) For the verb ἀναγγέλλω see also 4: 25; 5: 15 (the reading of Vaticanus); and 1 John 1: 5. There are only a few examples in Paul and 1 Peter; but it is more common in Acts for the reports of missionaries or for proclaiming God's will (14: 27; 15: 4; 19: 18; 20: 20, 27). It is not, however, a word that gives any peculiarity to style.

(5) ὁδηγέω might be considered more likely to stamp a writer's manner, though it could have come to mind from Ps. 22: 3 (23: 2); and Wisd. Sol. 9: 11. Luke uses it in the

Gospel 6: 39[1] and in Acts 8: 31 where Philip is invited to provide an exegesis of Isaiah. It is hardly necessary to derive the use in John 16: 13 from Luke. The idea of the 'way' had already appeared at 14: 4–6, and this may have had widespread currency in the earliest churches.

If Luke were the editor who inserted the spirit–paraclete sayings, why did he select λαλεῖν ἀπό for imitation, since this occurs but four times in John? and why insert λαμβάνειν ἐκ into 16: 13–15 (or 1: 16) although he is never tempted to use this in his own compositions? The same applies to the use of τὰ ἐρχόμενα.

One would have expected that, had he in truth been intent on interpolating material into the Gospel of John, Luke could not have refrained from bringing in somewhere the full title 'the holy spirit'. The most serious objection to this entire proposal is that there is nothing in the Lucan writings to indicate why 'the spirit of truth' should have been introduced nor why this spirit should further be defined as a 'paraclete'. It would be piling hypothesis on hypothesis to speculate that Luke interpolated merely the reference to the former, and that some other editor (the ecclesiastical sacramentalist?) later added the reference to the paraclete.

If a NT source is to be sought for these unusual ideas, the single obvious place is the First Epistle of John.[2] But before we consider that possibility in more detail, we wish to look at the larger context of the spirit–paraclete texts, to see whether there is any great loss of meaning if they are removed, and to find out how well they fit as they stand.

III

Even a cursory glance at the literary structure of John shows major divisions at 1: 18, 51; 12: 50; 18: 1 *a* and 20: 31. As we seek to show in the appended notes, it is possible to regard 12: 44–50 as part of the 'bridge' between the 'Book of Signs' (2: 1–11: 54) and the 'Book of the Secret Ministry' (13: 1–20: 31). Alternatively it may be incorporated into the latter

---

[1] J. Jeremias considers Luke 6: 39–40 a 'Lucan insertion into the Sermon on the Plain' (*The Parables of Jesus* (1955), p. 30, n. 41).

[2] See below, pp. 75–9.

67

part of the Gospel, along with 11: 55–12: 43. For 12: 47–50 in particular, dealing with the words of Jesus and the authority behind them, form an excellent introduction to the Farewell Discourses and the Prayer of Royal Intercession (chs. 13–17).

The essential business of the words, appropriately to the incarnate Logos as the emissary of the Father, is to communicate the Name of the Father; that is, the meaning and purpose of the one, true God. Jesus amply fulfils this ministry (15: 15; 17: 6, 8). It should be noted how 12: 50 is echoed in 14: 31, where a major break occurs: 'As the Father has told me, *so I speak*...As the Father has instructed me, *so I act.*' Within the Secret Ministry word and act are united 'sacramentally'.

Another point has to be made: the immediate audience is the circle of disciples in the Supper Room, but far beyond them one should envisage their converts, and even their converts' converts (cf. 15: 20; 17: 20). Hence it is permissible to hold that the celebration of the (Last) Supper in 13: 1 ff. is meant to mirror the contemporary celebration of the Lord's Supper, the Eucharist, in the Johannine Church. For at such an act the Lord's last will and testament would constantly be remembered under the influence of the spirit of God (cf. 1 Cor. 11: 26b).[1]

Since the Johannine mind is very subtle, as Dr C. H. Dodd has so often reminded us, we are emboldened to make two suggestions about the relation of the spirit to the disciples in this Book of the Secret Ministry:

(a) The first concerns *cleansing and consecration*:

At 11: 55 it is said that 'the Passover...was at hand', the festival of salvation. In the context of Jesus' life, however, this was 'the Passover when the Son was glorified'. For such an occasion many went up to Jerusalem 'to purify' themselves (ἵνα ἁγνίσωσιν).[2] So it is not surprising that we watch a scene of purification in 13: 4–11 (cf. 15: 3), one of the necessary preludes to the Christian Passover and the ministry that awaits the disciples thereafter (15: 16; 20: 21 f.). Can we fail to detect beneath the language and imagery allusion to the cleansing work of the divine spirit? That Jesus 'washes' with holy spirit may be one meaning of 1: 33.

---

[1] Cf. W. D. Davies, *Invitation to the New Testament* (1963), p. 467.

[2] Cf. 1 John 3: 3, and 1 Pet. 1: 22, 'purified...by your obedience to the truth for genuine love of the brothers, love one another...'.

Now, in the Footwashing scene Peter is told, 'What I am doing you do not know now, but afterward you will understand' (13: 7). This will recall 2: 22 and 12: 16; but it should direct us first to 14: 26 and 16: 14, for it is the function of the spirit of truth as paraclete to teach disciples the meaning of what Jesus did and what Jesus said.

Moreover, the purification theme in the Passover context will further lead one to 17: 19, where he who is to become the sacrifice 'consecrates' himself. One is tempted to suggest that the original text of 11: 55 may have been: 'many were going up in order to consecrate themselves' (ἵνα ἁγιάσωσιν ἑαυτούς). At any rate there is an intimate relationship between cleansing and consecration. May we not see how significant it is that for dedication to the service of the Holy Father (17: 11) a gift of 'holy' spirit is required (20: 22)? The promise of the abiding communion of the spirit in 14: 16 precisely fits the situation of the disciples. As the Father 'consecrated' Jesus and 'sent' him into the world (10: 36, ὃν ὁ πατὴρ ἡγίασεν καὶ ἀπέστειλεν εἰς τὸν κόσμον), so the disciples will be sanctified (17: 17: note that the 'word' both cleanses and consecrates; and the word of Jesus is drenched in spirit, 6: 63).

(b) The second suggestion is that the disciples in the Supper Room are being constituted as *the Body of Christ* and prepared for *worship in spirit and truth*.

Already at 2: 21 the new 'Temple' that is to be raised by Jesus is at one level of meaning his own resurrection 'body' and at another level the 'body' of his Church. Such ideas need not have been limited to St Paul and the Pauline churches; John *may* have received the image, however, from a Pauline source. Now in the place where the supper was enjoyed Jesus and his disciples were assembled as the 'Vine' of God, the Lord being the stem, his friends being the branches. Together they are the Children of God, the Son with his brothers, the true congregation.

Outside stood the magnificent Temple in the process of building by human hands; inside, Jesus and his community are becoming in ever more intimate and 'spiritual' fellowship that New Temple where prayer is truly offered to the Father (17: 1 ff.; cf. 4: 20). When Jesus departs out of this world, as he does very soon, as has happened by the time any reader comes on the Gospel account, how can the community worship the Father 'in spirit and truth' (4: 23 f.) unless by compensation it is blessed with his spirit? The true Messiah came, and he has inaugurated the new age of the spirit.

Viewed in the light of Johannine theology as a whole, it is not conceivable that the constitutive Word of the Church should have been spoken without explicit promise concerning the coming of the divine spirit. Because there is such rich teaching in chs. 14–16, we may be less puzzled by the absence of any explicit petition for the gift of the spirit in ch. 17.[1]

IV

Let us now examine carefully the contents of chs. 13–17: we soon discover that they have a character of their own and can be the product only of a single mind.

For example, they are marked by the use of a formula: 'These things I say (or, I have said), so that...' Three of the examples begin the second clause with 'so that when...' There is a variant in 16: 25, 'These things I have said to you in riddles; a time is coming when...'. 14: 25 begins in the customary fashion but continues: 'whilst abiding with you; but the paraclete...he will teach you...'.

The formula list is as follows:

13: 19.

14: 25. For the μένων clause, cf. 16: 4b.

14: 29, another version of 13: 19. We shall meet it again, in slightly different dress, at 16: 4a.

15: 11. This is virtually repeated in 17: 13; and cf. 1 John 1: 4.

16: 1. Cf. 1 John 2: 1.

16: 4a. The idea of 'remembering' is a link with 14: 26. 16: 6–8 soon follows. Both 14: 26 and 16: 6–8 relate to the spirit–paraclete.

16: 25. This should be contrasted with 14: 7–14. Have we evidence here of duplicate speeches or simply a failure to revise?

16: 33. Cf. 14: 27, 30 f.

---

[1] In his *Jesu letzter Wille nach Johannes 17*, Ernst Käsemann discusses three key themes of this chapter: the glory of Christ, the Church under the Word, and Christian Unity. It is a study that repays attention.

70

17: 13. Cf. 14: 28; 15: 11; 16: 6.[1]

There are two basic notes to be heard in this entire section of the Gospel, one is warning, the other is consolation. First, one hears *the voice of warning*:

Jesus is going away (13: 33; 14: 19; 16: 5, 16, 28; 17: 11). There is matter for sadness and pain here.

Peter will deny his Master and *all the disciples will be scattered* (13: 38; 16: 32).

The 'ruler of this world' (the Devil) *is about to come*, and there will be tribulation and lamenting (14: 30; 16: 33).

Trials and anxieties await the faithful friends of Jesus, both in Jerusalem on the night in which he was betrayed, and in the remaining time of the world (15: 18–20; 16: 1 f.; 17: 11–18).

In the (immediate) future *grave disunity threatens* the apostolic community (17: 11, 21–3).

These forecasts fit well into the general pattern of John's Gospel, for the muttering of enemies and the threat of death for the Incarnate Word are omnipresent.

Second, there is also *a voice of consolation and promise:*

Jesus will come again (14: 3, 18, 23, 28; 16: 22). There is matter here only for exultant joy!

If they are obedient, *the disciples will be protected* (13: 34 f.; 14: 21, 27; 15: 1–17; 17: 11).

Prayers will be answered (14: 13; 15: 16; 16: 24).

Disciples will accomplish 'still greater works' than Jesus himself (14: 12).

Disciples will go to the Father's home where they will see their Lord 'glorified' with his pre-existent glory (14: 2 f.; 17: 24).

There is one other promise that is so important it is reiterated four times: the spirit will be sent to fortify and assist the disciples when they continue the work of Jesus. This promise was foreshadowed in the first part of the book at 1: 33 and 7: 39, and its fulfilment must be seen in 20: 19–23. No strange supplement this! On the contrary, if John had left out any reference to the spirit-endowment precisely at this point, he would have demonstrated a violent departure from Christian tradition (see Mark 13: 11 and parallels; and Luke 21: 15).

---

[1] Bultmann, *Komm.* p. 365, n. 2, does not see the full range of the formula, but notes the connexion with 8: 24. He asks whether Isa. 46: 10 may lie behind the predictions of Jesus.

V

There are problems in the arrangement of the material within John 13–17, and several efforts have been made to produce a more reasonable order. The key problem is 14: 31, 'Rise, let us go hence', followed by two or three long speeches. As an alternative to the current theories I propose to regard them as a sequence of dramatic scenes, although one has to admit that the 'stage directions' are not at all clear. This may be accounted for by the unfinished state of the book at the time of the author's death; some of the scenes may have been alternative 'drafts'. Taking them as they are, however, one can discover a satisfactory picture if 14: 31 be considered as merely a 'stage exit', not marking a departure of the little company from the Room in the matter-of-fact history. Hence the next scenes take place, *on the stage before us only*, on the road, near the Holy Place of the Temple (cf. 15: 1), and then close to one of the city gates from which the way ran down toward the Kedron and the Garden of Gethsemane.[1] When 18: 1a arrives, we reach an exit that is both dramatic and realistic: that is, we are to understand that Jesus with his disciples then left Jerusalem for the place of his arrest. The action proceeds inexorably to his death.

These scenes in the Supper Room are intended to let us overhear a conversation between Jesus and 'his own folk' and penetrate deeply into the secrets of their communion; at another dimension of meaning, however, they become a conversation between the eternal, divine Logos and his listening Church: first the Church of John's age, next the Church of John's readers until the world comes to an end.

It is perhaps best to analyse the chapters into three speeches: (*a*) 13: 31–14: 31, having the form of a dialogue that becomes a monologue. (*b*) 15: 1–16: 4a, which is all monologue.[2] (*c*) 16: 4b–33, where we get some relief from the rather monotonous monologue at 16: 17, 29.[3]

---

[1] My proposal is very tentative. 17: 1 may be translated, 'lifting up his eyes to the sky'; cf. Luke 6: 20, but also John 4: 35 for the language.

[2] 15: 18–25 requires the addition of 16: 1–4a *ad sensum*. A new start is made at 16: 4b.

[3] Some scholars prefer to take 15: 1–16: 33 as an alternative version of the first address.

At first sight one might argue that 14: 16 f., 26 could be omitted from the first speech without irreparable damage. But this is to ignore all that we have discussed already in this chapter, and not to see the subtle cross-references in the text of the Gospel.

It is most impressive, and certainly it is astonishing, to hear the promise of 14: 12, 'he that believes in me will also perform the works that I do; and he will do (even) greater things than these, because I am going to my Father'. How can that be? The works of Jesus in this Gospel are awe-inspiring: he brings the dead Lazarus to life, heals the fevered boy at a distance, cures the cripple and the man born blind; and he does marvellous things with water and bread.

There is a parallel at 5: 19 f. which may be a concealed parable.[1] 'The Father loves the Son, and shows him all that he himself is doing; and greater works than these will he show him, that you may wonder.' There is always more for a son or apprentice to learn from his father or from the master crafts-man. So is it with the Son and his servants, who are now re-named 'friends' (15: 15). Jesus, the man in whom the Logos-son appeared among us, had to be consecrated for doing his works (3: 34; 10: 36). Surely the disciples too must receive the divine power of the spirit!

The words 'because I am going to my Father' in 14: 12 are repeated in a spirit–paraclete context at 16: 10.

The coming again of Jesus is paralleled not only by a coming of the Father and the Son (14: 23), but also by the coming of the spirit (14: 16 f., 26).

The teaching function of the spirit in 14: 26 recalls all that is said about the words and commandments of Jesus in 14: 10, 15, 21 and 24.

If there be interpolation here, we must register astonishment at the amazing neatness of the editorial genius involved!

When we turn to the second address, we get similar results: e.g. in the matter of witnessing which has already been dis-cussed. 15: 26, 'when the paraclete comes…', has a parallel at 16: 4a, 'when the hour comes…'. This makes it abundantly clear that John is alerting us to what happens after the Cruci-

---

[1] C. H. Dodd, 'Une parabole cachée dans le quatrième Évangile', *Revue d'Histoire et Philosophie religieuses*, XLII, Nos. 2–3 (1962), 107–15. E.T. in *More New Testament Studies* (1968), pp. 30–40.

fixion in regard to the disciples; for it was historical record that the Church sprang from the loins of the dead Christ. There was no enduring crisis or calamity. The community of believers was not stranded in the hostile environment of the world, for the power of the spirit came.

John looks at the issues both from the point of view of Peter, Andrew, Philip and Thomas and the others on the night of betrayal, and from that of the contemporary Church. He knew that the Church had been equipped and made ready for any succession of perils, until at length an hour should strike that would put an end to all times and would fulfil the ultimate triumph of God and his Christ. His message to the people of his own day and to ours is plain: there is and will be for ever a divine presence, a spirit, a protagonist that assures the faithful about God and about victory.

Such a message emerged inevitably from the Johannine doctrine of God becoming man in Jesus of Nazareth.

Whether or no 16: 4b ff. constitute a second version of the first speech, both, we observe, contain spirit–paraclete sayings. Yet there are some remarkable differences:

(a) 14: 16, the Father 'will give' the spirit; 14: 26, he 'will send' the spirit. Contrast 16: 7, 'I will send the spirit', says Jesus, as in 15: 26.

(b) In 14: 16 f., 26 the verbs of the spirit's action are abide, teach, remind. In 16: 13, 'he will guide into all truth' is equivalent to 'teaching'; but each of the other verbs in 16 makes a fresh point: will convict, will speak, will make predictions, will glorify.

On the assumption of interpolation, how are we to account for the rich, manifold nature of these new ideas? Far more is being said now than may be found in all the Synoptic parallels. Yet nothing in 16: 4b ff. is out of harmony with the other promises in chs. 14 and 15.

One of the functions that must belong to the spirit is that of *consolation*, for 14: 1, 27; 16: 6, 20–2, all speak of sorrow that is unavoidable. It has been suggested by several scholars that we may well find the background for this function in second Isaiah.[1] The more significant texts are these:

[1] See e.g. J. G. Davies, 'The Primary Meaning of ΠΑΡΑΚΛΗΤΟΣ', *J.T.S.* (New Series), IV, Part I (April 1953), 35–8.

41: 10, 17c: 'Fear not, for I am with you...I the God of Israel will not forsake them.'

41: 26: 'For who will declare what is from the beginning that we may know it; and the former things, and we shall say that they are true?' (LXX).

44: 3: 'For I will pour water on the thirsty land...I will pour my spirit on your seed.'

61: 1–3: 'The spirit of the Lord God is upon me...to comfort.'

61: 10f.: 'I will greatly rejoice in the Lord...so the Lord God will cause righteousness to spring forth...'

66: 9: 'Shall I bring to the birth and not cause to bring forth?'

66: 13: 'As one whom his mother comforts, so will I comfort you; you shall be comforted in Jerusalem.'

Such comfort is very precious; but it must be remembered that in John the activity of the spirit–paraclete covers much more than consolation.

VI

The analysis of Johannine language, style, doctrine and literary workmanship kept driving us to see the hand of the writer of I John, not that of St Luke.

Such a position would have been almost taken for granted in British and American circles some years ago. But the work of C. H. Dodd in his commentary on the Johannine Epistles in the Moffatt series has powerfully influenced many to abandon that view. Today it is popular to think of a Johannine 'school' out of which may have come not only the letters but also the Apocalypse.

We cannot discover any decisive reasons for rejecting the traditional position. The differences are intelligible if we allow for the situation to which the Epistle was addressed; its length; and its date, some time *before* the Gospel.[1] Part of the evidence consists of the following numerous parallels:

I John 1: 6, οὐ ποιοῦμεν τὴν ἀλήθειαν
Gospel 3: 21, ὁ δὲ ποιῶν τὴν ἀλήθειαν
(For the style cf. I John 3: 7f.)

I John 2: 1, πρὸς τὸν πατέρα
Gospel 1: 1, πρὸς τὸν Θεόν

---

[1] See my discussion in *Peake's Commentary*, ed. M. Black and H. H. Rowley, 905b; F. C. Grant in *H.D.B.* rev. ed. by F. C. Grant and H. H. Rowley, pp. 510–13; and R. Bultmann's article in *R.G.G.* III, cols. 836 ff.

1 John 2: 3, ἐὰν τὰς ἐντολὰς αὐτοῦ τηρῶμεν.
Gospel 14: 15, τὰς ἐντολὰς τὰς ἐμὰς τηρήσετε
    (Cf. Epistle 3: 23–4; Gospel 14: 21; 15: 10, 12.)

1 John 2: 6, ἐν αὐτῷ μένειν (Cf. 4: 13.)
Gospel 15: 4, ἐὰν μὴ ἐν ἐμοὶ μένητε.
    (Cf. Epistle 4: 16; Gospel 15: 6–7.)

1 John 2: 7–8, ἐντολὴν καινήν
Gospel 13: 34, ἐντολὴν καινὴν δίδωμι ὑμῖν

1 John 2: 13, νενικήκατε τὸν πονηρόν.
Gospel 16: 33, ἐγὼ νενίκηκα τὸν κόσμον.

1 John 2: 15, μὴ ἀγαπᾶτε τὸν κόσμον
Gospel 15: 18f., εἰ ὁ κόσμος ὑμᾶς μισεῖ...ἐκ τοῦ κόσμου οὐκ ἐστέ
    (Cf. Epistle 3: 1; 4: 4–5; Gospel 16: 8; 17: 6ff.)

1 John 3: 1, τέκνα θεοῦ κληθῶμεν
Gospel 1: 12, τέκνα θεοῦ γενέσθαι

1 John 3: 8, ὁ ποιῶν τὴν ἁμαρτίαν ἐκ τοῦ διαβόλου ἐστίν, ὅτι ἀπ᾽ ἀρχῆς ὁ διάβολος ἁμαρτάνει.
Gospel 8: 44, ὑμεῖς ἐκ τοῦ πατρὸς τοῦ διαβόλου ἐστέ...ἐκεῖνος ἀνθρωποκτόνος ἦν ἀπ᾽ ἀρχῆς

1 John 3: 14, μεταβεβήκαμεν ἐκ τοῦ θανάτου εἰς τὴν ζωήν
Gospel 5: 24, μεταβέβηκεν ἐκ τοῦ θανάτου εἰς τὴν ζωήν.

1 John 3: 16, ἐκεῖνος ὑπὲρ ἡμῶν τὴν ψυχὴν αὐτοῦ ἔθηκεν
Gospel 10: 17, ἐγὼ τίθημι τὴν ψυχήν μου
    (Cf. Gospel 15: 13.)

1 John 3: 23, ἵνα πιστεύσωμεν τῷ ὀνόματι τοῦ υἱοῦ αὐτοῦ Ἰησοῦ Χριστοῦ
Gospel 3: 18, ὅτι μὴ πεπίστευκεν εἰς τὸ ὄνομα τοῦ μονογενοῦς υἱοῦ τοῦ θεοῦ.

1 John 4: 2, Χριστὸν ἐν σαρκὶ ἐληλυθότα
Gospel 1: 14, ὁ λόγος σὰρξ ἐγένετο
    (Cf. Gospel 6: 51.)

1 John 4: 4, 6, ἐκ τοῦ θεοῦ εἶναι
Gospel 8: 47, ὁ ὢν ἐκ τοῦ θεοῦ τὰ ῥήματα τοῦ θεοῦ ἀκούει
    (Cf. Epistle 5: 19; Gospel 10: 26.)

1 John 4: 9, ἐν τούτῳ ἐφανερώθη ἡ ἀγάπη τοῦ θεοῦ ἐν ἡμῖν, ὅτι τὸν υἱὸν αὐτοῦ τὸν μονογενῆ ἀπέσταλκεν ὁ θεὸς εἰς τὸν κόσμον ἵνα ζήσωμεν δι᾽ αὐτοῦ.
Gospel 3: 16, οὕτως γὰρ ἠγάπησεν ὁ θεὸς τὸν κόσμον, ὥστε τὸν υἱὸν τὸν μονογενῆ ἔδωκεν, ἵνα πᾶς ὁ πιστεύων εἰς αὐτὸν...ἔχῃ ζωὴν αἰώνιον.
    (Cf. Gospel 10: 36; 15: 19; 17: 3, 18; 20: 21, 31.)

1 John 4: 12, θεὸν οὐδεὶς πώποτε τεθέαται

Gospel 1: 18, θεὸν οὐδεὶς ἑώρακεν πώποτε

(Cf. Gospel 5: 37, οὔτε φωνὴν αὐτοῦ πώποτε ἀκηκόατε οὔτε εἶδος αὐτοῦ ἑωράκατε, and 6: 46, οὐχ ὅτι τὸν πατέρα ἑωράκέν τις κτλ.)

1 John 4: 14, ὁ πατὴρ ἀπέσταλκεν τὸν υἱὸν σωτῆρα τοῦ κόσμου.

Gospel 4: 42, οὗτός ἐστιν ἀληθῶς ὁ σωτὴρ τοῦ κόσμου.

1 John 5: 1, πᾶς ὁ πιστεύων ὅτι Ἰησοῦς ἐστιν ὁ χριστός

Gospel 20: 31, ἵνα πιστεύητε ὅτι Ἰησοῦς ἐστιν ὁ χριστὸς ὁ υἱὸς τοῦ θεοῦ.

1 John 5: 9, ἡ μαρτυρία τοῦ θεοῦ

Gospel 5: 37, καὶ ὁ πέμψας με πατήρ, ἐκεῖνος μεμαρτύρηκεν περὶ ἐμοῦ.

1 John 5: 11, καὶ αὕτη ἡ ζωὴ ἐν τῷ υἱῷ αὐτοῦ ἐστιν.

Gospel 1: 3–4, ὃ γέγονεν ἐν αὐτῷ ζωὴ ἦν

(Cf. Gospel 5: 26.)

1 John 5: 14, ἐάν τι αἰτώμεθα κατὰ τὸ θέλημα αὐτοῦ, ἀκούει ἡμῶν.

Gospel 14: 13f., καὶ ὅ τι ἂν αἰτήσητε ἐν τῷ ὀνόματί μου, τοῦτο ποιήσω (Cf. 16: 23.)

15: 7, ὃ ἐὰν θέλητε αἰτήσασθε καὶ γενήσεται ὑμῖν.

1 John 5: 20, οὗτός ἐστιν ὁ ἀληθινὸς θεὸς καὶ ζωὴ αἰώνιος.

Gospel 17: 3, αὕτη δέ ἐστιν ἡ αἰώνιος ζωή, ἵνα γινώσκωσιν σὲ τὸν μόνον ἀληθινὸν θεόν κτλ.

(Cf. Gospel 20: 31.)

We may also allude to the common use of ἐκεῖνος in relation to God or the Son or the spirit.

We have of course omitted the references in John and 1 John to the 'paraclete' and to 'spirit'.

Given the close relation posited by this mass of material, one is strongly inclined to define 'another paraclete' in John 14: 16 by reference to 1 John 2: 1, 'we have a paraclete with the Father'. The appearance of this idea in the Gospel is too casual, too much taken for granted, not to be regarded as a concept that must have been familiar in the circles for whom the book was meant, or at least it could not have been felt by the Evangelist to be wholly unintelligible to the general public amongst whom his book might circulate.[1]

Admittedly, there is one remaining difficulty that made

[1] One must always be cautious in trying to define precisely for whom the Fourth Gospel was intended. Some of it seems very esoteric, and yet 20: 31 can be interpreted as having non-believers in view. See further F. Hahn, *Mission in the New Testament*, pp. 152–60.

Windisch feel that the spirit–paraclete sayings must have been interpolations: *there is no association in 1 John of 'spirit' and 'paraclete'*.

Before this be fastened on as a mortal blow at the theory that John's Gospel was inscribed by the hand that wrote the First Epistle, we had better enquire exactly what the latter document has to say about the functions of the spirit. Is the pneumatology to be dismissed as 'undeveloped' and therefore by no means the forerunner to the Gospel doctrine?

(1)   The spirit is an *instrument of assurance*: 'We know that he (Christ?) abides in us by the spirit which he has given to us' (1 John 3: 24). At the same time, this communion is made dependent on moral obedience: 'All who keep his commandments abide in him, and he in them.'

Despite the differences, this function is akin to what is taught in John 14: 16 f.; 16: 13, 15.

(2)   The spirit *inspires a right Christian confession*, either in the ecstasy of initiation (cf. 1 Cor. 12: 3) or in the exalted mood and words of prophetic teaching (1 John 4: 1–6). As such it must oppose false prophets and heretics who are the embodiment of the spirit of antichrist, i.e. the Devil. Accordingly, in the lives of the faithful, the 'orthodox', is to be found 'the spirit of truth', which is either the power of God himself effecting true belief and right living, or is an angelic being antagonistic to the Devil, the angel of darkness and falseness.

In this paragraph of 1 John 4 we have astonishing parallels to John 14: 17; 15: 26; 16: 13. They must not be undervalued.

(3)   'And the spirit is the witness, because the spirit is the truth. There are three witnesses, the spirit, the water and the blood; and these three agree' (1 John 5: 7 f.).

It is not clear how 'spirit' is to be understood in these verses: (i) the spirit that rested on the Messiah at baptism; (ii) the spirit that the Son breathed into his disciples after the resurrection; (iii) the power in the Christians when they were summoned to courts of law. That apart, we have to note the predication of *the witness function* to the spirit, as in John 15: 26 and perhaps 16: 8.

A great deal is missing, it is true. But if we may see in the writer of 1 John a man who later wrote a Gospel in order to expound and defend the true faith in the Son of God, we must hold that he claimed 'apostolic authority' (1 John 1: 1–4), and he wrote as an inspired prophet and teacher. In fact he acted as 'a paraclete', a representative of the 'spirit of truth'. He is at war with the 'antichrists' (2: 18). His community has been consecrated and is the home of the divine spirit (2: 27; 3: 24).

So we find nothing in the Epistle that is alien to the Gospel teaching about the spirit, however elementary it may appear in the light of the brilliant message of the Gospel.

VII

To conclude:

In the drama of the Secret Ministry there are four chief assertions of the Christian faith:

(i) The revelation of the Father's nature and purpose did take place in the historic mission of Jesus Christ.

(ii) The Gospel is a message not of defeat but of victory: 'Be of good cheer. I have overcome the world!' (16: 33).

(iii) Provision was made for divine witness to the Saviour Christ in all time to come.

(iv) To accomplish (iii) provision was made, *mirabile dictu*, for human witness to this Christ in all time coming, by sending to the disciples divine, personal power, that is to say, the spirit–paraclete.

In very simple but profound terms, John proclaims in his Gospel that Jesus began to do something which his Church is called to continue. Without the spirit-sayings all this would be evacuated of meaning.

Nevertheless, we have not yet discovered why the 'spirit' in the Fourth Gospel is described as 'the spirit of truth', nor why it is also 'the paraclete'. Recent study has sought to answer these questions, so we must next proceed to take its measure.

CHAPTER 7

RECENT STUDIES ON PARACLETE
AND THE SPIRIT OF TRUTH

Without any doubt the most significant recent contribution to the investigation of this subject has been made by Otto Betz.[1] Since his book is not available in English, a careful review and critique of it may be most useful for our purpose. We do not intend to provide another detailed word study of παράκλητος,[2] nor to write a history of spirit–paraclete research.[3]

I. THE PROBLEM AND THE METHOD OF STUDY

Dr Betz begins by defining the problem as follows:

(i) The title ὁ παράκλητος has its roots in the legal sphere. An example of the word in Hellenistic Greek can be found in the second-century A.D. Mimus fragment referred to by A. Deissmann.[4] A paraclete is some sort of *advocate*.

(ii) On the other hand, it is quite clear that the Paraclete of

---

[1] *Der Paraklet. Fürsprecher im häretischen Spätjudentum, im Johannes-Evangelium und in neu gefundenen gnostischen Schriften*, 1963.

[2] For this see the articles by Behm and Schweizer in *T.W.N.T.* and J. G. Davies, 'The Primary Meaning of ΠΑΡΑΚΛΗΤΟΣ', in *J.T.S.* (New Series), IV (1953), 35–8, arguing for an active sense 'comforter' on the basis of the LXX usage of the *verb* παρακαλεῖν and its connexion with the themes of *glory*, *peace*, *joy* and *sorrow*, *river* and *water*, and (it is said) *spirit*: but of course precisely *not* with '*the spirit of truth*'! This thesis therefore cannot be accepted, though the stress on the 'comforter' idea is sound so far as it goes.

[3] Betz, *Der Paraklet*, pp. 4–35, offers a brief history. Apparently, he knew little of British and American literature on the subject. Hence I should like to list *honoris causa* the following: James Denney, 'Holy Spirit', *H.D.C.G.* (1906), I, 731–44; James Hastings, 'Paraclete', *H.D.B.* (1900), III, 665–8; A. J. Macdonald, *The Interpreter Spirit and Human Life* (1944); T. Rees, *The Holy Spirit* (1915; with useful bibliography); H. W. Robinson, *The Christian Experience of the Holy Spirit* (1928); E. F. Scott, *The Spirit in the New Testament* (n.d. [1923]); G. B. Stevens, *Johannine Theology* (1894); H. B. Swete, 'Holy Spirit', *H.D.B.* (1899), II, 402–11; idem, *The Holy Spirit in the New Testament* (1909); E. W. Winstanley, *Spirit in the New Testament* (1908); I. F. Wood, *The Spirit of God in Biblical Literature* (1904).

[4] *Licht vom Osten* (1908), pp. 285–6.

the Farewell Discourses in John does not perform a legal office corresponding to his title. Certainly he is a speaker, but he is not an intercessor. Rather, he is a prophetic teacher who verifies and completes Jesus' revelation. Only in the difficult passage 16: 8–11 is any suggestion of a lawsuit found. But there the Paraclete is not the advocate for the disciples. He is a prosecuting counsel, listing the charges against the *cosmos* at the judgment seat of God and securing a conviction.

(iii) Note the *nature* of this Paraclete: (*a*) he is a *person*, the successor to Jesus, the first paraclete (John 14: 16; cf. 1 John 2: 1); (*b*) the paraclete is also a *heavenly power*, and it is implied that this is *impersonal*, for πνεῦμα is neuter.

Betz points therefore to the way in which John's descriptions 'seesaw' between the personal and the impersonal: the Paraclete is to be *with* the disciples or *in* them; he is to *abide* with them (14: 16 f.). He is sent as the *envoy* or *apostle* of God (14: 26; 15: 26; 16: 7). On the other hand, as power it is *given and received* (14: 16 f.). In the account of the event which is to be regarded as the fulfilment of the paraclete promises it is *breathed into* the disciples, for they are now to work as apostles (20: 21 f.).

(iv) Finally, it may be asked whether the 'other Paraclete' is really necessary, since Jesus announces that he himself will soon come back. Was H. Windisch perhaps correct in calling the spirit–paraclete a *donum superadditum*? (14: 3, 18 f., 23; 16: 16, 22).

Before proceeding farther, some comments must be made on this presentation of the issues. Item (iv) may be ignored, for we have already dealt with the theory that the spirit–paraclete sayings are interpolations, and the relation of Jesus' return to the coming of the spirit will have to be discussed later.

Objection must first be made to the assumption without further ado that in John 'paraclete' is the title of a person and that it is proper to speak about 'the Paraclete'. The present book intends to challenge this assumption, which is widespread; and the rest of this section will be relevant to the point.

Assuming this, Betz simply goes on to assess the views of W. Bauer (who was impressed by parallels in Philo and the Hermetic literature, but chiefly by those in the Mandaean texts); C. H. Dodd (who is anti-Mandaean and thinks of the paraclete as 'Christ prolonged'); and C. K. Barrett (who defines the paraclete as 'the Spirit of the Apostolic proclamation' of the

Gospel during 'the eschatological continuum' between the beginning and the ultimate fulfilment of Christ's revelation). These three scholars, in Betz's view, take the paraclete title too lightly. 'The Paraclete has got swallowed up in teaching about the spirit.'[1]

After a short review of G. Bornkamm's essay[2] in the 1949 *Festschrift* for R. Bultmann, Betz himself jumps at once into the material from the Dead Sea Scrolls, although it is admitted that still no proved Hebrew or Aramaic equivalent for παράκλητος can be produced from the Scrolls or from the intertestamental literature.

What justifies Betz's concentration on the Qumrân documents?

(*a*) He cannot accept the views of Rudolf Bultmann on the Mandaean parallels (see below). He does agree that the concept of the paraclete is mythological, and originally it was non-Christian.

(*b*) He follows the lead of S. Mowinckel and N. Johannson in looking for the most fruitful sources of the paraclete idea in the literature of early Judaism, especially the apocalypses, for it abounds in advocate-intercessor language.[3]

(*c*) He takes it for granted that the Dead Sea Scrolls are pre-Johannine.

(*d*) He notes the appearance in those Scrolls of 'the spirit of truth', and this makes up for the absence of 'paraclete'. 'Es handelt sich dabei vor allem um die am Toten Meer gefundenen Qumranschriften, in dener zwar nicht der Titel, "Paraklet", jedoch der Name "Geist der Wahrheit" vorkommt.'[4]

It must surely be said that this methodology is highly

---

[1] *Der Paraklet*, p. 25. See W. Bauer, *Das Johannesevangelium* (3rd ed. 1933), pp. 182 ff.; C. H. Dodd, *Interpretation*, pp. 124 f., 223 f., 414; C. K. Barrett, *John*, pp. 75–7, 385 f.

[2] 'Der Paraklet im Johannesevangelium.'

[3] See e.g. Job 5: 1; Tobit 12: 12, 15; Test. Levi 3: 5; 5: 6 f.; 1 Enoch 9: 3; 1QS 2: 9. We may add that angelic intercession is possible in 1QS 2: 9, 'May no intercessor plead for thy welfare' (E. F. Sutcliffe, *The Monks of Qumran*, London, 1960, p. 156). Possible Accadian and Aramaic background is discussed by Wernberg-Møller, *Vetus Testamentum*, III (1953), 196 f. and *The Manual of Discipline*, p. 53. (For a different kind of parallel, the *tumu* of Easter Island, see Thor Heyerdahl, *Aku-Aku*, p. 293.)

[4] *Der Paraklet*, p. 3. He discusses the Qumrân material on pp. 36 ff.

questionable, for the ground has not been laid by careful study of primitive Christian pneumatology and in particular of the Johannine documents themselves. Our own investigations into the Fourth Gospel suggest that the spirit–paraclete passages must not be isolated from John's Christology, and quite certainly not from everything he has to say about 'spirit'.

It is not even certain that the Qumrân scrolls are to be dated prior to John, although in our judgment it is probable.[1]

It is also dubious procedure for Betz, in spite of his recognition that most of the paraclete's work according to John is simply not forensic at all, to move on in Part B of his book to an elaborate investigation of precisely the *legal* character of Jewish thought as it is seen in Qumrânian and other pre-Christian literature!

The basic justification offered is the contention that ὁ παράκλητος is a legal term and title and so we must first disregard the non-forensic elements in the Johannine picture and try to discover a source for an advocate-intercessor who is active both in heaven and on earth.

Is this not swallowing up in a forensic paraclete the vast preponderance of John's evidence for a *teacher, interpreter, prophetic and prosecuting counsel?*

We must start with the Johannine material itself. What is then disclosed?

The only ground for holding that the members of the Johannine Church thought of Jesus, the risen Lord, as the 'first paraclete' is the phrase 'another paraclete' in John 14: 16. Did they perhaps think of him as a heavenly High Priest, a fulfiller of the Elijah expectation, just as the author of Hebrews did? (and cf. Rom. 8: 34, Christ 'intercedes for us', following 8: 27, 'the spirit intercedes for the saints').[2] If so, such a concept is not necessarily forensic. It may also be questioned whether 1 John 2: 1, 'we have an advocate with the Father, Jesus Christ the Just One', is to be understood wholly in a legal meaning. For in 1 John sin is an uncleanness (1: 7) that requires expiation or propitiation (2: 2). Virtue is more than

---

[1] For another view see Sir G. R. Driver, *The Judaean Scrolls*, who assigns dates as follows: 1QS, A.D. 46–66; 1QpHab., A.D. 70–3; 1QH, A.D. 73–5; 1QM, A.D. 100–15; and CD, A.D. 125–30.

[2] Cf. Philo, *Vit. Mos.* II, 134.

obedience, since it is firmly settled on rebirth as children of God (3: 1, 9; 4: 7; 5: 1, 4).[1]

Next, in the Supper discourses there are four instances of *paraclete*, and three of *spirit of truth*.[2] These all belong within a Gospel that employs *spirit* in the meanings considered above in Part 1: six times, *power* or *force* is the primary sense (1: 32 f.; 3: 5–7, 34; 6: 63; 7: 39; 20: 22). God is the giver according to 3: 34; while in 20: 22 the vital power is the breath of the living Lord. When we remember these, as well as the 'God is spirit' of 4: 24, we realize that the spirit cannot be described by the modern word 'impersonal'.

The facts lead one to believe that *spirit*, *spirit of God*, or even *holy spirit*, were far more familiar and much more important than *paraclete* in Greek or in its Semitic equivalent (if it had any). *Spirit* is intimately associated with *God's* creative, providential and redemptive activity; whereas *paraclete* merely denotes a particular kind of *functionary*.

Just as 1 John encourages sinners by reminding them that Jesus Christ *acts as their heavenly paraclete*, so the Gospel tells disciples that 'the spirit of truth' *acts as their paraclete* because it resides within the Church, and does so in the time of Jesus' absence.

The conclusion seems to be inescapable that '*the paraclete*' *is secondary to* '*the spirit of truth*'.

This can be tested in 14: 16 f. where John writes ἄλλον παράκλητον. He does not write τὸν ἕτερον παράκλητον, as if Christian readers would at once exclaim with glad recognition, 'Of course, the *second* Paraclete!' It is probably incorrect to translate here: 'and he will give to you Another as your paraclete'. Nevertheless, prolonged examination of John compels the present writer to take these words to mean: 'and he will give to you as another paraclete...the spirit of truth'.

Thus ἄλλον παράκλητον are adjectival to τὸ πνεῦμα τῆς ἀληθείας.[3]

It follows that paraclete in 14: 26; 15: 26 and 16: 7 has in Greek the definite article, not because 'the Paraclete' is a title for a personal Figure, but for good grammatical reasons: the

---

[1] Legal ideas are to be found in 1 John 3: 4 and 5: 2.
[2] We omit 'the holy spirit' from 14: 26 on textual grounds.
[3] Cf. Behm in *T.W.N.T.* v, 799, n. 1.

article is a virtual demonstrative, and the reference is to the preceding 'another paraclete'. The same consideration applies to the use of ἐκεῖνος. This pronoun does not turn the spirit–paraclete into a second heavenly ambassador, or a manifest teacher, or another revealer who is the Successor to Jesus.[1] If 20: 22 be truly the fulfilment of the paraclete promises, we should have to identify this Successor as Christ's own Breath! It cannot be said too firmly that *no satisfactory elucidation is forthcoming in that way.*

Let us now look more closely at the functions to be performed by the spirit–paraclete.

Betz is correct in stating that most of them are non-forensic.

To 16: 8–11, however, we may add the witnessing of 15: 26, because the immediate context is the hostility of the world. So the spirit as paraclete bears a testimony concerning Jesus before the world that hated him and killed him. And yet one cannot be sure that the Evangelist intended this witness theme to be only or primarily legal. For testimony is given by preaching the Gospel and by writing a Gospel-book, as well as by giving evidence in some court of law.

In any case, both witness and prosecution raise very interesting questions. For example, at what judgment will such functions be performed by the spirit–paraclete? The Last Judgment is ruled out, probably, because these functions are said to be done '*when he comes*' or '*when it comes*'; not at some distant future on the Last Day.[2] There is a profound sense in which the Devil has

---

[1] Cf. 12: 48, ὁ λόγος ὃν ἐλάλησα ἐκεῖνος κρινεῖ κτλ. This does not imply that Jesus' *word* has now become an autonomous Person! No more is the paraclete.

[2] C. H. Dodd, *Interpretation*, p. 414, seems to miss the force of ἐλθὼν ἐκεῖνος ἐλέγξει κτλ., which describes what the spirit–paraclete will begin to do once Jesus returns to the Father and God sends or Christ sends it. Dodd notes the parallel to 9: 35–41 and writes: 'Thus the coming of Christ after his death, which for the disciples means the attainment of eternal life, means for the world the Last Judgment. As this coming is mediated for them by the Spirit, so the Last Judgment also is mediated by the Spirit.' But, however true it is that Jesus' life, death and resurrection constituted a judgment on the world, John had survived two generations of ups and downs. The Devil had not ceased to be a troubler (8: 44; 12: 31; 17: 11–18). John's adventism and his concept of a Last Day should not be forgotten because of his stress on present life and a continuing process of judgment (cf. 3: 19; 12: 48).

been condemned already, before the time of the spirit–paraclete in the Church (16: 11), and the fact is to be made known through the Church so long as it endures.

The legal functions are thus performed in time and on earth, yet no such visible figure as the spirit–paraclete is to be seen. What men see are the disciples.[1]

Are we perhaps faced with an example of the Semitic genius for personification? is this spirit–paraclete simply a name for the Community of witnessing disciples and a symbol for the supernatural power at work in them? The answers must be in the negative, because the power is 'supernatural'; that is, it truly (in the belief of John and his Church) proceeds from the Living God. John is speaking about the Presence of God in the Christian Church.

At this point it will be well to set out concisely the other non-forensic functions:

A 14: 16–17: PRESENCE

After Jesus' departure the spirit of truth will come to help the faithful and to represent their Lord. For the presence of the spirit–paraclete makes up for the absence of Christ.

B 14: 26; 16: 13, 15: COMMUNICATION

Five different verbs explain what is to take place: there will be a ministry of *teaching*, *reminding*, *guiding* into all truth, *speaking*, and *announcing*. Each of these, we noted in Part I, is related to the Christ, for there is no new ministry of revelation.

C 16: 14: DOXOLOGY

The spirit of truth will glorify Jesus Christ. In this saying all the others are clarified. It is not by measure that God 'gives the spirit' to the Logos incarnate (3: 34; cf. 5: 20–3). 'All that the Father has is mine' (16: 15). These tremendous claims do not assert that the Son is the Father, nor that the Christ is God (ὁ θεός). But they do insist that spiritual powers and influence flow from God and from the risen Christ into the Church (14: 16, 26; 15: 26). Jesus has not come in his own name, to

---

[1] So Barrett, correctly, *John*, p. 406.

seek honour at the hands of men (5: 41, 43). Yet the same Jesus can say, 'I and the Father are one' (10: 30).

So the words that unfold the wealth of Johannine teaching about the spirit of truth and the paraclete are *comforter, interpreter* or exegete, *teacher, prophet, legal counsel*: and the right method of study is to begin from them, not from any non-Christian etymology and not with the non-Johannine use of paraclete in its Greek or Hebrew form.

It follows too that the distinction between the paraclete as a person and the spirit as a power or force seriously distorts the issues from the beginning.[1] Would 'personal' and 'impersonal' have been intelligible to the primitive Christian mind?

Raymond E. Brown is correct when he says that the attempt to apply impersonal concepts to the spirit and personal ones to the paraclete 'is a bad over-simplification'.[2] Brown points to the development in pneumatology from 'the aspect of a God-given prophetic force or impetus' to a more personal concept (e.g. in 1 Cor. 12: 11; Rom. 8: 16), and asserts that John's use of 'the masculine title παράκλητος and...masculine personal pronouns...was making more specific an attitude that already existed'. He also notes that 'Jesus, who is clearly a person, is also given (iii. 16) and received (v. 43), without the slightest loss of personality'.

Our first thesis then is this: *the proper starting-point is exegesis of the Johannine texts.* And on this basis we can formulate a working definition that may act as a principle of criticism: *the spirit of truth, as paraclete, acts on behalf of Christ and for the advantage of the disciples. The most useful word in English to cover all the meanings of the Greek* παράκλητος *is the word 'representative'.*

We are now ready to consider some of the chief contributions made to our subject in recent times.

[1] Betz, *Der Paraklet*, pp. 159–64, deals with the evidence more fully.

[2] 'The Paraclete in the Fourth Gospel', *N.T.S.* xiii, No. 2 (Jan. 1967), 124. See also my earlier article 'Spirit' in *A Theological Word Book of the Bible*, ed. A. Richardson, p. 245.

II. THE PARACLETE AS A REVEALER:
R. BULTMANN'S VIEW

In his massive and justly renowned commentary on the Gospel of John, Rudolf Bultmann argues that the Paraclete is neither an intercessor nor a comforter. This is true enough if either be proposed as in itself an adequate translation of παράκλητος in all its Johannine meanings. It is to be noticed at the outset that Bultmann assumes that we can speak about the Paraclete as some sort of Personage.

He will have nothing to do with Mowinckel's attempt to derive understanding from certain texts in Job and the Testament of Judah, and thus to see behind the use of 'paraclete' an angelic mediator. For Dr Bultmann, recourse to Jewish sources is useless.

The alternative that he offers is Gnosticism, and in particular the Mandaean concept of the *Jawar* or *Jawar-Ziwa*, a *helper* of men. According to Bultmann, Jesus and the Paraclete are presented in John under gnostic terminology: both are Revealers.[1]

We must begin the discussion with Bultmann, therefore, by asking if this is a correct presentation of the evidence.

(1) In John 14: 17 the 'other paraclete' is quite simply identified as 'the spirit of truth' with no further definition of what either expression means. The readers of the Gospel, like the disciples who are addressed, are supposed to know.

Some assistance is to be had, as we have suggested above, from 1 John 4: 1–6: this paraclete is from God, it inspires true prophets, it compels Christians to make the confession that Jesus was the Christ who did come in the flesh. Hence it might be argued that as spirit of truth the paraclete is an agency that promotes the orthodoxy of a definitive revelation in Jesus.

There would seem to be nothing here, however, to indicate a gnostic-type of one who reveals the secrets of God to a select few. The divine commission of Jesus of Nazareth as 'a man anointed with holy spirit and power' (Acts 10: 38) was in so

[1] R. Bultmann, *Das Evangelium des Johannes*, pp. 424–39. See too the valuable remarks in W. A. Meeks, *The Prophet-King: Moses Traditions and the Johannine Christology*, pp. 258 ff. On the Mandaeans, K. Rudolph, *Die Mandäer* (1960).

many words the public proclamation of the Church from the start of its mission. From the standpoint of the author of 1 John, the spirit might be described as 'the true spirit', because it bears witness to a revelation already made. And there are good grounds for finding a similar attitude in the Evangelist (see e.g. John 6: 25 ff.).

To call the paraclete of John 14: 16 f. a Revealer seems to underplay and misunderstand the binding nature of the tie that associates it with the historic Jesus.[1]

The first Gospel text further excludes any thought of the paraclete's being a revealer to the world of unbelieving men and women (cf. 14: 22–4). But what is revelation if there is no unveiling to those who do not know or refuse to believe? The paraclete is in some sense a helper of those who are already the disciples of Jesus, although it must be admitted that John is not entirely clear about the stages of faith and knowledge in the case of Andrew, Simon Peter, Thomas and their fellows. There seem to be certain elements in the truth about Jesus that had to remain unknown or unclear until after the Crucifixion (in spite of 6: 68 f.). Full disclosure is attributed to the interpreter-spirit which is also the remembrancer-spirit, and functions in these ways as 'another paraclete'.

(2) This becomes specific at 14: 26. For this paraclete is sent in the Name of Jesus Christ, that is, with his *imprimatur* and in dependence on him. 'All the words spoken by Jesus' thus form the reservoir out of which the spirit–paraclete draws.

Surely this points not to 'revelation' but to 'exegesis'?

(3) It is not otherwise with the witness to Jesus (περὶ ἐμοῦ) of 15: 26.

If its application is not to a court of jurisdiction like Pliny the Younger's, one may think of a procession of biblical witnesses, including John the Baptist (1: 7 f., 19, 29 ff.; 3: 27–30; 5: 33–5), Isaiah (12: 38, 41), Moses (5: 45–7) and all the way back to Father Abraham (8: 56).[2] Every one of these plays such a rôle because he is an instrument of God himself; for 'the Father himself has given witness to me' (5: 37). Even Caiaphas, God's

---

[1] By 'historic' is meant that Jesus is an historical figure like others, e.g. Caesar or Captain Cook; but also that he is like these two men, only in superlative degree, in that after him things in history could never be the same again. [2] See above, p. 32.

supposed High Priest, in an irony of divine election, is allowed to make a true prediction about Jesus' sacrifice and so become a witness (11: 49–51).

This is not how one expects a gnostic revelation of deep mysteries to take place.

(4) How can anyone miss the connexion between the saying of Jesus, 'sorrow has filled your hearts', and the manifold promise of what the spirit—paraclete will accomplish vis-à-vis the world? This is *consolation*: and therefore one cannot deny to this presence the happy word *Comforter*. With this may be compared 14: 17, where an assurance is given to the disciples in the same situation (13: 33; 14: 1) that this paraclete will never leave them nor forsake them. Nothing less could be expected from the God Jesus revealed as *Abba*. Nothing less was the urgent necessity of a disciple's life.

It may reasonably be doubted that all this was said to the disciples that last evening in the Supper Room, or that they could have accepted it. What cannot be denied, however, is that this is *the promise of a Comforter*.

(5) When we turn to the charge-sheet of 16: 8–11, we see that *sin* is related to a religious profession of belief, and *righteousness* to a verdict about the historic Jesus. Did he or did he not enter human life as the divine Son who fulfils the Messianic hopes of Jews and Samaritans (1: 41, 49; 4: 25 f.; 18: 37; 19: 21 f.)? Did he or did he not win a strange triumph by welcoming his death-destiny (10: 17 f.), so that for him the road to the Roman cross was also the way to God his Father and to everlasting glory?

Similarly, the *condemnation of the Devil*, 'the ruler of this world', is to be connected with the emancipation proclaimed at 8: 34–6. Several questions have to be faced: Are men and women indeed set free because of their belief in Jesus as the Christ, the Son of God (20: 31), the saviour of the world (4: 42)? Has the disappearance of Jesus the significance of his return to the Father, which is a principal affirmation of the Church's faith in his Resurrection? and if so, has it not also the character of the condemnation of evil and the Evil One? (Cf. 1 Cor. 15: 54–7; Heb. 2: 14 f.)

According to Johannine theology, affirmative answers to such questions do not exclude what may be called 'revelation'. No one can come to Jesus as the Christ or Lamb or Son 'unless the Father draw him' (6: 44). As we have noted, there is to the act and submission of belief a considerable mystery, and so to any statement of the Gospel that somehow enables it to find other people through the witness of the apostles or that of their evangelical successors. One cannot quarrel with the claim that the paraclete sent by the Father or the Son has to do with 'mystery and meaning'; but is the gnostic view of revelation merely a matter of communicating the meaning of a mystery?

(6) A similar line of argument must be followed in the view one takes of 16: 13, 'the spirit of truth will guide you into all truth...and will declare to you the things that are to come'.

The former function (guidance into truth) belongs to the *exegete* or *teacher*, the latter to the *prophet*, one who casts light on future events. It may be unwise to emphasize unduly any predictive ministry, because the truth is in Jesus (cf. 14: 6) and the entire business of the spirit–paraclete is to glorify the Christ.[1] We are back to the concept of an agency that promotes orthodoxy. *All future revelations*, one may say, *are keyed to a past incarnation*.

There are additional arguments against Bultmann's general disposition to relate John's Gospel to Gnosticism which need not be listed here.[2] Otto Betz devotes some space to criticisms made by W. Michaelis in his 1947 article, 'Zur Herkunft des johanneischen Paraklet-Titels', in *Coniectanea Neotestamentica*, Uppsala, pp. 147–62.[3] Behm too in the *T.W.N.T.* is critical. All these are succinctly summarized for us by Raymond E. Brown[4] as follows:

(1) There are not in John a large number of heavenly revealers as there are in Mandaean thought; there are at most two: Jesus himself, who is departing, and the Spirit of Truth, who remains with the disciples (xiv. 17). (2) The Mandaean revealers are simultaneous, not in tandem as Jesus and the Paraclete are. (3) The Mandaean revealers do not present a forensic aspect in the same way that the Johannine Paraclete does. (4) The Mandaean 'Yawar'

[1] See below, pp. 137–41.
[2] See C. H. Dodd, *Interpretation*, pp. 97–130; R. McL. Wilson, *Gnosis and the New Testament*, pp. 34 f., 45–8.
[3] O. Betz, *Der Paraklet*, pp. 28–30.
[4] *N.T.S.* xiii, No. 2 (Jan. 1967), 119 f.

occurs as a name for a particular revealer, frequently in the combination Yawar Ziwa. To describe the other helpers different words are used. Thus the case for Yawar as an equivalent for the *title* Paraclete is not clear at all. Moreover, one must insist that παράκλητος does not primarily or obviously mean 'helper' or 'friend' in Greek: βοηθός would have been a much more natural translation of a term meaning 'helper'. (5) To these objections may be added the contention of Lady Drower[1] that Yawar does not mean 'helper' at all but 'one who glows', so that Yawar Ziwa would be the 'Glower of Heavenly Light'. Her derivation is not without philological difficulty, but one very important factor favours her theory: the Mandaeans glorified Yawar Ziwa as a figure of heavenly light.

The case against a gnostic or Mandaean explanation must therefore be rated as extremely strong.

One may retort to Bultmann that recourse to Mandaean sources is simply useless.

III. THE SPIRIT–PARACLETE AS THE ALTER EGO OF JESUS CHRIST:
R. E. BROWN AND THE BRITISH SCHOOL

There is a view of the relationship between the spirit (or Holy Spirit or Spirit of God) to Jesus Christ in the Gospel of John that has long been influential among British scholars. Recently it seems to have attracted Professor Raymond E. Brown to its support.

Briefly, it is to the effect that the risen Christ comes back to his disciples and is ever present to them as the spirit or through the spirit.[2] So it is not surprising that E. F. Scott held that the spirit is tautological in Johannine thought and is a mere accommodation to traditional theology.[3] Does this do justice, one

---

[1] ' *The Secret Adam* (Oxford, 1960), pp. 62–3. Also *The Canonical Prayer Book of the Mandaeans*, pp. 252–3. She takes יאואר as a peal participle active of the root יור (cf. Hebrew אור).' [In addition, cf. W. A. Meeks, *The Prophet-King*, pp. 264–6.]

[2] Parallels with Matt. 28: 19 f.; 1 Cor. 15: 45 and 2 Cor. 3: 17 f. come to mind at once. E. Schweizer too thinks that the Spirit is Jesus Christ himself as proclaimed in the Christian community, *Neotestamentica*, p. 178.

[3] *The Fourth Gospel: Its Purpose and Theology*, pp. 345–52; *The Spirit in the New Testament*, pp. 206–8. It is doubtful if C. H. Dodd could subscribe to this, since he regards John as a theologian of Father, Son and Paraclete

must ask, to the relationship of the spirit to God the Father according to John 3: 34; 14: 16, 26; 15: 26? or to the communion that is to be enjoyed with the Father as well as the Son (14: 23)? Why not go the next logical step and identify the Father and the Son?

There is no doubt, however, that the theory expresses well the intimate nature of the spirit's relationship to Jesus, and it is this that has recommended it to Brown.[1] He is not uncritical of certain forms that it takes, quoting specifically the statement by Ian Simpson 'that those passages in John that reflect distinction between Jesus and the Paraclete are merely John's way of saying that the Paraclete is Jesus present in another form'.[2] Here too much violence is done, says Brown, to the Johannine presentation, for 'the patent thrust of the Paraclete passages is that the Paraclete and the risen Jesus have distinct rôles in that Jesus will be above with the Father while the Paraclete continues the work on earth'.

What has impressed Brown is the almost exact correspondence between what John says about Jesus and what he says about the Paraclete:

(a) Jesus has *come* into the world (5: 43; 16: 28; 18: 37). He *came forth* (ἐξέρχεσθαι) from the Father; and the Paraclete does so too (only, the verb is ἐκπορεύεσθαι). The Father *gave* the Son (3: 16). Jesus *was sent* by the Father (3: 17 and *passim*). As the Paraclete is to be sent in the Name of Jesus, so Jesus came *in the Name of his Father* (5: 43). 'In many ways the Paraclete is to Jesus as Jesus is to the Father.'

It is not necessary to list the Paraclete references.

(b) Jesus is the *first Paraclete* (14: 17; 1 John 2: 1). Brown infers that he acted in this capacity during his earthly ministry, because the exactly parallel ministry of the second Paraclete will be accomplished on earth.[3]

(*Interpretation*, p. 226). Hence Betz errs in ascribing to Dodd the idea that the spirit–paraclete is 'der Christus prolongatus' (*Der Paraklet*, p. 24). The spirit rather takes the place of Jesus and is in fact another advocate.

[1] *N.T.S.* XIII, No. 2 (Jan. 1967), 126–8.

[2] 'The Holy Spirit in the Fourth Gospel', *The Expositor*, 9th series, IV (1925), 292–9.

[3] *Loc. cit.* p. 127, n. 1, arguing against M. Miguéns, *El Paráclito*, p. 158 n., whose position is that Jesus is a Paraclete in heaven after the Resurrection. Cf. Dodd, *Interpretation*, p. 414.

Jesus is the truth (14: 6), as the Paraclete is the Spirit of Truth. He is the Holy One of God (6: 69), as the Paraclete is the Holy Spirit (accepting this reading in 14: 26). Hence the Holy Spirit in John, as in the New Testament generally, is the Spirit of Jesus: it rested on him as he began his ministry (1: 32) and he breathed it forth at its close (20: 22; 'perhaps 19: 30', adds Brown).

(*c*) It is a special privilege for the disciples to *know* and *recognize* Jesus (14: 7, 9). Jesus remains *in* and *with* his disciples, making his dwelling with them (14: 20; 17: 23, 26; 15: 4 f.; 14: 23). He taught those who would listen (6: 59; 7: 14, 28; 8: 20). He is the *way* and the truth (14: 6; cf. 16: 13, 'the Paraclete will *guide* the disciples *along the way* of all truth'). Jesus as the Messiah *announces* or *reveals* all things (4: 25 f.). He bore witness (8: 14, i.e. *to himself*, for he knows the secret of his coming and going). Jesus did *not* speak *on his own authority* (8: 28, and *passim*); he *glorified* the Father (12: 27 f.; 14: 13; 17: 4), as the Paraclete will glorify him.

(*d*) The *world* of evil men did not *accept* Jesus (5: 43; cf. 12: 48). It will soon *cease to see* him (16: 16; although he was visible during the public ministry, and the Paraclete will *not* so be visible). Men do not *know* nor *recognize* Jesus (16: 3; cf. 7: 28; 8: 14, 19; 14: 7). Jesus bore *witness against the world* (7: 7).

'The Paraclete will prove the world wrong concerning the trial of Jesus, a trial that colours John's whole portrait of the ministry of Jesus' (*loc. cit.* p. 127).

Prof. Brown cannot regard such parallelism as coincidental, and he is perfectly correct. His conclusion is that 'as "another Paraclete" the Paraclete is, as it were, another Jesus...and the Paraclete is *the presence of Jesus when Jesus is absent*' (my italics): and so is fulfilled Jesus' promise to dwell with the disciples. In a footnote (p. 128, n. 2) the reservation is made 'that, even in this final form of Johannine thought, some of Jesus' words about his return to his disciples may refer to his coming at the end of time, because a belief in the return of Jesus in and through the Paraclete and a belief in the parousia seem to have coexisted in Johannine thought'.

This is an impressive statement, and with much of it one cannot disagree.

But (i) there is constant reference to the spirit–paraclete as if

94

it were a figure comparable to Jesus in all respects except that on earth it is invisible!

(ii) On p. 123 of the article cited Brown concludes his summary of research into the Jewish background by accepting the idea that in the Johannine picture there are two 'salvific figures'. Jesus and the Paraclete are harnessed 'in tandem' like Moses and Joshua or Elijah and Elisha. For the chief figure passes on his 'spirit' to a Successor.[1]

But Jesus did not pass on his spirit to a Successor. There is not one word of such a suggestion in John. The only conceivable parallel to the OT predecessors would have been a succession of James the Great to Jesus; or of Peter; or of Paul. Nothing of this appears in the Fourth Gospel.

A better parallel would have been Moses sharing his spirit with the seventy elders (Num. 11: 16 ff.).

It is part of the paraclete's function, as we observed in Part I, to demonstrate that there is one only Saviour of the world, Jesus the Christ, Son of God, Logos become man. How can such a person have a Successor? John rather seems to be concerned to prove that he has successors, and that they are bound by divine necessity to witness to his sufficiency. The possibility of any other mediators of salvation is ruled out by the doctrine of Incarnation.[2]

It was no fantastic, inconceivable possibility that another claimant might arise to dispute the pre-eminent place of Jesus Christ. Less than a century later, the charismatic Montanus seems to have asserted that the Paraclete, the Holy Spirit of God, had become incarnate in himself; John's great promises were fulfilled, and the end of the ages would take place very soon.[3]

Hence in our judgment our attention must be given, not to a Successor however invisible, but to the apostolic Church to which promises of divine power were made.

There is thus an admitted parallel between the spirit that animated Jesus of Nazareth to do the Father's will, and the

---

[1] Fr Brown has informed me that for him the tandem idea 'means one comes after the other, but not as a second revealer'.

[2] Cf. Col. 2: 18 f.; 1 Tim. 2: 5; Heb. 7: 27 f.; 9: 12, 15, 26; 10: 10; 1 Pet. 3: 18 ('once and for all').

[3] The prophecies of Montanus have been collected in P. de Labriolle, *La Crise montaniste* (Paris, 1913).

spirit–paraclete that is to be given to the disciples. The Church cannot displace or replace Jesus; and yet it can perform 'greater works'. The Church is the visible community that continues the ministry and mission of Jesus to the world, by proclaiming his name and function, by discovering within its own life the measure of his love, wisdom and grace. So the succession theme is to be defined in terms of God's spirit at work in and through the Church.

IV. LIGHT FROM THE JEWISH BACKGROUND:
A. S. MOWINCKEL AND N. JOHANNSON

The examination of the Jewish background of the Fourth Gospel has proved most fruitful during the past forty years, and it has to be studied under two periods: before and after the discovery of the Qumrân scrolls. We begin therefore with the first period, which is dominated by the names of Sigmund Mowinckel and Nils Johannson. At this point we are following the lead of Otto Betz, who has to consider these two scholars carefully: they are his own immediate predecessors.[1]

Instead of seeking illumination on the paraclete problem from literary criticism or from Philo, Josephus and rabbinic literature, Mowinckel turned to the Old Testament and in particular to the apocalypticism of the intertestamental era.[2]

There he found the primary clue in the מֵלִיץ (mēlits) concept in Job: 'Even now, behold, my witness is in heaven, and he that vouches for me is on high' (16: 19); 'I know that my vindicator lives' (19: 25); 'If there be for him an angel, a mediator, one of the thousand, to declare to man what is right for him...Then man prays to God, and he accepts him...' (33: 23, 26).

Here the Scandinavian scholar found the angelic intercessor, a 'spirit', an idea that had entered Judaism from Babylonian and Persian sources. Further evidence to link this to the holy spirit of God was seen in '*the spirit of truth*' of Test. of Judah 20 (quoted earlier) and in the way *wisdom* is related to the spirit in Wisd. Sol. 1: 7–9.

---

[1] *Der Paraklet*, pp. 14–22.

[2] 'Die Vorstellung des Spätjudentums vom heiligen Geist als Fürsprecher und der johanneische Paraklet', *Z.N.T.W.* xxxii (1933), 97–130.

The paraclete sayings in John, according to Mowinckel, go well beyond the comparable words in Mark 13: 11 and its Synoptic parallels; and beyond Rom. 8: 26. For in John the spirit–paraclete is an inspiring and revealing Power which is active in the apostolic preaching.

Johannson accepted this thesis and proceeded to widen the range of the investigation.[1]

In the Old Testament, for example, the function of intercession is exercised by Abraham, Moses,[2] Samuel and various prophets. Moreover there is evidence for heavenly intercessors in passages like Zech. 1: 12; 3: 1–7. Johannson wishes to see the Servant of the Lord in Isaiah as a representative of the people of Israel; he pleads for the nation, and acts as its guide and witness. Hence the Servant, according to Johannson, is a figure rather like Job's angel mediator.

In early Judaism there is still more evidence for regarding the patriarchs, Moses and the angels, including the great angel Michael, as intercessors. There the spirit of God or the spirit of truth may accuse men (Wisd. Sol. 1: 6–8; Test. of Judah 20) or lead them in the right way (Wisd. Sol. 7: 27 f.; 9: 17 f.; Test. of Levi 2: 3 f.; Ps. 143: 10).

Special attention should be paid, Johannson believed, to the Enoch literature, where the Enoch–Son of Man is a character of many parts: a revealer of secrets, a guide, a witness, a judge, a mediator, and a defender (סָנֵיגוֹר).[3] Rabbinic material in support of this is cited from Paul Billerbeck: in it one should note references to Elijah and Phineas as heavenly high priests.[4]

Johannson observed that the Targum on Job translated מֵלִיץ by the Greek loan-word 'paraclete' (פְּרַקְלֵיטָא) and so he was prepared to believe that Jesus himself might have uttered the spirit–paraclete sayings, using the loan-word פרקליטא, through which he could express the substance of his own missionary self-awareness.

---

[1] *Parakletoi* (Lund, 1940).

[2] The Moses traditions have been studied more recently in W. A. Meeks, *The Prophet-King*, pp. 118, 137, 159–61, 174, 200–4, 254 f.

[3] Bultmann too notes the use of סניגור in relation to the spirit in *Lev. R.* 6 (109a); *Midr. Cant.* 8, 9 f. (132b); cf. Strack–Billerbeck, *K.T.M.* II, 562; Meeks, *The Prophet-King*, pp. 201 f.

[4] Strack–Billerbeck, *K.T.M.* III, 696, 812; IV, 457 ff., 789 ff. Cf. J. Jeremias in Kittel–Friedrich, *T.W.N.T.* II, 934 f.

The criticisms which Betz makes of Johannson's work are acute: e.g. from texts like 1 Sam. 12: 23 he makes the false deduction that guidance necessarily belonged to a ministry of intercession; he was far too ready to interpret Isaiah's Servant along the lines of the angelic mediator in Job; he regards Satan as the court Accuser who degenerated into being God's enemy, despite rabbinic evidence;[1] he neglected the book of Jubilees. Finally, says Betz,

(1) Johannson's détour into rabbinic literature caused him to lose sight of two important elements in apocalypticism, dualism and the eschatological expectation.

(2) It is to encumber unduly the Intercessor's function to bind it as closely as Johannson did to the idea of guidance and to the sacrificial cult.

(3) There is too much insistence on the intercessor ideas; probably Johannson had a weak case to argue.

(4) Betz simply cannot agree that in the New Testament the office of the Intercessor was tied to a single historic person, by no means mythical; or that this must therefore be regarded as precisely and in the highest degree God's proper work.

Betz is much less severe on Mowinckel, because he holds that it was he who pointed to the most significant source for the Johannine Paraclete and so he came very close to the correct solution. There are said to be three basic flaws in Mowinckel's case:

(a) None of the examples brought forward really shows that the Holy Spirit was known as Paraclete. This was inferred only by combining some quite heterogeneous citations. Mowinckel was so overjoyed by his discovery that he was unwilling to face up to the difficulties. (Yet Betz has to admit that Mowinckel did try to correct the impression that the Holy Spirit was actually known as Paraclete.)

(b) Mowinckel simply paid no attention to the dualism in John, and this is fatal.

(c) Above all, he did not see that 'the spirit of truth' and 'the holy spirit' were originally two different realities.

According to Betz,[2] the spirit of truth came out of Iranian dualism, whereas the holy spirit belongs to the monist tradition

---

[1] See Strack–Billerbeck, *K.T.M.* 1, 136–49.
[2] For this point see especially *Der Paraklet*, pp. 165–9.

of the Old Testament. So in the Gospel of John the Holy Spirit is to be regarded as distinct from the Spirit of Truth. John 20:22 means that the disciples are reborn and given power for the new apostolic service of God in a re-creation scene. In that scene the Evangelist saw the fulfilment of the promises to send the Paraclete, for it is the genius of John that he combined the *Person* (Paraclete, probably an angel) with the divine impersonal *power*. The former he took from heretical Judaism, the latter from more conventional biblical traditions.

But that is to anticipate!

My own position is that Dr Betz does not give Mowinckel his due. The identification of מֵלִיץ as the most likely Hebrew prototype for παράκλητος seems to be the greatest contribution made by any scholar in the pre-Qumrân period.

It is therefore surprising that, when Betz comes in his turn to examine the Hebrew terms used in the Qumrân scrolls for witness, interpreter, accuser, and intercessor, he finds there this very word מֵלִיץ in 1QH 2: 13, 31; 4: 7, 9; 6: 13, for the *interpreter* of knowledge or the *teacher*, but rejects it as the *Vorbild* of paraclete, (*a*) because it seems to have no forensic meaning, and Betz must at all costs have a legal term; and (*b*) because an interpreter is not required once the Community of the sons of light has attained to union with the angels (cf. 1QH 6: 13). Neither reason is weighty. The Johannine paraclete, as he has admitted, seldom performs as an advocate but does act as a teacher and interpreter.

I suggest therefore that Mowinckel is to be followed with less reserve, and also that we should mark with much gratitude Johannson's reference to the use of פְּרַקְלֵיטָא for מֵלִיץ in the Targum. For this means that παράκλητος is almost certain to have had wide currency in Greek Judaism as well as in Palestinian Judaism during the first century A.D. and later. The Johannine public, Christian or not, would not be taken wholly by surprise when *the spirit of truth* and the *other paraclete* appeared in the Fourth Gospel or the First Epistle.[1]

---

[1] There is a useful list of examples of παράκλητος in Philo in Bauer's *Dictionary* (E.T. by Arndt and Gingrich): see *adv. Flacc.* 13, 22, 151, 181; *Joseph.* 239; *de. opif. mundi,* 23, 165; *Exsecr.* 166; *Vit. Mos.* II, 134; *Spec. Leg.* I, 237. Usually it means *intercessor.* The technical meaning *lawyer* or *attorney* is rare in Greek. The active sense is notable in view of the formation. It may

The meaning 'interpreter' for מֵלִיץ is supported by fourth-century B.C. Cypriot inscriptions (*C.I.S.* I, 44, 88) and some of the biblical examples.

In Gen. 42: 23 it simply means 'translator' and the LXX uses ἑρμηνευτής; one should not exaggerate the stance of 'go-between' that is implied in בֵּינֹתָם in that text. *Envoys* is the meaning in 2 Chron. 32: 31. More obscure is Isa. 43: 27, where the best rendering is perhaps '*spokesmen*' rather than 'mediators'.[1]

The most illuminating cases, however, are those in Job:
(i) 16: 20: מליצי רעי אל־אלוה דלפה עיני RSV, 'My friends scorn me; my eye pours out tears to God'. LXX, ἀφίκοιτό μου ἡ δέησις πρὸς κύριον, ἔναντι δὲ αὐτοῦ στάζοι μου ὁ ὀφθαλμός. Onkelos, 'My paracletes are my friends'. A modern Jewish version is, 'My spokesmen are my thoughts'.[2]

In this text the pointing of מליצי and the reference of אל are difficult. On the basis of the LXX, or emendation, or both, various solutions have been proposed by W. B. Stevenson,[3] Jean Steinmann,[4] and N. H. Tur-Sinai (Torczyner).[5]

The last-named reads מליציו, 'his spokesmen', i.e. God's. He derives the word not from לוּץ or לֵץ, but from מֶלַץ, 'to speak smoothly', and insists that מֵלִיץ does not mean defence counsel. Rather, it means 'interpreter' or 'intermediary'.[6] This view depends partly on the exegesis of Job 33: 23 (see below). So Tur-Sinai takes the reference to be to an angel mediator, which is in fact 'one of the voices talking to man out of his own conscience'.[7]

be added that paraclete is found frequently in later rabbinic literature, and often in the plural, until the time of Ibn Ezra. The word can be used of good deeds, repentance, or angelic mediation; all before God, the Holy One. The history of the usage both in Hebrew and Greek points to *a continuous meaning of spokesman*. (For assistance with the rabbinic period I am much indebted to my colleague, Mr David Rome, Lecturer in Jewish Studies, McGill University.)

[1] Nils Johannson suggested *Fürsprecher* (*Parakletoi*, p. 47); cf. James Muilenburg, *I.B.* v, 500. George Adam Smith's '*representative men*' makes excellent sense, *The Book of Isaiah*, II, 156.

[2] According to Mr David Rome.   [3] *The Poem of Job* (1951), p. 71.

[4] *Le Livre de Job* (1955), p. 150.   [5] *The Book of Job* (1957), p. 269.

[6] *Ibid.* p. 472.

[7] The 'vindicator' (kinsman and spokesman) of Job 19: 25 may be the same angel helper.

Probably the most attractive and satisfying solution is Marvin Pope's, who attaches אל to verse 20*a*, supplies a lost אלי in 20*b* and reads the singular מליץ: 'Interpreter of my thoughts to God toward whom my eye drips.'[1] This interpreter is the heavenly witness of verse 19.

The derivation from מֶלַץ denoting 'sweet rhetoric' nicely suits the original meaning in παρακαλέω, παράκλησις and παράκλητος: and it may be noted that the one who appeared as 'spokesman' on behalf of the High Priest and the elders before Felix at Caesarea in the case of Paul of Tarsus is called a ῥήτωρ (Acts 24: 1).

(ii) Job 33: 23 is especially important:

אִם־יֵשׁ עָלָיו מַלְאָךְ מֵלִיץ, לְהַגִּיד לְאָדָם יָשְׁרוּ: RSV, 'If there be for him an angel, a mediator...to declare to man what is right for him'.

This angel interprets God's will and also intercedes for man: 'I have found a ransom' (verse 24).

At this point the evidence of 1QH 6: 13 f. must be cited: 'and in the lot together with the angels of the Presence. And there is no intercessor (מליץ בנים) [to thy holy ones]...an (angel) announ[cer]...' (Mansoor's trans.). Mansoor[2] quotes from Canney in *A.J.S.L.* XL (1924), 137; Kissane, *The Book of Job* (1939), p. 225; and H. N. Richardson, 'Some Notes on ליץ and its derivatives', in *Vetus Testamentum*, V (1955), 169, who there argues that the angel's function is simply to inform man about his rights.

It is at this stage, apparently, that the words מֵלִיץ and παράκλητος become virtual titles for such angels. They are of course far more 'personal' than the other media of intercession to which 'paraclete' could be applied, namely the cry of a man, or a cup of cold water given in mercy, or some act of repentance. It is easy to understand too how one of the patriarchs or Moses or one of the prophets could be thought to assume the rôle of a paraclete.[3] The usage is clear: *mēlits* or

---

[1] *Job* (Anchor Bible, 1965), pp. 115, 118.

[2] *The Thanksgiving Hymns* (1961), p. 143. Clearly the derivation of מליץ is still not agreed on by the philologists.

[3] Gen. 18: 23–33 and Exod. 32: 11–14; 33: 12–17 are moving examples of such intercession.

paracletos denotes a function. Neither Jews nor Christians could have thought of a figure called 'the Paraclete'.

All this consorts well with the reference to *the angel of the Lord* in Zech. 1: 11; 3: 1 ff. (note there too the evil spirit, Satan the adversary and accuser), and to *Gabriel*, the interpreter-angel of Dan. 8: 16 ff.; 9: 21 ff.; 10: 21 ('I will tell you what is inscribed in the book of truth'). It is no great leap from such an *angel*, the heavenly *mēlits*, to *the spirit of truth* (Test. of Judah 20), because *spirit* can mean *angel*.

Now, it was Sigmund Mowinckel who gave the signal to explore these passages about an angelic mediator and one cannot be too grateful.

V. LIGHT FROM THE JEWISH BACKGROUND: B. O. BETZ

We come now to a more detailed review and critique of Otto Betz's *Der Paraklet*. In this section his material that deals with Israelite law-court procedure, the various intercessors according to Qumrân ideas, and the function of intercession (pp. 36–116) will be expounded and criticized.

As was stated earlier (p. 82), Betz plunges into the Qumrânian and related intertestamental evidence after a brief account of those who pioneered the way in paraclete research; and his first target is the context of the law-court (pp. 36–55).

Of old in an Israelite court a judge, perhaps the king, behaved like an attorney who seeks to do justice and help the oppressed. So a great man like Job in his heyday would be heard with due respect, for he was 'eyes to the blind, feet to the lame, a father to the poor'. He sat at the city gate 'like a king among his troops, or as one that comforts mourners' (Job 29: 15 f., 25).

God too is One who seeks for justice. In his court the accuser was Satan, and an angel might be the defence attorney. Such ideas coloured the eschatological hopes of sects like that of Qumrân, which envisaged a union of angels and men in a single community at the end of the times.

Betz goes on (pp. 56–72) to consider the various *Intercessors* according to the teaching of Qumrân.

They included the patriarchs and Moses (so too in the book

of Jubilees), but it is to the angels that special attention must be paid.

From Jubilees 1: 29 and Test. of Levi 5: 6 it is deduced that the supreme Helper is the archangel Michael (ἐγώ εἰμι ὁ ἄγγελος ὁ παραιτούμενος τὸ γένος 'Ἰσραήλ), while Satan is the leader of the wicked demons. This leads on to the present plight of the sons of light, the faithful who realize that there is war between the light and the darkness.

Quite correctly, in my opinion, Betz wishes to identify *Belial* as the angel of darkness and therefore the Satan (CD 5: 18; 1QS 1: 17 f.; 3: 20–4; 1QM 13: 10 f.); and *Michael* as the angel of truth and prince of lights (CD 5: 17–19; 1QS 3: 24 f.; 1QM 13: 10; 17: 6 f.). These mighty angels have therefore some very close connexion with '*the spirit of error*' and '*the spirit of truth*' (1QS 3: 13–4: 26; cf. Test. of Judah 20; John 14: 17).[1]

Nevertheless, Betz goes on, 'in no text of the three documents,

---

[1] The basic texts include CD 3: 24; 5: 17–19, the prince of lights, and

1QS 3: 24   ואל ישראל ומלאך אמתו

3: 25   והואה ברא רוחות אור וחושך

4: 21   ויז עליו רוח אמת כמי נדה, and בשרו ולטהרו ברוח קודש

1QM 13: 10   לאמתכה ושר מאור מאז פקדתה לעוזרנו

17: 6–8, 'He will send eternal assistance to the lot of the redeemed by Him through the might of an angel: He hath magnified the authority of Michael through eternal light to light up in joy the house of Israel, peace and blessing for the lot of God, so as to raise amongst the angels the authority of Michael and the dominion of Israel amongst all flesh' (Yadin's edition, E.T.).

It was noted above (pp. 5–7) that considerable caution is required in the exegesis of these texts, especially the essay on the two spirits in man. The 'spiritual' characteristics of men answer to the presence and power in them, not simply of abstract qualities or endowments, but also and more significantly of influences from good angels and wicked demons; above all, from Michael or Belial, according to a preordained measure.

It is a plausible interpretation that Michael, as the angel of truth and light, may sometimes be meant by God's 'holy spirit'. Here too caution is in order. According to late OT books and the intertestamental literature, including the scrolls, God works through several angels, e.g. Uriel and Raphael. On the basis of the texts in Daniel, Gabriel would be the interpreter angel and so the 'paraclete', the spirit that communicates eschatological truth. Yet, if this was true in the early Maccabaean period, it need not have been so in the later, more developed teaching of Qumrân. Hence, by the time 1QM was composed, Michael may indeed have become for the Sect the holy spirit of God.

The Rule of the Community (Sektenkanon), the *War of the Sons of Light* (Kriegsrolle) and the *Damascus Document*, do the two angels appear as intercessors or accusers; the same holds good for the *Hodayot'*. This does not mean that such functions were not known, merely that others held the stage (p. 69). Thus, in 1QH 2: 31–3; 3: 19–23; 5: 20–2; 7: 6 ff., 'God himself and his holy spirit are the power and protection of the suppliant' (p. 72).

Intercession (Fürbitte) is the topic of the next section in *Der Paraklet* (pp. 73–116). It is scarcely to be distinguished from Witnessing, according to Betz.

Besides a divine revelation, an historic event (ein geschichtliches Ereignis) may be a witness (Neh. 9: 26, 30, 'thou didst bear with them, and didst warn them by thy spirit through thy prophets'; Jubilees 30: 7–11). At the Judgment, the Servant of the Lord would bear witness (Isa. 42: 1; 43: 10, 12; 44: 8); but this might be the function of the Qumrân Community itself, for it saw itself as closely linked to the Servant (1QS 8: 6).

In *God's* court a spokesman is inevitably an intercessor and his action has a set 'form': praise, calling to remembrance, and petition (p. 86; cf. 1QS 9: 26; 10: 6 f.; CD 20: 18 f.; 1QH 1: 24; and the liturgical text from Cave Four, ed. M. Baillet: see *R.B.* LXVIII (1961), 195–250).

Other texts are cited to make the same point (e.g. Deut. 32: 7; Jub. 30: 22; Wisd. Sol. 18: 21 f., of Aaron the Priest).

In relation to petitioners who struggle against evil and seek their way in the darkness, the function of the spokesman may be described as guiding into truth. Hence we find angels as mystagogues: Uriel, Raphael and Michael (in Eth. Enoch 21: 5; 22: 3; 71: 3 f.; cf. Test. of Levi 2–5). Angels were the teachers of the Law (Test. of Levi 9: 6; cf. Paul to the Galatians, 3: 19). Michael taught Abraham (Jub. 12: 1–7, 25–7) and revealed the Book of Jubilees at Sinai (Jub. 2: 1 ff.; Apoc. of Moses 1: 1). According to 1QS 3: 20, 24; 4: 2 f., on Betz's exegesis, Michael and the Spirit of Truth connected with him are such guides (cf. Jub. 41: 24).

It is said to be an interesting fact that the *Hodayot* do not mention either Michael or the Spirit of Truth.

The poet prays to God himself, so that here God is both teacher and leader (1QH 2: 23, 33; 7: 14; cf. 1QS 11: 2, 10 f.

and 4Q Test. of Levi 12, 17, where the priestly Levi prays that God will show him the way of truth and prevent Satan's ruling over him).[1]

Another form that intercessary mediation takes is convicting (הוֹכִיחַ; cf. the use of the verb ἐλέγχω, John 16: 8). The sons of light share in the divine judging of the nations (1QpHab. 5: 4 f.) and therefore they wait without fear for the great Day (cf. 1 John 4: 17). Belial according to Jub. 1: 20, and Michael according to Eth. Enoch 89: 61 ff., are accusers then.

In summary, Betz writes:

The Qumrân sect, by its exegesis of the OT material, shows how vital for them is the Spokesman who contends for the embattled saints before the throne of God. A great drama is going on in the universe: between God and man stand the puissant powers, Light and Darkness, embodied in a host of good and murdering spirits, and led by the two angelic princes, Michael and Belial. Spokesmanship is tied to this dualism.

Here too old biblical ideas are, as it were, re-mythologized because in the OT itself there is no such picture of 'gods' or angels in conflict (cf. 1QM 1: 10 f.; 14: 15 f.; 1QH 7: 28; 10: 8; cf. John 10: 34 f.).

When one moves to the earthly scene, the mythical elements are reduced. For it is evident that on earth it is not Belial but the power called *the spirit of error* that is at work; it is not Michael but the power known as *the spirit of truth*. These two spiritual powers are attached to men, whose 'spirit' they control (deren Geist sie regieren) and whose situation they determine.

The eschatological framework is not to be passed over. God has not abdicated, for in fact a judicial process is going on. The Community at Qumrân praise God and remind him of his wondrous works; they bless the good and curse the wicked. In this manner they are anticipating the Last Judgment and the witness–intercession function that must then be fulfilled; that function proleptically is being shared out among themselves, the true and holy People of God who make atonement and follow the interpretations of their inspired priests (1QS 5: 9;

---

[1] See J. T. Milik, 'Le Testament de Lévi en araméen', *R.B.* LXII (1955), 398–406; Betz, *Der Paraklet*, p. 105, n. 2.

1QpHab. 2: 8–10). They are thus the only genuine custodians of God's covenant and law.[1]

In the eighty pages of Part B of *Der Paraklet* Dr Betz has assembled a remarkable amount of evidence from Qumrân. He has examined it in full view of the Old Testament and the materials provided by intertestamental literature, especially the apocalyptic books.

The parallels to Johannine thought are striking, as W. G. Kümmel notes:[2] ethical dualism, the concept of creation, pre-destinarian concepts, witnessing to truth, the light of life, and so on. This accumulation certainly justifies the work of Betz, and yet the question must be put: do the parallels demand that there has been direct influence from Qumrân and related thought upon John?

Kümmel's reply is short and decisive: 'the alleged influence of Qumran upon the evangelist in Ephesus is completely a fabrication'. The dualism at Qumrân had a wholly different context from that of the Fourth Gospel. 'We must conclude, therefore, that John and the community at Qumran presuppose a common background, but that the thought-world of Qumran cannot be the native soil of the Johannine thought-forms (so Bultmann, Baumbach, Teeple, NovT 1960, H. Braun).'[3]

R. E. Brown allows that there is dependence of John on Qumrân, but the line is 'indirect'.[4]

It must be granted that Betz is vulnerable at this point, for he failed to lay the ground adequately for bringing together his massive collection of Jewish evidence. In spite of that, the present writer agrees with Betz that the affinities are so numerous and striking, leaving aside the spirit–paraclete idea, that it is both legitimate and essential to turn to the scrolls for fresh understanding of the Johannine teaching. The vocabulary and ideas that are primary in this regard are:

   (i)   spirit of truth; spirit of error.
   (ii) light; darkness.

[1] Betz, *Der Paraklet*, pp. 113–16.
[2] Feine–Behm, *Introduction to the New Testament* (E.T., 1966), p. 157. Cf. O. Böcher, *Der johanneische Dualismus im Zusammenhang des nachbiblischen Judentums* (1965).   [3] *Ibid.* p. 158.
[4] *New Testament Essays* (1965), pp. 102–31; 'The Paraclete in the Fourth Gospel', *N.T.S.* XIII, No. 2, 126, n. 1.

(iii) the doctrine of election.

(iv) the acclamation of Jesus as the Prophet who should come, a Jesus who is also in some sense a King (John 6: 14).[1]

(v) the three testings of John the Baptist in John 1: 20 f.[2]

Betz would appear to be vulnerable in another area.

He is forced to admit that neither Michael nor Belial is entitled a 'spokesman' or 'accuser' in the primary Qumrân documents (p. 69). Now this, we submit, is quite crucial if his intention, based on assumptions he has not challenged, is to identify a Personage known as 'the Paraclete'. One has to assume that the title and sub-title of his book give away this limitation of his purpose. Later it will be seen that his only route to identifying the paraclete of John's Gospel with the angel Michael is via another John's apocalypse (Rev. 12)![3]

It may be admitted, however, if only in a provisional way at this stage, that what has been collected thus far does permit the investigator to conclude either that the spirit of truth in the Fourth Gospel is the angel Michael or that it has Michael associations. If so, one might add that John seems to mean that Jesus Christ ascended to the Father and sent the Guardian Angel of Israel, Michael, to console, to guide, to teach and to enliven the little company of God's 'true Israel', the Companions of Jesus (cf. the allegory of the True Vine in John 15).

VI

Before any attempt be made to develop such a finding, however, it is first necessary to see how in fact Dr Betz resolves his problems. We therefore turn to Part C of *Der Paraklet* (pp. 117–212), and then to his closing section on 'Revealers, Helpers and Paracletes in the Newly Discovered Gnostic Texts' (pp. 213–36).

Space does not permit any large précis of Part C, hence it must suffice to state the outline of the discussion and then consider carefully the conclusions reached.

---

[1] W. A. Meeks claims that the relation beteeen the Prophet and the King had not been explored before his own study. He has discovered Jewish and Samaritan elements and considerable influence from 'traditions which the church inherited from the Moses piety' (*The Prophet-King*, p. 319).

[2] See above, pp. 52–5.   [3] Betz would object to 'another John's'.

The outline is clear: (*a*) the dualistic and legal *Sitz im Leben* (pp. 117–26); then (*b*) Jesus the Intercessor and the 'Other Paraclete' (pp. 127–75), a section where at last he deals with the origin and nature of the Johannine paracletes; and finally (*c*) the office or ministry (Dienst) of the Johannine paracletes (pp. 176–212).

His findings, which we must now set forth, are on pp. 206–12:

(A) Pre-Johannine Judaism knew the Greek expression παράκλητος and later employed it as a loan-word. John took over traditions that are found in the apocalyptic literature of early Judaism and in the Qumrân documents, and he gave them new meaning.

(B) (1) For the paraclete promise John had Michael before him, Michael who is the spokesman for the elect, prince in the kingdom of light, helper against Satan. For Satan is the tempter, the accuser and murderer of man. Satan works through evil, blinded men like Judas, Caiaphas and Pilate.

The Michael–Satan myth can be seen in Jude and the Revelation of John, a document that must belong somehow to the other Johannine literature.

(2) It was John who equated the angelic Advocate with the spirit of truth which is the protector of the faithful against the insidious attacks of the spirit of error.

John could do this because *ruaḥ* can mean angel as well as spirit, and because the Advocate, Michael, had already been linked with the spirit of truth at Qumrân.

(3) This explains why the Johannine spirit–paraclete is exhibited both as Person and power.

(C) (1) The Fourth Evangelist relates the Michael-spirit of truth phenomenon to Christ the exalted Logos. The Christ returns to heaven and there does as Advocate what had been predicated both of Michael and of the spirit of truth.

(2) This victory of Christ involved the expulsion of Satan from heaven (John 12: 31), so that he could harass and persecute Christ's followers on earth by means of the spirit of error, a diabolical power.

The wicked team of Satan and the spirit of error must meet its match; and this is arranged through a happy exchange. The second paraclete exchanges places with Christ at Easter and comes to earth, where it joins forces with the spirit of truth. This other paraclete glorifies God in Christ, and it is part of its (his) function to remind the saints of Christ and his work (not to remind God, as in the pre-Christian traditions).

(D) New Testament texts that can be cited to support this theory are: Matt. 10: 20, 32 f.; 1 John 2: 1; Rev. 12; 20. In keeping with the primitive creed, e.g. in Phil. 2: 10 f., Jesus Christ is exalted over all principalities and angelic powers, Michael included.

Of course, Qumrân knew nothing about any revelation in the incarnate Logos, or about his atoning death, or about the out-pouring of the Holy Spirit, all of which are eschatological events.

The paraclete who appears as spirit of truth is approximated to the Holy Spirit, and indeed is finally identified with it.[1]

(E) John did not derive the paraclete sayings from a written source, for he and his readers knew these traditions. They are integral to his whole Gospel.

But we are to note that John's interpretative genius has been at work.

His task was to bring together in a meaningful way the heritage from early Judaism and the Christian message.[2] For the danger had already appeared that the place of Jesus might be usurped (cf. Gal. 1: 8; Col. 2: 18). In Jewish-Christian circles Michael could be regarded as the equal of Christ (Hermas, *Sim.* IX, xii, 7; VIII, iii, 3; *Clem. Hom.* 18: 4; and the *Gospel according to the Hebrews*).[3]

Betz argues that John divided the originally twofold function of the paraclete as a heavenly defence counsel, and as a protecting power on earth in the life of the people of God; with the result that Christ, 'the first paraclete', now acts as Advocate in heaven, while Michael, God's true angel, works on earth through 'the spirit of truth'. In fact, contrary to the belief of Qumrân, John identified Michael with the spirit of truth (p. 156).

[1] A. R. C. Leaney thinks it unnecessary to follow Betz in identifying the paraclete with the archangel Michael. It is the existing concept of 'the spirit of truth' that has been deliberately identified with the Holy Spirit by John (*The Rule of Qumran and its Meaning* (1966), pp. 53, 207 ff.).

[2] At this point I add material from *Der Paraklet*, pp. 154 ff., to the summary of the conclusions.

[3] *Der Paraklet*, p. 155, n. 2, with citation of Jean Daniélou, *La théologie du Judéo-Christianisme* (Tournai, 1958), pp. 173–5.

Before we go farther with the conclusions of Betz's book, it may be helpful to make some comment at this point:

Betz can tell us nothing more than what was summarized in the paragraph from p. 156 concerning this peculiar formation of John's 'other paraclete' out of two disparate entities. It is necessary to be clear that this is *a speculation made by Betz*. Like others before him, he has noted the ease with which an idea like *Wisdom* (sophia) could be personified in Hebrew thought; and this is only one of the kind. Alongside these virtual hypostatizations Betz has also seen reference to what he regards as impersonal *power* (dynamis) in relation to the divine and supernatural.

One of his primary clues is found in the Revelation of John with its mythological framework. It is true that it does not speak of a paraclete, but it does feature Michael, the warrior angel. It is equally true that the Gospel of John never mentions Michael but does speak about the paraclete.[1] Believing that Revelation comes from the same 'School' if not from John the Evangelist himself, Betz ingeniously proposes that the whole picture is clarified if Michael in the Apocalypse be given his title, 'paraclete', and if in John's Gospel the paraclete be given his 'name', Michael.

To state this theory is to condemn it as inconceivable. John is to be saddled with the idea that he has robbed the paraclete of a proper name he knew very well; and he has omitted from his Gospel all the spiritual phenomena associated with an angelic intercessor and advocate: the visions, alarums and excursions of the typical apocalypse.[2]

To resume the conclusions offered by Otto Betz; lastly,

(F) The paraclete promise and the parousia hope go together of necessity, for the activity of the two paracletes will cease at the parousia. In John 16: 22, 25–7, 'that day', with its revelations and its joy, means the Day of the parousia.

[1] John the Evangelist, I wish to add, makes nothing of any angelic servants of God, in spite of 1: 51; 12: 29; 20: 12. (The best texts do not include 5: 4, though it has some good early Western support.)

[2] Contrast the Baptist's vision (1: 32) with the gift of sight (9: 37) and the *bath qol* (12: 28) with Peter's confession (6: 68 f.). It is the historic life of Jesus that becomes for the elect a 'staircase' to heaven. And that life is presented to men in the form of John's narrative.

These six paragraphs A to F constitute, then, the major findings of *Der Paraklet*. But we must defer full discussion of them, because at this point in the book the author adds what at first sight must seem a quite unexpected comment. He has found, he claims, the true solution to the paraclete problem. Yet there remains an unexplained element, namely, *the gnostic overtones of the Johannine writings*. 'The manner in which John describes the revelation of Christ and sees salvation validated in correct knowing reminds us of Gnosticism.' Scholars like Barrett, Bauer, Bultmann and Dodd have already done much in this field, but there are newly discovered texts from Nag Hammadi: they must be examined to see what light they may have to shed on our subject.[1]

As an historian I find this procedure highly questionable.

(1) With virtually no exceptions, the new documents thus far published come from a time much later than that of the Fourth Gospel, which can hardly be dated later than A.D. 100. At best, the originals of the Coptic texts do not go farther back than approximately the middle of the second century A.D.

(2) Although the whole subject is obscure and there is little agreement among the specialists, it is rather clear that Gnosticism should be defined as a syncretistic and highly mythological system that emerged during the second Christian century. Various elements, ideas and vocabulary, however, circulated at earlier periods and over a very wide area: roughly that of Alexander the Great's empire. Thus we can detect pre-gnostic phenomena throughout the three hundred years from 200 B.C. to A.D. 100; it is also possible, in the judgment of some scholars, to identify what are to be called 'proto-gnostic' elements that developed over the course of time and became absorbed into the different kinds of gnostic systems.

(3) One cannot be certain which features should be expected, as it were, during the first Christian century. Perhaps (i) a central use of *cosmological speculations*, under the influence of Genesis; (ii) a *dualism* in which the Creator is neither good nor

---

[1] There is a useful summary of the state of the question in Feine–Behm–Kümmel, *I.N.T.* pp. 155–61. Cf. I. de la Potterie, 'L'arrière-fond du thème johannique de vérité', in *Studia Evangelica*, ed. Aland, Cross, Daniélou, Riesenfeld and van Unnik (1959), pp. 277–94; R. McL. Wilson, *Gnosis and the New Testament* (1968).

competent, or in which two eternal 'principles' wage war; (iii) a *pre-mundane fall*; (iv) a view of sin as fundamentally '*ignorance*' which can be removed through *the gnosis of a secret revelation*.

But the utmost caution and reserve have to be exercised when dealing with actual New Testament documents dating from this time.

(4) The Nag Hammadi texts seem to be largely from what is generally regarded as heretical Christianity.

(5) It is dangerous in history to read back, because the element of speculation is then inevitable. Robin Wilson has well said:

It is evident that if we approach from the side of the second Christian century, and interpret in the light of the later Gnostic systems, there is much in the New Testament that may be claimed as 'Gnostic'. When we begin at the other end, however, and endeavour to trace the historical development, it is another matter. In most cases the 'Gnostic' features admit of another explanation, and seldom if ever is the Gnostic explanation absolutely demanded as the one explanation which alone is possible.[1]

(6) The Gospel of John does not show any marked interest in cosmology, whatever the association between the Prologue and the Genesis creation story. There is one true God who loves the world.

It does have some dualistic ideas, but they are by no means overtly gnostic: they *may* be proto-gnostic.

Sin appears to be a power that enslaves man (8: 34), but John offers no consistent doctrine. There is a self-righteousness that is sinful and guilty (9: 41); and it is presumably a disobedience of God's will and an opposition to his love (cf. chs. 14–17 on the life of virtue). It is also, as we have seen, a kind of 'unbelief' (16: 9).

Believers are saved only by *gnosis* in the sense that they must 'know the true God and him whom God sent' (17: 3). The actual noun *gnosis* is never used. The coming to God is by way of revelation, true; but also by divine 'drawing' of men to Christ. Nothing suggests that this election is to be related to a secret communication and apocalypse of God's Name.

---

[1] *Gnosis and the New Testament*, p. 58.

In other words, the Gospel itself requires no system of gnostic practice and belief to account for its primary teaching. It is probably to be interpreted as anti-docetic (in spite of Käsemann). And the fact that we ascribe it to the author of the First Epistle does not lessen either its anti-gnostic or its anti-docetic character; in spite of the views held by several scholars that 1 John shows signs of 'incipient Gnosticism'.

One cannot quarrel, of course, with the right of Otto Betz to investigate the Nag Hammadi documents, but one suspects that he did so on the presupposition that John is correctly regarded as to some degree a gnostic Gospel. Moreover, it is odd that he should not have considered their evidence before he listed the conclusions of his research.

At any rate, the present writer is not surprised by the results of Betz's reading of the gnostic texts from Nag Hammadi (*Der Paraklet*, pp. 234–6):

(*a*) No reality comparable to the Johannine paraclete can be found in them.

(*b*) They cannot provide the pattern or model for the paraclete.

(*c*) John did not know a fully developed Gnosis which he cut in pieces. The most that can be said is that the road struck out by the fourth Evangelist goes farther in the new documents, till their syncretistic philosophy becomes quite irreconcilable with John's theology.[1]

VII

This review and summary of Dr Betz's book has not done justice to the industry, thoroughness, and critical acumen he has brought to the paraclete problem. Attention should be drawn especially to pp. 176–206 which discuss the ministry of the paracletes in witnessing, glorifying, calling to memory, interceding, guiding into truth, announcing things to come, and convicting the world. There is a wealth of material here that repays study, and the book should certainly be translated from German.

---

[1] Bertil Gärtner, *The Theology of the Gospel according to Thomas* (London, 1961), pp. 26, 171, 180 f., thinks that John originated in a gnosticizing milieu. John believed in a genuine Resurrection, the Gnostics did not. This partly explains the question-and-answer 'form' of 13: 36–14: 24. Yet even pre-gnostic Jewish teachers and Jesus himself had employed such a device!

I wish now to make the following constructive criticisms:

(1) The recognition that there is an old concept of an angelic representative behind the 'other paraclete' and 'the spirit of truth' means that John was not interested in the succession motif as illustrated in Noah–Abraham, Moses–Joshua, Elijah–Elisha (*Der Paraklet*, pp. 127 ff.). This should have been recognized as a by-path. For it would have been preposterous for John to have presented any spirit as the Successor to the Logos incarnate in Jesus, the only One who should attract to himself the whole world.[1]

(2) The contention that John has restated the myth that is supposed to underlie the relation of Jesus Christ to the spirit of truth is not successful.

For one thing, the exegesis of 12: 31 is dubious: 'Now shall the ruler of this world be cast out.'[2] Betz thinks this means that, at that moment in the life of Jesus, Satan was expelled from heaven and came down to earth to carry on his wicked devices. The only ground for holding that during the mission of the Logos on earth Satan was in heaven before the throne of God is the postulated myth that the angel Belial or Satan operated (so to speak) in heaven; whereas on earth the evil power at work was the spirit of error.

In my opinion, Belial is present on earth, an evil influence that fosters error and wickedness in men, i.e. 'a spirit of untruth and ungodliness'. There is no need to separate Belial from the latter, as though he were a personal demon and the latter only an impersonal power.

Again, John's Gospel does not portray the Christ as returning to heaven to act as a paraclete and to remain there until the Second Advent, although that *may* be true of 1 John (see 2: 1, 28; 3: 2; 4: 17). How distant is the 'will come again' of 14: 3? How near is the 'we will come to him' of 14: 23? The latter is more related to ethical and faithful loving than to time. John has the kind of mentality that holds together the assurance of 5: 24 (the believers have emigrated from death to life) and the hope of 5: 28 f. (the believers will be raised to life eternal).[3]

---

[1] Betz himself writes (p. 137), 'Aber das Verhältnis Jesus-Paraklet geht in der Bestimmung "Vorgänger-Nachfolger" nicht auf'.

[2] Bultmann, *Komm.* p. 330 says 'aus seinem bisherigen Herrschaftsgebiet'; F. Godet, *Commentary*, III, 77, 'out of the world, his ancient realm'.

[3] Cf. John 6: 40 and 11: 25 f.; and in Paul, Rom. 6: 6–11; 8: 2–10; Gal. 2: 20; Col. 2: 12 f.; 3: 1–4.

Consequently it is not a simple matter of the Christ departing and then sending his Representative, for he is both absent and present. Behind the mystery here may lie the Hebrew attempt to speak of Yahweh's utter invisibility and at the same time his revealing theophanies.[1] We cannot accept the thesis of R. E. Brown that 'the Paraclete is the presence of Jesus when Jesus is absent'.

(3) What we have said above about gnostic vocabulary and ideas means that we cannot acquiesce in Betz's posing of the spirit–paraclete problem in the context of a 'radical dualism'.[2]

(4) Betz has noticed but has not sufficiently stressed the polemical dimensions of the Fourth Gospel.[3]

The angelic mediator of earlier views is firmly subordinated to Jesus as the Christ.

The subordination begins [Betz writes] with the sending of Michael to earth after the exaltation of Christ and his being there equated with the spirit of truth. His person, his name, his leading rôle among the angels, are now obscured and only the title ὁ παράκλητος still directs us to the original situation intended. One may perhaps see in this meaning a determined attack on the belief of apocalypticism and the Qumrân sect in angels. No angel but Christ is the Redeemer and the true Revealer of God.

Hence for Betz too the spirit of truth ought not to be regarded as the *alter ego* of Christ. Only the first paraclete appeared on earth as a man; the other paraclete is on earth as a spirit.[4]

When this polemical purpose of John is given full weight, further light on the paraclete question is forthcoming.

(5) We should examine more fully the position taken by Betz that Belial is not the spirit of error and that Michael is not the spirit of truth.

The central argument is renewed on pp. 147–9 where, following F. Spitta, H. Delafosse, H. Windisch, H. Sasse and R. Bultmann, Betz asserts that the paraclete and the spirit were different realities. For him, the paraclete is an angel and there-

---

[1] See Gen. 1: 3; Exod. 24: 15–25: 1; I Kings, 19: 12.

[2] The gracious, holy, and innocent character of God the Father is fully reflected in his Son's (1: 18; 3: 16, etc.). Contrast 1QS 3: 15, 25.

[3] *Der Paraklet*, p. 164, for example.

[4] Such a spirituality is scarcely kin to the incarnational type of Christology John offers in the Logos doctrine!

fore spirit of a sort (er ist Geist von Art). 'For the angels in the time of early Judaism appear (gelten) as "spirits" (רוּחוֹת, πνεύματα), that is, as spiritual beings in contrast to mankind which is fleshly' (p. 148). In a footnote we are told: 'Of course in Qumrân documents individual angels are not described by רוּחַ; this expression remains pre-empted for the wind as the power of God.'

These statements are simply not accurate. We have seen already that *ruaḥ* in 1QH 3: 23; 8: 12 does mean angel; hence it is probable that in the famous essay of 1QS 3: 13–4: 26 we must allow for 'spirit of error' and 'spirit of truth' sometimes having a psychological meaning, but always as having an indirect reference to angelic presences.[1]

Angels were believed to be invisible, but they encountered man in unusual experiences like trances and visions, and they mysteriously communicated messages, truths, and interpretations of texts to chosen prophets and teachers. Hence there was no difficulty in ascribing to their influence and presence:

(i) wicked impulses, perverse desires, sullenness and depression, and the like; and

(ii) good longings, holy desires, serene emotions and so on.

The spirit, mood or disposition resulting in a man was therefore put quite correctly into Hebrew with רוּחַ and into Greek with πνεῦμα, although these did not exhaust the resources available in one language area or the other.

(6) A final criticism that has to be made is that the attempt to explain the unnamed paraclete of the Fourth Gospel by the Michael of Revelation 12: 7 must be judged unsatisfactory for the following reasons:

It is true that certain evidences can be produced to link the Gospel and the Apocalypse with what is nowadays called 'the Johannine school'.

For example, the following verses in Revelation:

1: 2, ὃς ἐμαρτύρησεν τὸν λόγον τοῦ θεοῦ καὶ τὴν μαρτυρίαν Ἰησοῦ Χριστοῦ

2: 28, ὡς κἀγὼ εἴληφα παρὰ τοῦ πατρός μου

---

[1] See M. Mansoor, *The Thanksgiving Hymns*, pp. 74 f. *Ruaḥ* in Qumrân literature seldom means 'wind'. R. E. Brown in his *N.T.S.* article, p. 126, seems to misunderstand Betz on this issue.

3: 10, ὅτι ἐτήρησας τὸν λόγον τῆς ὑπομονῆς μου
3: 20, εἰσελεύσομαι πρὸς αὐτὸν καὶ δειπνήσω μετ' αὐτοῦ
(Cf. John 14: 23.)
5: 6, ἀρνίον [but not ἀμνός, as in the Gospel] ἑστηκὸς ὡς ἐσφαγμένον
6: 16, ἀπὸ τῆς ὀργῆς τοῦ ἀρνίου
(Cf. John 3: 36.)
14: 7, προσκυνήσατε
(Cf. John 4: 20–2; 9: 38.)
14: 15, θέρισον, ὅτι ἦλθεν ἡ ὥρα θερίσαι
(Cf. John 4: 35 f., but this harvesting in Rev. is one of judgment—cf. Joel 3: 13—not of salvation.)
21: 6, ἐγὼ τῷ διψῶντι δώσω ἐκ τῆς πηγῆς τοῦ ὕδατος τῆς ζωῆς δωρεάν.

These similarities, which are not particularly impressive separately or together, need to be posted against the background of significant differences in the theology, Christology, angelology, millenarianism, and general attitude of the Apocalypse. We note:

1: 1, διὰ τοῦ ἀγγέλου αὐτοῦ and *passim*.
1: 20, ἄγγελοι τῶν ἑπτὰ ἐκκλησιῶν
1: 5, ὁ μάρτυς ὁ πιστός, ὁ πρωτότοκος τῶν νεκρῶν καὶ ὁ ἄρχων τῶν βασιλέων τῆς γῆς.
1: 16, καὶ ἐκ τοῦ στόματος αὐτοῦ ῥομφαία δίστομος ὀξεῖα ἐκπορευομένη
3: 3, μετανόησον...ἥξω ὡς κλέπτης
7: 17, ὅτι τὸ ἀρνίον τὸ ἀνὰ μέσον τοῦ θρόνου ποιμανεῖ αὐτοὺς καὶ ὁδηγήσει αὐτούς
(The OT background is quite explicit.)
19: 7, ὁ γάμος τοῦ ἀρνίου
22: 12, ἰδοὺ ἔρχομαι ταχύ, καὶ ὁ μισθός μου μετ' ἐμοῦ, ἀποδοῦναι ἑκάστῳ ὡς τὸ ἔργον ἐστὶν αὐτοῦ.
(This is not quite the same as the teaching of John 5: 29! Indeed, if divine judgment is according to man's work, who can stand? It is not justice men need at the hands of God, it is mercy.)
1: 8; 11: 17; 21: 22, the God of the Apocalypse is ὁ παντοκράτωρ; cf. 15: 3, ὁ βασιλεὺς τῶν αἰώνων [v.l. ἐθνῶν]. The lineaments of the Father are all of majesty and power.
Hence we need not be astonished at
6: 10, ἕως πότε, ὁ δεσπότης ὁ ἅγιος καὶ ἀληθινός, οὐ κρίνεις καὶ ἐκδικεῖς τὸ αἷμα ἡμῶν κτλ.; nor by the picture of Rome ('Babylon') fallen to fiery ruin (ch. 18), nor by the invitation to the carrion birds

of 19: 17f., 'to eat the flesh of kings...of captains...of mighty men...of horses and their riders, and the flesh of all men, both free and slave, both small and great'.

The punishment of the apostates who conformed to the cult of Rome and the Emperor is just as terrible: to be 'tormented with fire and brimstone in the presence of the holy angels and of the Lamb...they have no rest, day or night, these worshippers of the beast and its image, and whoever receives the mark of its name' (14: 10 f.).

Unfamiliar to the Gospel are the following in Revelation: καιρός (1: 3), λύειν ἐκ τῶν ἁμαρτιῶν (1: 5), πνεῦμα ʒωῆς (11: 11), κατήγωρ (12: 10), εὐαγγέλιον (14: 6), and the millenarian vision of 20: 1–6.

These differences must not be glossed over, for together they make a powerful case against accepting the Revelation as coming from the mind or school of the fourth Evangelist.

It is therefore impossible for me to believe that John knew his spirit–paraclete as the kind of angel Michael is in the Apocalypse. Michael there is a fair colleague for its Christ, terrible in the panoply of a warrior Messiah. Michael too is a warrior. He is no consoler, no teacher, no prophet like the spirit–paraclete of the Gospel. Not even in 16: 4b–11 of the Gospel can one detect the militant and almost bitter attitude that informs Revelation.

Accordingly, in a way that is not intended by Dr Betz, it is indeed to be marked as significant that the name Michael is missing from the Gospel of John, and that his military functions are confined to Revelation. The one cause that is adequate to explain this fact is that the Evangelist has deliberately omitted to mention Michael by name, although one can hardly doubt that the name was familiar to him. The omission is part of his polemical intention. To develop this point it is necessary that we should now pass from the history of recent research and present our own hypothesis.

CHAPTER 8

THE SPIRIT–PARACLETE IN THE JOHANNINE POLEMICS

In the remaining chapters of this book the theses to be stated and defended are (1) that the author of the Fourth Gospel combined 'spirit of truth' with 'paraclete' in a deliberate rebuttal of heretical claims for an angel-intercessor as the spiritual guide and guardian of the Christian Church; and (2) that the spirit–paraclete is the Spirit of God, which is also the Spirit of Christ, and thus an active divine power that becomes embodied in certain outstanding leaders within the catholic Church: the exegete, the teacher and evangelist, the prophet, the consoler out of sorrow, and the witness for the defence in times of persecution.

I

We may begin by rehearsing some of the positions already occupied (see above, pp. 84–7 and also Part 1 as a whole).

To discover the full range of Johannine meaning in the case of the 'spirit' we must begin with exegesis of the Johannine text; and in so doing we have found that the basic sense of 'spirit' is divine power. It is effective in the life of the universe, for it is creative. It is effective in the life of humanity, but by way of mystery, since it shares in all the wonder and grace of God himself from whom it proceeds, God the loving Father proclaimed by the Lord Jesus: so some men see but do not perceive, they hear but do not understand (Isa. 6: 10; John 12: 40). Yet the spirit moves in the midst of their time to accomplish the purposes of God and, as it were, 'blows' where it will. It is effective as a cleansing agent, purifying man from the stain and control of sin if he is humble, believing and penitent; and it is like a creative breath of life that fires the elect faithful with new capacities for the service of God and his Christ. John can thus imagine it as the life-giving breath that issued from the 'mouth' of the resurrected Jesus. For the spirit is the power with which the Son of God, the Logos made man, was equipped for his Messianic ministry.

We hold too that in the dramatic discourses when Jesus bade his men farewell and *shalom*, the focus is primarily on the spirit of truth, and that 'paraclete' should be interpreted as a secondary term denoting a variety of functions.

This word '*paraclete*', already used in the First Epistle, is best translated by the English '*representative*', which is wide enough and accurate enough to cover the actual Johannine usage and also the meanings in Jewish and Greek literature: advocate in a legal setting, intercessor, mediator, and spokesman.

We accept the view of Sigmund Mowinckel that the Hebrew rootage should be found in מֵלִיץ and that this was applied to an *angel intercessor*.

The fact that the Fourth Gospel introduces the spirit promises during the private communion of Jesus with his disciples in the Supper Room is right and proper, for the unanimous Christian tradition was that Jesus had given to his men just such a promise that in time of persecution and grave danger they would be assisted by a divine spokesman. It was a promise for the time of Jesus' absence and it had a consoling power.

'*The spirit of truth*', also used in one particular meaning in I John, appears to be a new expression within Christian literature, but it can now be traced in the intertestamental literature and in the Dead Sea Scrolls. It belongs with a dualism that had become deep-rooted in early Judaism, doubtless with considerable influence from Iranian and other sources, the extent of which is still debatable.

The work of Otto Betz and of others who have investigated the Qumrân evidence makes it reasonable to believe that the spirit of truth had been identified in pre-Christian Judaism with the angel of truth, the prince of lights, *Michael*. This angelic guardian, a product of the religious imagination and to some extent a relic of ancient polytheism in Israel, was conceived under various guises as the helper of the covenant nation, and the chieftain of the 'lot' of God, that is, the predestined community or *yaḥadh* which in the desert was preparing the way of the Lord.

Even if the scrolls from the Dead Sea caves had to be dated in the first half of the first century A.D. (a position we cannot accept but which is not yet to be ruled out of court), it would remain true that the angelic meaning of the spirit of truth had been domesticated in the synagogues and sects of Judaism long before the Fourth Gospel was composed.

It is therefore essential to consider how such ideas are to be connected with the spirit–paraclete promises in John.

Otto Betz came to the conclusion that John identified (*a*) the spirit of God, 'the Holy Spirit', (*b*) the angelic spirit of truth (although he thinks that this term was understood impersonally as an operative power),[1] and (*c*) the archangel Michael. The process by which this moulding took place is not well explained by Betz, and our complaint is that it is really his own speculation.[2] He summarizes by saying that as Person this Spirit is the 'other Paraclete', and that he performs his work as 'a spiritual power'.

We should prefer to say that this motif of an angelic spirit should be studied in the light of John's absolute insistence that it is a spirit sent from the Father in the name of Jesus Christ or sent by the victor Christ himself. So John implies without any question that for him the spirit of truth is the spirit of Christ or the spirit of God.[3] He must have had good reason for thus adopting a phrase that has quite different meaning in early Judaism.

We reiterate that John cannot be speaking about an angel, for he could have said so explicitly if that had been his exegesis of the promise recorded in the Synoptic Gospels. Nor does he mean to describe Michael without putting the name to him! What then was his reason?

It is a polemical one.

The Gospel of John has several polemical aims: e.g. in reaction to those who elevated John the Baptist unduly; to the Synagogue with its veneration for Moses and the old Law; and to those who propagated docetic views of Christ. It is no surprise to have the teaching on the spirit linked with such a basic attitude.

[1] Raymond Brown comments on this: 'We would rather say that in QS (the reference should be 1QS) the term "spirit of truth" has both personal and impersonal application; when it is used of a personal being, then the Spirit of Truth is Michael' (article cited from *N.T.S.* XIII, No. 2, 122, n. 5).

[2] Brown, *ibid.* p. 125, n. 3, notes that Betz is not simple and that sometimes he thinks the amalgamation was pre-Johannine.

[3] 'The Holy Spirit' is also possible.

We suggest that the identification of the angel Michael with the true spirit of God is pre-Johannine and that it had become a menace to the 'orthodox' faith in Jesus as the Christ, the Son of God and saviour of the world. Hints that certain sectarian groups within the Church were toying with the ideas and worship of angelic mediators are given, as many have noted before us, in Gal. 1: 8; 3: 19; Col. 2: 18 ff.; and Heb. 1: 4 ff. By making skilful use of terminology that was current in such groups, John turned the tables on his opponents and safeguarded the primacy of Jesus.

The development given to this heretical terminology in the interests of his own teaching and the needs of his Church is brilliant and profound.

II

From the few authentic sayings of Jesus in the Synoptics on the Spirit of God, from the much fuller evidence of the Acts, and from the letters of Paul, it is certain that the Church of the first two generations cherished the conviction that God had verified the claims of Jesus and the apostolic proclamation of his Gospel by the distribution of spirit-gifts, the results in the minds and hearts of the baptized of God's own spirit at work: 'God also bore witness by signs and wonders and various miracles and by gifts of the holy spirit distributed according to his own will' (Heb. 2: 4; cf. 1 Cor. 12: 4–11; Acts 2: 43–4: 31, etc.). The spirit had indeed come to rest on the disciples (John 14: 17). The oft-repeated prayer of Ps. 51: 10–12 was being fulfilled far beyond all expectation or desert:

> Create in me a clean heart, O God,
>   and put a new and right spirit within me.
> Cast me not away from thy presence,
>   and take not thy holy spirit from me.
> Restore to me the joy of thy salvation,
>   and uphold me with a willing spirit.

From this we may infer that John's theology assigned full deity to the Father, and a unique place to the incarnate Word in Jesus of Nazareth; but the spirit apparently was not regarded by him as other than the power and influence that proceeded from God in creative and redemptive mission. Certainly we cannot accept the idea that his spirit should be thought of as a third hypostasis denominated as 'the Paraclete'.[1] This does not imply, however, that the spirit in John was merely an impersonal energy. The word πνεῦμα, like רוּחַ, fluctuated between the sense of a *divine power* which could in Hebrew minds be personified, like 'word', 'wisdom', 'hand of God'; and that of *dynamic energy immanently at work* within men and women.[2] This made it easy enough for John to speak of τὸ πνεῦμα τῆς ἀληθείας as ἄλλος παράκλητος and to employ ἐκεῖνος and αὐτός, as well as to use many verbs of personal activity. The masculine attributes come, not from Michael the angel, but from Jesus Christ the Logos or from the Father who is ὁ θεός.[3]

We welcome therefore the recognition by Barrett, Bultmann, Schweizer and Mowinckel that the Johannine spirit—paraclete is the spirit at work in the apostolic preaching. We propose (see the next chapter) to extend this insight to other aspects of the life of the Johannine Church in a time of danger and crisis near the end of the first century: namely, teaching, interpreting what Jesus had said, prophesying, witnessing, and doing battle with the 'world' in the law-courts of Rome or the *beth din* of the synagogue.

III

The *Sitz im Leben* proposed here for the Johannine sayings differs markedly from that suggested by Raymond Brown. It will be helpful if we discuss his views now.

John's paraclete teaching, according to Brown, answered two problems: (1) 'the uneasy confusion caused by the death of the apostolic eyewitnesses', and (2) 'the delay of the parousia'.[4]

As to the first, Brown thinks that the first edition of John's Gospel should be dated about A.D. 70–85, after the martyrdoms of James the son of Zebedee, James the brother of the Lord,

---

[1] This raises questions for the systematic theologian but does not in itself solve the trinitarian issue.

[2] On personification in Hellenistic Judaism, see H. Ringgren, *Word and Wisdom: Studies in the Hypostatization of Divine Qualities and Functions in the Ancient Near East* (1947).

[3] It is pedantic to use only 'it' of the spirit; but the use of 'He' unduly befogs the study of John's doctrine. Since the spirit is God's and Christ's, we may sometimes employ the pronoun 'he' without causing confusion.

[4] *N.T.S.* XIII, No. 2, 128, 130.

Peter and Paul, and the deaths of most of the eyewitnesses. The final edition, as we now have it, is dated between 90 and 100, just after the death of the Beloved Disciple, as implied in 21 : 22 f.[1] The paraclete promise was meant for a much wider circle than the Eleven or any others called apostles (cf. 1 John 2: 20, 27).[2] John is an example of reinterpretation done some fifty to sixty years after Jesus under the inspiration of the paraclete, with the Beloved Disciple as the principal authority.[3] For that disciple and his followers were the ideal agents of the spirit–paraclete.

There is, however, nothing in John 1–20 that seems to have in mind any such event as the passing of all the eyewitnesses. The setting seems rather to correspond with that of the First Epistle, the crisis caused by docetic heresy; and there is much to be said for the view that relations with the Synagogue were very strained (as Louis Martyn argues in his *History and Theology in the Fourth Gospel*).

John's doctrine of Incarnation, itself an inevitable growth in christological thought, demanded a constant memory of the historic Jesus and therefore the 'remembrancer' rôle of the spirit. The apostles and their successors relay to all generations the word that is Christ (13: 20; 15: 20; 17: 20; 20: 21).

To what extent, next, does the delay of the parousia occasion the appearance of the Gospel of John?

Brown insists that John never dispensed with the hope of Jesus' final return in visible glory, and so he dissents from Bultmann, who attributes to an editor all passages about futurist eschatology, and from Betz, who says that the coming of the spirit–paraclete and the arrival of the parousia belong together.[4] Brown thinks that such sayings as Mark 13: 30; Matt. 10: 23 (also Mark 9: 1?) seemed to say that the parousia would take place during the lifetime of Jesus' hearers; that the

---

[1] *Ibid.* p. 129.

[2] Brown disagrees with F. Mussner (cf. p. 51 above) that the gift was only for the Twelve Apostles (*sic.*) But Mussner is on the right track, and he makes an excellent case. The Church in John is an *apostolic* community commissioned to witness.

[3] The Beloved Disciple remains an enigma to us!

[4] This is not quite accurate. Betz makes the point that on earth the ever-abiding paraclete works side by side with the exalted Lord Christ who is in heaven; but this Christ will return soon: he is the 'bald wiederkommende Herr'. *Der Paraklet*, pp. 149–53.

Fall of Jerusalem had been considered to be the sign of the End (Mark 13: 14 and pars.); but the apostolic generation had died, Jerusalem had fallen, and still Christ had not come back. John 21: 23 demonstrates the hope in Johannine circles that the return would take place at least before the death of the Beloved Disciple. Yet this too had happened, and the parousia had not come.

In the midst of his bewilderment because of this, a disciple (Brown suggests) would be consoled by the message that 'Jesus is already present to the Christian in and through the paraclete'. The judgment had come (3: 19) but it was in the future still (5: 28 f.). The Last Judgment had come in a sense proleptically, because the presence of the paraclete 'puts the world on trial and proves the world wrong about Jesus'.[1]

What does Fr Brown think a Christian about A.D. 90 was invited to 'see' when he was reassured by the authorities of the Church that 'the paraclete is present among us'? Is an invisible spirit much of a reassurance?

The argument of Brown fits John 21 but is much less successful with the rest of the Gospel. I can find nothing to indicate that this book had fearful saints in mind who needed to be told that, after the death of all the Apostles, the Church had not been abandoned. Adventism was by no means a dead issue by the end of the first century; and the so-called Johannine school produced about that time a tract admirably suited to certain adventist hopes.

It would seem more credible that John, like St Paul, had learned not to be anxious about the date of the parousia and to concentrate on the need for growth in wisdom, love and truth (cf. Phil. 1: 9–11).

It is somewhat doubtful if John 16: 7–11 should be taken along with 3: 19 as part of an 'inaugurated eschatology', in the sense that it is to be regarded also as a foretaste of the Last Judgment. The emphasis is on the present situation of the Church, and the End is very much in the background.

[1] N.T.S. xiii, No. 2, 132. On this page, note 1, κέκριται (John 16: 11) is taken to mean 'was actually destroyed', a quite impossible rendering. Christians knew only too well that the power of Satan had *not* been destroyed. It had been *condemned*.

IV

In summary:

The spirit of God in John 14–16 is defined as the spirit of Jesus the Christ, and so its ministry is related intimately and fruitfully to the historic ministry of Jesus.

It is described also as the spirit of truth that acts as another paraclete, in one sense therefore taking the place of Jesus who has ascended to enjoy the glory that had been the glory of the eternal Logos. Yet the spirit could never challenge Jesus' title as Saviour and his unique duty to reveal the Father and perform the Father's will. This teaching is in opposition to any who would seek to displace Jesus and impose another spirit or introduce as true mediator and intercessor such an angel as Michael.

As paraclete, the spirit is the representative of Jesus and it should not therefore be considered 'another Jesus' or 'the presence of Jesus when Jesus is absent'. Rather, this concept directs attention to the evidence in the life of the apostolic Church of wisdom, vitality, virtue, and graces that Christians could explain only as the signs of divine power and God's very presence.

Within the churches the influence and the gifts of the spirit–paraclete were mediated to certain persons who fulfilled precisely those functions that are ascribed in the Farewell Discourses to the spirit itself. They are therefore to be identified as the agents of the divine spirit. John the Evangelist must be regarded as one such agent, and it would not be improper to honour him with the title of 'paraclete of the Christians', one that was in fact bestowed about a hundred years later on young Vettius Epagathus, a martyr witness during the persecution terror at Vienne.[1]

---

[1] Eus. *H.E.* v, i, 10. G. A. Williamson's translation is in the Penguin Classics (1965), p. 195.

CHAPTER 9

THE PRESENCE OF THE
SPIRIT-PARACLETE IN THE CHURCH

'No one has ever seen God; the only Son...has made him known' (John 1: 18). God is spirit; so we may go on to say that no one has ever seen the spirit. It is like the wind and therefore mysterious; but it is no less 'real' in the world. Our final thesis is that the apostolic Church, according to the author of the Fourth Gospel, is the society of men that makes the spirit known.

Jesus of Nazareth, of whom people could say, 'Don't we know his father and mother?' (John 6: 42), is for John no mere man, though he was that too, a man subjected to fierce ignominy and disgrace (18: 28–19: 5). Jesus is the embodiment in man of the Logos, 'the Word that was with God, the Word that is God'; and at the last even doubting Thomas must fall down in the adoration of 'My Lord and my God!' (20: 28). Once visible, now he is hidden from human sight in the glory of the Father's throne. He too as the God–man is spirit and the source of spiritual life. No one in John's era could see Jesus the Son of God with the eye of the flesh; but they could see his embodiment in the Church of his disciples.

How true then was James Denney's remark that 'to understand what is meant by the Spirit is to understand these two things—the N.T. and the Christian Church'![1]

It is not altogether a thankless task to seek among the words of Jesus in the Gospel of John, and especially in the Farewell Discourses, for authentic logia of the historic teacher from Nazareth.[2] It is certainly a much more rewarding one to penetrate beneath the outward form of the spirit–paraclete sayings to the contemporary realities within the Johannine Church that helped to give them a habitation and a name.

[1] 'Holy Spirit', *H.D.C.G.* I, 731 a.
[2] C. H. Dodd, *Historical Tradition in the Fourth Gospel,* shows the progress that can be made by applying form-critical methods. Genuine traditions do form the basis for the elaborate Johannine discourses.

So, on the assumption that the apostolic Church was for the fourth Evangelist the genuine Successor to Jesus and that divine spiritual power kept it alive and qualified its great leaders and its obscure members alike, we proceed now to test our thesis by the evidence of the New Testament; for it may be taken for granted that much of the literature in the New Testament will provide useful source material for the life-situation of the churches in the apostolic and the sub-apostolic period of Church History.

I. THE INSPIRED TEACHER

The first function of the spirit–paraclete to be discussed is that of the interpreter or exegete: 'he will teach you all things, and bring to your remembrance all that I have said to you' (14: 26); 'he will bear witness to me' (15: 26); and 'whatever he hears he will speak...he will take what is mine and declare it to you' (16: 13 f.). 'He will guide you into all the truth.'

(1) For John the unseen spirit of Christ is the reality behind the appearance of inspired teachers in the congregations of Christians. Such a teacher is a paraclete of his fellows and truly a representative of Jesus: 'I have given them the words which thou gavest me...' (17: 8).

It is a very interesting fact that several authors in the New Testament had satisfied themselves that ideally a church had such spiritual insight and such a capacity for self-teaching that it needed no special teacher. 'You are all sons of light and sons of the day...therefore let each one encourage and edify his fellow' (1 Thess. 5: 5, 11). The appearance of the verb παρα-καλῶ there means that each member is to act as a *paraclete* to the others![1] Compare Heb. 10: 24 f., 'take thought to provoke one another to the good works of love...encourage each other (παρακαλοῦντες)'; 1 John 2: 20, 27, you need no teacher, really, because the Holy One has anointed you; Jude 22, 'convict some (or, convince some) (ἐλέγχετε), who doubt'. On the Jude text, where the reading is uncertain, Michael Green comments: '"Argue some out of their error while they are still in two minds." *Elenchein* means to overcome error by truth.

---

[1] διὸ παρακαλεῖτε ἀλλήλους καὶ οἰκοδομεῖτε εἰς τὸν ἕνα κτλ.

When men are beginning to waver, that is the time for a well-taught Christian to come alongside them and help.'[1]

From the evidence of St Paul's letters, e.g. 1 Cor. 12, it could be deduced that the Apostle to the Gentiles believed that every baptized member of the Body of Christ had been enriched with his own distinctive spiritual gift for the common good; and this is almost sure to be pardonable exaggeration. For Paul himself knew well how much help the Christians of just such a church as Corinth required from an inspired man like himself! (Cf. 2 Tim. 2: 14; Tit. 3: 1.)

According to the Acts of the Apostles (in this matter a reasonably trustworthy source), certain men became leading teachers for the first congregations:

Peter (5: 1 ff.); Barnabas (11: 22); at Antioch, Symeon Niger, Lucius of Cyrene, and Manaen (13: 1); and Paul (19: 9 f.; 20: 20, 27, 35). For example in his Miletus speech:

Paul defined his ministry as a proclaiming (ἀναγγεῖλαι) and teaching (διδάξαι) as well as a witnessing (διαμαρτυρόμενος). He had, he says, endeavoured to declare the whole counsel of God (οὐ γὰρ ὑπεστειλάμην τοῦ μὴ ἀναγγεῖλαι πᾶσαν τὴν βουλὴν τοῦ θεοῦ ὑμῖν). At one point in his address he *reminded* the Ephesian elders of what Jesus himself had taught about the blessing of generosity.

When we turn to Paul's correspondence for corroboration, we find it in luxuriant abundance. A few passages may be cited:

2 Thess. 3: 10–12, Christians should work to earn their living; note especially the words, παραγγέλλομεν καὶ παρακαλοῦμεν ἐν κυρίῳ Ἰησοῦ Χριστῷ.

1 Thess. 2: 11 f., the Christian's life must be worthy of the God professed and of the hope for his glorious kingdom; note παρακαλοῦντες... καὶ παραμυθούμενοι.

1 Thess. 3: 2, Timothy had been sent to Salonica as a teacher εἰς τὸ στηρίξαι ὑμᾶς καὶ παρακαλέσαι ὑπὲρ τῆς πίστεως ὑμῶν.

Similar language is used in the teaching about the parousia in 1 Thess. 4: 15, τοῦτο γὰρ ὑμῖν λέγομεν ἐν λόγῳ κυρίου: that is, the Apostle communicates this belief as an inspired representative of the Lord (or is this to be taken perhaps as an example of Pauline 'prophecy' rather than 'teaching'?). The

---

[1] *The Second Epistle of Peter and the Epistle of Jude* (The Tyndale New Testament Commentaries, 1968), p. 187.

same is true of his Gospel as a whole and his interpretation or exegesis of the conditions to be laid down for membership and 'full communion' in the Jewish–Gentile churches (Gal. 1: 11 f.; 2: 11–21). Christians were forced to choose Paul, Peter or James as the true paraclete, the authorized spokesman; and this led to bitter schism (1 Cor. 1: 10 ff.; Gal. 2: 11–14; Acts 15: 39 f.).

A good part of Paul's case arose from his exegesis of scripture, and this is illustrated in Gal. 3: 6–20; 4: 22–5: 1; 5: 13–15. In this he followed the example of Jesus, for he is represented in Mark 10: 2–9, 17–21; 12: 18–34 as such an exegete.[1]

The vocation to biblical interpretation was to be expected, since both the Old Testament scriptures and the Words of the Lord Jesus were authoritative in the churches. The business of the teacher was linked to a *charisma* of the spirit, e.g. in 1 Cor. 12: 8 (wisdom and knowledge) and 28, 'God has appointed in the Church first apostles, second prophets, third teachers...' Similarly, deutero-Pauline Ephesians 4: 11: 'And his gifts were that some should be apostles, some prophets, some evangelists, some teaching pastors...'; and 1 Pet. 4: 10 f., ἕκαστος καθὼς ἔλαβεν χάρισμα...εἴ τις λαλεῖ, ὡς λόγια θεοῦ.

In Hebrews there is Christian exegesis of the Psalter (1: 5–13) and of Jer. 31: 31–3 (8: 8–13); see also 5: 5 f., 11 ff.; 6: 1–3. The author calls his document a word of exhortation (λόγος τῆς παρακλήσεως, 13: 22; cf. Acts 15: 31, describing the letter despatched by the so-called Apostolic Council).

The writer of James advises his readers against the ambition to become teachers (3: 1), but obviously belongs to this rank himself (cf. 2: 8–13 on the 'royal law'). Compare too 1 Pet. 2: 6–10; 1 Tim. 2: 7; 3: 2; 4: 1 ('the spirit expressly says'), 11; 2 Tim. 2: 2; 3: 15 f.

In the history of the first missions and within the life of the earliest congregations the spirit did not have free rein and its messages did not, it would appear, come through without

---

[1] Form criticism has shown how teachers in the post-Resurrection Church reinterpreted the words of Jesus to suit their situation and even put words in his mouth. See now a useful essay, 'Sayings of the Risen Jesus in the Synoptic Tradition...' by F. W. Beare in *Christian History and Interpretation*, eds. W. R. Farmer, C. F. D. Moule and R. R. Niebuhr, pp. 161–81 (a volume incidentally that is to be greatly welcomed as a tribute to Dr John Knox; it is full of meat).

ambiguity. Hence the controversies and dissension that arose. Paul's letters contain harsh passages in which he denounces false apostles as the agents of Satan: they might have been called 'paracletes of the Devil'. Fraudulent documents were circulated, and deceptive rumour (2 Thess. 2: 2; cf. 1 Cor. 16: 21, 'I Paul write this greeting with my own hand', and other authenticating statements of this kind). 'Do not be led away by diverse and strange teachings' (Heb. 13: 9. The Pastorals are full of warnings to the same effect). 'Beloved, do not believe every spirit!' (1 John 4: 1).

(2) Within the Fourth Gospel the two or three speeches contained within 13: 31 and 16: 33 may be regarded as dramatic (eucharistic?) homilies of a teacher, built up on the basis of certain sayings of Jesus and enlarged by the writer's own inspired complement. It was entirely natural, therefore, that H. Sasse wished to consider John the Evangelist as the embodiment of the paraclete; but the evidence for this should be sought in the Gospel discourses and not, as Sasse did, in the visions of Revelation.[1]

Other examples of the inspired teacher at work may be found in 3: 11–21, revelation and judgment; 4: 7–38, the water of life; 5: 19–47, the true witness to Jesus Christ; 8: 12–20, the light of the world; 8: 34–59, emancipation from evil; and 10: 1–18, the good shepherd.

Of special interest is 6: 31–58, the living bread, and it should have fuller notice in view of Dr Peder Borgen's stimulating thesis.[2]

Borgen treats this pericope as a homily on the heavenly manna. Its text is stated in verse 31 *b* from Exod. 16: 4, after a haggadic fragment, 'Our fathers ate the manna in the wilderness'.

The particular homiletical 'form' here was discovered by examining similar sermons in Philo and in the Palestinian *midrashim*. According to Borgen, there is however no dependence of John on Philo. John represents a parallel usage, and his is distinctive because the central theme is Jesus, the son of Joseph, the incarnate Word.

---

[1] 'Der Paraklet im Johannesevangelium', *Z.N.T.W.* xxiv (1925), 260 ff.
[2] *Bread from Heaven* (1965). See also the remarks of Wayne Meeks in *The Prophet-King*, pp. 91 ff.

After the text is given, there is a paraphrase of it and of similar texts. This is then combined with traditions from the haggadah, and in the case of John 6 with traditions that related to the Christian Eucharist.

Dr Borgen illuminates the homily by appealing to the LXX and to rabbinic teaching: e.g. ἑλκύω in 6: 44 is a legal term which means, 'I take possession of my property'. Here it is related to Jesus' function as the envoy or representative of the Father who is entitled to possess all Israel. Its people are 'his own' because they are God's. (This sheds light also on ch. 15.)

In the current fashion Borgen supposes that this reinterpretation of a familiar idea came from a Johannine School after the breach between the Church and the Synagogue. He thinks that this School was close to and perhaps strongly influenced by the *Merkabah* mysticism of Judaism, a sort of gnostic theosophy influenced by Ezekiel.[1]

Besides the emphasis in 6: 31 ff. on Jesus as the *shaliaḥ* (apostle or representative) of God, the following are significant:

(*a*) Reference to the gift of the Torah at Sinai, for the Torah was likened to heavenly manna (6: 32, 46; cf. 1: 17 f.).

(*b*) Allusion to the Wisdom of God, for it too could be identified with the manna, and rabbinic Judaism sometimes identified Wisdom and Torah.

(*c*) The I AM formula of 6: 35, 41, 51 'is a midrashic formula by which words from the Old Testament (and the tradition) are identified with persons (such) as Jesus, John the Baptist, and (the Emperor) Trajan, in the first person singular'.[2]

(*d*) The comments made have parallels in the Qumrân scrolls as well as Philo and the rabbis, so that there must be due recognition that the Gospel of John stands fully within the framework of Jewish tradition.

(*e*) τρώγειν, which is used instead of ἐσθίειν in 6: 54–8, and again in 13: 18, probably comes from a peculiar translation of Ps. 41: 9 ('My bosom friend...who ate of my bread, has lifted his heel against me') that appeared in the eucharistic material. But no special theological meaning is intended.

(*f*) Some other elements of the vocabulary point to the

---

[1] Cf. G. Scholem, *Jewish Gnosticism, Merkabah Mysticism, and Talmudic Tradition* (1960); and the comments of R. McL. Wilson, *Gnosis and the New Testament*, pp. 20 f., 26 f. [2] Borgen, *Bread from Heaven*, p. 78.

Wisdom tradition familiar from Prov. 8 and Wisd. Sol., e.g. 'come', 'hunger' and 'thirst' as in 6: 35, 'He that comes to me will (certainly) not hunger, and he that believes on me will (certainly) never thirst'; and again, 'eat' and 'drink' the flesh and blood of Christ, the Son of Man (6: 51–5).

(g) John's docetic opponents may have quoted Isa. 54: 13, 'And they shall all be taught of God', to support their claims.

(h) True believers are in spiritual continuity with the fathers in Israel. Like Nathanael, they are Israelites in whom Jacob's guile is not found (1: 47). John here agrees with Paul.

How then, according to Borgen, is the manna-miracle of the Old Testament related to the feeding of the thousands in the Gospel tradition? Is the former a 'type'? Borgen emphatically and persuasively denies that it is.

The debate between the Johannine Jesus and the Jews about the manna-scripture finds its centre in Jewish failure to see that the historical miracle points away from Moses to Moses' God. Employing the midrashic technique (6: 32), Jesus argues: 'Do not read the text as "Moses gave", but rather as "God the Father gives".' In the same way, the feeding of the thousands had not been properly recognized as a sign (6: 26). It too was external, historical, and it points away from Jesus the son of Joseph to God the Father who feeds men.

This very insight leads to the scandal of the Gospel that the Father's blessings come in and through this martyr who gives his flesh and blood to be consumed in death. John's eucharistic practice, we infer, used 'flesh and blood', as did that of St Ignatius of Antioch and St Justin Martyr, not 'body' as in the other traditions. The mode of feeding in the post-resurrection Church was sacramental.

The reason for this remarkable sermon was polemical, for John had to combat the docetism of his gnostic and spiritualist opponents. This explains some apparent inconsistencies:

(i) 6: 32 a, it was not Moses who gave; 6: 52, how can this man give us?

(ii) 6: 25–7, do not work for food that perishes; and 6: 34, Lord, give us this bread always.

(iii) 5: 39, the scriptures bear witness to me; and 6: 42, is not this Jesus, the son of Joseph?

'John tries to show that the docetic spiritualists in the Church
are like "Jewish" externalists, because both reject the Incarnate
One as the only mediator between God and man.'[1] Hence
Borgen could accept Bultmann's view that 6: 63 b, 'It is spirit
that gives life, flesh is of no avail', is quoted from the teaching of
John's opponents. 'Agreed,' says John, 'yet spirit was enfleshed
in Jesus of Nazareth, the historical prophet we proclaim!'

Two criticisms of this thesis may be made:

The first is that the language of hungering and thirsting for
God, which was familiar of old in the Old Testament world,
need not be related to Wisdom speculations. It is more likely
that the paraclete-preacher (whether the Evangelist or some
source he is using) has built his homily on a genuine word of
Jesus like the beatitude of Luke 6: 21 or Matt. 5: 6. It must be
recalled that John everywhere insists that the truly inspired
teacher will recall the teaching of Jesus himself.

The second is that Borgen does not attend to the difference
between the manna-miracle which has come down in a narrative within the Torah, and the feeding of thousands miracle
which is assumed to be a real event of history. Only if the latter
was described for John and his Church in a narrative possessing
equal scriptural authority could it be compared on all fours to the
manna story.

If it was not, one must make it plain that the two miracles
seem to be treated by John as if *both* were (so to say) simple *acts
of God in history*. But this would appear to be ruled out by
Borgen's initial premise and by his exegesis of John 6: 32.

Should we merely say that the genius of John as a paraclete-
teacher is seen in the way he handles the familiar sign of a
feeding miracle (Mark 6: 30–44) by making use of a contemporary homiletical method? He is not afraid of new terminology, and he does not disdain forms that are current elsewhere,
but he never abandons the central message of Incarnation
and its redeeming mission. Thus we learn something here
about the Johannine Jesus as an interpreter, but also about
John as a Christian teacher. The same spirit rested on John as
on Jesus.

There are lessons to be learned from all this for the ongoing

---

[1] Borgen, *Bread from Heaven*, p. 184.

function of the teacher in a time when it is said that 'the medium is the message' and there is danger of giving up the essential core of the Gospel in order to accommodate it to the drift of public opinion about creation and providence understood in the context of modern scientific discovery.

II. THE INSPIRED PREACHER

The second function of the spirit–paraclete is posited on 15: 26 f., 'he will bear witness...and you also are witnesses', and 16: 14 f., 'he will glorify me, for he will take what is mine and declare it to you'.

(1) From the Fourth Gospel itself one can collect an array of material in which Jesus defines the message of salvation in the strictest christological manner (his self-witness).

He reveals himself to the Samaritan woman as the Messiah and then to her fellow-townspeople in such wise that they confess him to be the saviour of the world (4: 26–42). He reveals himself to the blind man cured as the Son of Man, a figure to be worshipped (9: 37). To all who have ears to hear he reveals himself as the Son who enjoys perfect unity with the Father and may even claim the title 'god' (5: 17; 8: 18, 47, 54 f.; 10: 30, 33–8; 14: 9).

All this he does as One on whom the spirit rests, who speaks the words of God, whom the Father consecrated and sent into the world (1: 32 f.; 3: 34; 10: 36).

Others appear only as consentient witnesses, and we need not list them. John's entire book is a summary of what he held to be the true Gospel, the message of the Son of God in whom and by whom men and women may come to enjoy eternal life. 'Amen, amen, I tell you, we speak of what we know, and bear witness to what we have seen' (3: 11; cf. 1 John 1: 3). Who is the Speaker to Nicodemus? Jesus of Nazareth who had called to him his chosen disciples, 'a teacher come from God'? Yes. But also John the Evangelist as spokesman for the Church to all whom Nicodemus at this place in his book represents: the constituents of the synagogues and the rabbis. And not only John, but all the 'evangelists' of the Church in his day and in our own generation. For the 'we' of a book like John's has virtually no limit in time and space. When the spirit–paraclete comes, it comes to 'abide for ever' in the Church.

What John has done is to make his Jesus the prime theologian and evangelist of the Christian kerygma. And his book bears in all its parts a challenge concerning *the person and the authority of such a Jesus* as John can thus portray. Or, more briefly, for the fourth Evangelist Jesus himself is the Gospel.

(2) If John's is a Gospel about a pentecostal paraclete that enables the preaching of the saving Word, the Acts of the Apostles is a document of the Gospel-preaching in the power of the spirit, renewing Jerusalem, Samaria, Galilee, and going forth to the ends of the Roman world.

See, for instance, Acts 2: 14–42, which needs neither synopsis nor analysis; 3: 15; 4: 20, 33; 5: 32; 8: 25; 10: 41; 20: 21, 24; 22: 15; 23: 11 and 26: 16–18 for the *witness* theme.

In 28: 23 ff. we have a useful summary of the Lucan understanding of a preaching witness:

Paul under guard at Rome is able to continue his work as an inspired preacher, 'witnessing to the kingdom of God and trying to convince (the Roman Jews) *about Jesus* from the Old Testament (the law of Moses and the prophets)'. Then, the usual result of preaching to Jews having taken place, he quotes a favourite Christian proof-text from Isa. 6: 9 f., attributing it to 'the holy spirit', and formally renounces a mission to the Jews in favour of one to the Gentiles. So for two years he remains 'preaching the kingdom of God and teaching about the Lord, Messiah Jesus'. To the very end, Paul is the agent of the spirit–paraclete.

What is said in Acts 9: 31 might have been said about the Church at many turning points in its life: it enjoyed peace with God; it was growing in grace; and, as it made its pilgrim way 'in the fear of the Lord', it increased in numbers 'through the *paraclesis* of the holy spirit'.

It is not necessary to labour the point: Peter and Paul were two only out of a larger company of inspired preachers, through whose imagination, courage, eloquence, and martyrdoms this *paraclesis* was accomplished. Once again John 14: 12 is relevant: the Church and its ministering leaders were doing 'greater works'.

As for the remainder of the New Testament it will suffice to quote Heb. 2: 3 f., 'It (our great salvation) was declared at first by the Lord, and it was attested to us by those who heard him, while God also bore witness by signs and wonders and various miracles and by gifts of the holy spirit...' and to suggest a perusal of Rom. 10: 5–17; 1 Cor. 2: 1–5; Phil. 1: 15–18; Col. 1: 7; 1 Pet. 1: 12; 5: 1; and 2 Tim. 4: 5, 'do the work of an evangelist', one of the very few examples of the word 'evangelist' in the New Testament.[1]

III. THE INSPIRED PROPHET

According to John 16: 13 the spirit–paraclete will declare the things to come. This is a prophetic function.

(1)   In his self-disclosure to the woman at the well Jesus responds to her 'When the Messiah comes, he will declare to us all things' (ὅταν ἔλθῃ ἐκεῖνος, ἀναγγελεῖ ἡμῖν ἅπαντα) by saying, 'It is I, I that speak to you'; or, 'I am the One who was to come' (and also, 'I am the I AM in the flesh'?), John 4: 25 f. Jesus here claims to be the prophet of Samaritan hope, and this may refer to the second Moses.

Among his prophecies may be listed John 10: 18; 12: 32; 13: 38; 14: 12, 29; 15: 20; 16: 2–4, 7. Jesus can do this, of course, as the Word incarnate in whom the spirit rested. In the background may lie biblical material like Deut. 34: 10 f. and 18: 15–22, for the first Moses was full of the spirit (Num. 11: 17). His successor likewise was endowed with the spirit (Num. 27: 18).

John the Baptist too was 'a man sent from God' and this probably concedes that he was prophetic. In John and in some of his predecessors of the Hasmonaean period the work of the prophetic spirit had not ceased (as the later rabbis thought).[2] As we have seen, the Messianic age was to be one in which the spirit of God would be active in new and more wonderful ways for the people of his covenant, and the Christian evidence shows that the Church had prophecy in plenty.

[1] See the article 'Evangelist' in *H.D.B.*, rev. edn. F. C. Grant and H. H. Rowley, p. 276.
[2] b. Yoma 9*b*; Mish. Sotah 9: 12.

(2) St Paul[1] clearly rated the prophet along with the apostle and teacher as a charismatic of the first order (1 Cor. 12: 10, 28 f.), but he insisted that without love prophecy is nothing; and it is sure to pass away (1 Cor. 13: 2, 8).

It is notoriously difficult to be sure exactly what Paul meant by prophesying. In 1 Cor. 14 it is channelled through several speakers and seems to be one form of glossolalia (14: 6). It is however directed to believers (14: 22); and yet it may become an instrument for convicting (the verb is ἐλέγχειν) and blessing an outsider who may be present, for he may be led to discover the 'real presence' of God in the assembly (14: 24 f.).

Such ecstatic and intelligent discourse is more closely related to *teaching* than to prediction. Probably there was no sharp demarcation of the functions, for Paul himself acts as apostle (missionary preacher), prophet, and teacher. Light on this may be forthcoming from current research into the place of prophets in Pharisaism of the first and later centuries of the Christian era. W. D. Davies has examined the *Pirqê Aboth*, which begins, 'Moses received the Law from Sinai and committed it to Joshua, and Joshua to the elders, and the elders to the Prophets; and the Prophets committed it to the men of the Great Synagogue' (Danby's translation).[2]

He goes on to consider some of the issues raised and emphasizes that rabbinic sources regard the prophets as bearers or transmitters of the tradition, but also as creators of tradition.

Moses, the mediator of the Torah, is a man of the Spirit and the Spirit that was given to him was transmitted to the elders who accompanied him to Mount Sinai to receive the Torah. So far from there being any opposition between law and Spirit the opposite seems to have been the case: the transmitters of Torah are bearers of the Spirit.[3] But the Spirit is also *par excellence* the inspiration of prophecy. This assertion is so well attested that no details need be given in support of it... In Num. the giving of the Spirit to the elders, which means that they are given the gift of prophecy, precedes the giving of it to Joshua, and in Midrash Rabbah much is made of the

---

[1] See M.-A. Chevallier, *Esprit de Dieu, paroles d'homme*, pp. 195 f.

[2] 'Reflexions on Tradition: The Aboth Revisited', in the Studies presented to John Knox, *Christian History and Interpretation*, eds. W. R. Farmer, C. F. D. Moule and R. R. Niebuhr, pp. 127–59.

[3] 'In Num. R. on 11: 16–17...the elders are identified by R. Tanhuma (A.D. 427–68) with teachers.'

fact that, although Moses gives of his Spirit to the elders, it remains undiminished, and he is still able to endow Joshua with it (see Num. R. on 11: 17, Soncino translation, p. 672).[1]

In an addendum Dr Davies points out that 'the prophets are interpreters of the Law in 1QS 8: 14–16; and in Josephus, *Bell.* 2. 10. 12 there are prophets among the Essenes; part of their task is to read sacred books. Halakic activity is ascribed to prophets in Mishnah Yadaim 3: 4.'[2]

Is it permissible to conclude from this that in the Christian churches the spirit–paraclete energized not only the more unusual forms of predictive prophecy[3] but also the ethical directives of *prophetic teachers*? They would build on Christian tradition, but to this they would add guidance about the will of God in changing circumstances. There can be little doubt that in the Johannine area and in the Pauline too such guidance never lost sight of the words and acts of Jesus (cf. 1 Cor. 11: 2, 23; 15: 3; 1 Thess. 4: 1 f.; 5: 19–22; 2 Thess. 2: 13–15).

Hence prophesying may have included what we normally call 'preaching', the delivery of homilies that communicated the tradition and applied it to contemporary situations. People always have to be 'reminded' and 'encouraged' to practise what they know to be right.

We may by-pass such places as 1 Pet. 1: 10–12; Jude 17; 1 Tim. 4: 1 ff.; 2 Tim. 3: 1 ff.; and 1 John 4: 1–6 in order to consider the longest and most obvious example of prophecy in the New Testament.

The Revelation of John is a 'prophecy' (1: 3), for the Seer was told to 'write what you see, what is and what is to take place hereafter' (1: 19). God is called 'the God of the spirits of the prophets' (22: 6). So the revelation is given by God (1: 1), but its source and guarantor are in Jesus himself: 'I Jesus have sent my angel to you with this testimony for the churches...He who witnesses to these things says, "Yea, I am coming soon!" Amen. Come, Lord Jesus!' (22: 16, 20). Or, it may be claimed that all this took place because the writer was 'in the spirit on the Lord's day' (1: 10), and everything that is to be sent to the churches of Asia goes with the *imprimatur* of the spirit: 'He that

---

[1] *Christian History and Interpretation*, p. 133.
[2] *Ibid.* p. 159.
[3] See P. Ricca, *Die Eschatologie des vierten Evangeliums*, p. 171.

has an ear let him hear what the spirit is saying to the churches' (2: 7, 11, 17, 29; 3: 6, 13, 22). They are of course also 'the words of the exalted Christ', who is arrayed in all the titles of magnificent and divine glory: he holds the seven stars in his right hand, he is the Alpha and the Omega, he has a sharp two-edged sword, he is the Son of God with eyes like a flame of fire, he possesses the seven spirits of God and the seven stars... he is the True Witness (2: 1–3: 14 and 1: 13–18).

No doubt such an apocalypse may be a legitimate form of the predictive ecstasy, but it suffers from one damaging defect. Nothing is worse for such a document and its author than predictions that go unfulfilled, and that is what has happened to the Revelation of John. The Lord Jesus did not come soon.

During the second century it failed to win much support from the Church at large, though its millenarianism attracted Papias and its vision of a New Jerusalem descending to earth fascinated Montanus and his first disciples. Since the third century the Greek Church of the East has never accepted the book as fully canonical, and the Western Churches have had to accommodate themselves first to the persecutions of Rome, then to the Constantinian peace, and thereafter to the fluctuating fortunes of the Church in the civilization that came in the wake of new learning and new discoveries.

The association of charismatic exegesis and teaching with predictive prophecy has, nevertheless, continued to play a part in Christian preaching;[1] and the Church goes on repeating the ancient formulas about the speedy coming of the Lord Jesus as Judge and King.

The names of some prophets in the New Testament age, in addition to that of John of Patmos, are known: Agabus (Acts 11: 28; 21: 10); some of those listed in Acts 13: 1, Symeon Niger, Lucius of Cyrene, Manaen, Barnabas and Paul; and the four virgin daughters of Philip the evangelist (Acts 21: 9). The author of the Johannine epistles (if he was not the Evangelist) should perhaps also be included as a prophetic teacher.

The promise of the spirit–paraclete embodied in an inspired

---

[1] This could be documented from the history of preaching in the Church from Origen and Ambrose, the medieval friars, the martyr Savonarola and John Knox, to the moderns, D. L. Moody, General Booth and W. (Billy) Graham.

prophet is therefore no dead promise, so long as the Church believes in the energetic presence of God with his people in history. But its limitations should be marked. Long-range predictions about the future are just not consonant with a faith that God loves men and respects their autonomy (itself his gift); yet there must always be those (not necessarily acting as Churchmen) who see some way into the immediate future and warn or console their fellows. 'Would that all the Lord's people were prophets,' cried Moses, 'that the Lord would put his spirit upon them!' (Num. 11: 29).[1]

IV. THE INSPIRED ADVOCATE

At an earlier point we observed that one of the primary meanings, though not the only meaning, of a *paraclete* is that he is an intercessor in cases of law. So the spirit–paraclete in John is to be a witness to Jesus Christ, the Son of God (15: 26), and when he comes, 'he will convict the world of sin and righteousness and judgment' (16: 8–11).

(1) The context is 15: 18–16: 11, where it is said that suffering inevitably awaits the disciples of Jesus in this world, after his departure to the Father. They have to expect hatred, persecution, excommunication from the Synagogue, and death by murder or judicial process. For the world is a humanity of sinners that is easily deluded by the Devil and ruled by him.[2] The Gospel of the self-revealing Jesus in the book of the Evangelist John or in any similar book[3] has no easy passage in the traffic of men.

This context, we have insisted, is not to be regarded as forensic and nothing else. Behind the imagery one should see, in addition to the courts of the imperial rulers and of the Jewish rabbis:

[1] Interesting parallels to the Christian prophet abound; e.g. there is a Muslim view of the prophet as God's messenger and deputy, 'almost a human god'. See 'Avicenna's Theory of Prophecy in the Light of Ash'arite Theology', by M. E. Marmura in *The Seed of Wisdom* (*Festschrift* for T. J. Meek, Toronto, 1964), ed. W. S. McCullough, pp. 159–78.

[2] Whether or not a personal evil spirit, Satan or Belial, really exists is irrelevant to the belief stated in John.

[3] It may be assumed that such books preceded John's.

(i) the ceaseless warfare between good and evil in the hearts of men.

(ii) the kind of antagonism that is expressed merely in slander and gossip, catcalling and the petty pinpricks of social intercourse.

(iii) religious schisms, which can be of them all the most bitter (John 17 shows that the Evangelist was aware of disunity).

Beginning with the drama of John 9 and its reference to excommunication from the Synagogue (9: 22; cf. 12: 42; 16: 2), Louis Martyn thinks that there were in the Johannine Church Jewish disciples, some who were 'rulers' in the Jewish community, some who had been banned from the Synagogue and some who were secret believers. The formal separation between the Church and the Synagogue had been accomplished in John's area by means of the new benediction against heretics (*Berakoth* 28 f.) promulgated by the rabbinic leaders centred in Jamnia. It took place about A.D. 85 when a *Takkanah* was sent to the synagogues in Palestine and the Dispersion from Jamnia. In John 12: 42, Martyn 'the Pharisees' would explain as a reference to Jewish apostles or to members of the local Jewish *gerousia* in the Johannine city.[1]

This is a very persuasive thesis and more convincing than that of D. R. A. Hare, who holds that the test required of any suspected Jews, namely the recitation of the benediction against heretics, led only to self-exclusion and not to any formal excommunication from the Synagogue.[2] John's tone suggests that he has in mind the formal ban, something that is not at all likely to have been in force within the first thirty years of the Church.

(2) The New Testament evidence for the sufferings of Christians is so profuse that it can mostly be relegated to a footnote of references.[3] There were lashings in the Jewish synagogues, beatings, shipwreck, hunger and thirst, and all

---

[1] *History and Theology in the Fourth Gospel*, pp. 19, 22–41.

[2] *Jewish Persecution of Christians* (1967), p. 55.

[3] 2 Thess. 1: 4; 1 Thess. 2: 14–16; 3: 4; Gal. 1: 13; 6: 12; Rom. 15: 31; Phil. 1: 29 f., and esp. 2 Cor. 11: 23 ff.; 12: 10; Acts 5: 41; 8: 1; 9: 16, 29; 13: 50; 14: 19, 22; 16: 19–24; 17: 5; 18: 12–17; 19: 29; 20: 3, 23; 21: 11–14, 27 ff.; 23: 12–15; 25: 3; Heb. 10: 23–5; 1 Pet. 3: 14–17; 4: 1, 12–19; 5: 9; Rev. 2: 10; 3: 10; 6: 10; 2 Tim. 3: 12.

kinds of danger for a travelling missionary of the calibre and spirit of Paul. The whole brotherhood throughout the world is said to share a common suffering; and so on.

The death of disciples is alluded to in Acts 9: 1; 26: 9–11; Rev. 6: 9; 20: 4–6. Two witnesses are mentioned in the famous passage, Rev. 11: 3–13. They were prophets and had special powers, but they were killed by the beast from the bottomless pit, 'and their dead bodies will lie in the street of the great city which is allegorically called Sodom and Egypt, where their Lord was crucified (Jerusalem)'. They were however resurrected by 'a spirit of life that came from God' and then translated to heaven on a cloud. It is impossible to identify the characters of this strange tale. Enoch, Moses and Elijah were all translated to heaven, according to the Old Testament, but the corpses of none of them lay in Jerusalem. It is possible however that an obscure story about Moses *redivivus* and Elijah *redivivus* lies beneath the surface.

Specific names of three martyrs are known: Stephen, Acts 7: 54–60; James the son of Zebedee, Acts 12: 2; and Antipas of Pergamum, Rev. 2: 13. This information can be supplemented from various sources (e.g. Josephus and 1 Clement 5) on the death of James the Lord's brother and on the martyrdoms of Peter and Paul.[1]

To assist the disciples to face crisis situations they had *the Lord's Prayer*, with its petitions for deliverance from the 'tribulations' associated with the coming of the kingdom of God, and from the Devil (Matt. 6: 13; Luke 11: 4, Western text; cf. John 17: 15; 2 Thess. 3: 3).[2]

They had also the assurance that divine power (*dynamis*) was available to bring strength and liberation (cf. 1 Thess. 1: 5, the good news of Christ had come to Salonica 'in power and in holy spirit and with full conviction'; 1 Pet. 1: 5; 2 Tim. 1: 7 f., 'a spirit of power', 'the power of God'; 4: 17).

A vocation so divine laid on Christians an obligation to live with such fidelity and grace that it would become plain how in them

---

[1] Cf. O. Cullmann, *Peter: Disciple, Apostle, Martyr* (Philadelphia, 1953); Jocelyn Toynbee and J. B. Ward-Perkins, *The Shrine of St Peter and the Vatican Excavations* (London, 1956).

[2] Luke 11: 2 in Marcion's text would be fitting here: 'let thy holy spirit come upon us and cleanse us'.

God was at work to redeem them in holiness of spirit and belief in the truth (2 Thess. 2 : 13). The Timothy of the Pastoral Epistles is advised to 'guard the truth that has been entrusted to you by the holy spirit that dwells in us' (2 Tim. 1 : 14). This language reminds us of 'the spirit of truth' in the Johannine literature.

(3)   To the believing Church, one of the most consoling aspects of the spirit–paraclete's ministry, 'when he comes', must surely have been what is meant by his convicting the world: i.e. defeating the Opposition. For this was to be no merely defensive operation, holding disciples in the foxhole trenches and discouraging any adventurous forays into no-man's-land. The paraclete in this forensic rôle is a *prosecuting counsel*.

I suggest that the reality in the life of the Johannine Church which had demonstrated to our Evangelist how this promise had been fulfilled was the way in which Christians on trial for their life passed from apology to counter-offensive. This presumably had been going on within John's own area, but there was already a 'tradition' about it.[1]

It is this tradition that we see illustrated in the Acts of the Apostles: e.g. in Peter's bold front when he insists that he and his colleagues must obey God rather than men. Peter, it is said, spoke as a man 'filled full of holy spirit', and he pushes his attack by claiming that Jesus of Nazareth who had been rejected was now the Head Cornerstone (2: 22–4, 37; 3: 12–26; 4: 7–20; cf. Mark 12: 10; 1 Pet. 2: 7; *Barnabas* 6: 4; Ps. 118: 22). So the accusers are soon made to understand by what *power*, in what *Name*, with what *witness* the apostolic community of Jesus is ready to stand before the world (cf. 5: 27–32). Before God it is in fact the priests and rulers of the Jews that are on trial, for God had vindicated Jesus in resurrection by giving him his 'right place', his 'just due', at the Right Hand of Majesty on High!

Another dramatic example is to be seen in the sudden turn in the long speech of Stephen, when he cries out, 'You stiff-necked people that you are, you are the "uncircumcised" in heart and ear. For ever resisting *the holy spirit*! Just like your

---

[1] Its origin is in the trial of Jesus himself: see e.g. John 18: 4, 6, 21, 34, 37; 19: 11. Jesus was in command of the situation, and the faithful martyr follows his example!

fathers before you, for what *prophet* did they not persecute?' (Acts 7: 51–3). In the final description of the martyr's death the Christian apologist set a pattern that influenced many subsequent martyrologies, for he insisted on the holiness of spirit with which Stephen was filled even in his death-throes (7: 55–60).

Perhaps the richest source of material on the theme of *the prosecutor in the person of the accused* is found in Acts 22: 1–26: 32, where Paul, the paraclete of the Christians, is shown 'standing as a witness' before kings and governors (26: 22).

The voice of the Apostle is not the voice of craven fear; he is ready to challenge all comers. He can speak of an actual voice (a *bath qol?*) at his commissioning; he has the wit to take advantage of differences between Pharisees and Sadducees on the matter of resurrection and drive a wedge in that would discomfit his opponents. One hopes that this was not in sober fact his way of defending the Faith, for it short-changes the Christology that he defined and proclaimed, but it was very effective courtroom tactics and many a lesser man may have tried it as a means of escape and survival.

In Acts 24: 1–9 Tertullus, the professional pleader, makes a poor showing and Paul seems to ignore him with contempt. 'Where are the Jews from Asia?' he shouts. It was they who had claimed that Paul was guilty of profaning the Temple: why are they not present to press charges? We are not surprised that Paul will have nothing to do with a return to Jerusalem and that he asserts his right to appeal to Caesar. He is no criminal, he tells Festus, and he is not afraid to die.

The same tactics are employed in the appearance before Agrippa and Bernice, with the result that he is vindicated: 'He could have been released if only he had not appealed to Caesar' (26: 32).

It may be that these dramatic scenes owe much to the genius of an editor, possibly Luke the companion of Paul, but this cannot detract from the exhilaration with which the speeches stir the reader. The living Christ was providing to such witnesses 'a mouth and wisdom', so that the tables were turned by accused men who became inspired controversialists.[1]

---

[1] To be realistic, one must assume that, as Pliny told the Emperor Trajan, there had been Christian failures and apostates; on which see Heb. 6: 4–6; 1 John 5: 16; Mark 3: 29; *Shepherd* of Hermas, *Mand.* III, 1–3; IV, i, 8, iii, 1–7.

The topics in the Christian apology certainly included the credibility of Jesus as the Envoy of the Father and the long-awaited Messiah of Israel; there were *testimonia* in plenty to back the case. It would therefore be sin not to believe in him. One omission is perhaps the assertion that the Devil had been condemned, although one could cite Rev. 12: 7–12. But there are passages which claim that Jesus Christ is superior to all good and evil spirits.[1]

The spirit of endurance in the times of tribulation that lasted all through the first three centuries could not have been sustained, however, without a hope that God would finally call the unbelieving world, the persecuting Synagogue, the pagan Empire of Rome, and all the devils there are to a final reckoning. Hence the promises of John 16: 8–11 may have had the Last Judgment in mind too.

So long as any darkness endured, so long as men and women rejected Jesus as the Son of God, so long as the faithful conventicles were hated, made to suffer, and persecuted, it could never be said that the Evil One had been destroyed, far less redeemed. What could be said, in faith and hope if not always with love, was that the life of Jesus and the witness of the Christian martyrs proved that the Devil had been condemned. This too must have become one of the standard 'heads' in every Christian homily and each word of testimony in the pulpits of the public executioner.

V. THE INSPIRED COMMUNITY

This survey of the presence of the spirit–paraclete in the membership and leadership of churches during the pre-Johannine period and also in John's own time, or indeed immediately after John, would not be complete without some consideration of John 14: 16 f., 'that it may be with you always...it will dwell with you and will be in you'.

The power of the spirit, pouring into the Church in the name and with the authority of its Lord Christ, is a means to a profound communion grounded in divine love. For such power springs out of the loving unity in the life of the Father and the

[1] For example, 1 Cor. 15: 24 f.; Gal. 4: 9; Phil. 2: 9 f.; Col. 2: 8 ff.; Heb. 1: 4; Eph. 1: 21 f.; 6: 11 ff.

Son (3: 35; 10: 17; 14: 9; 15: 9; 17: 21, 23–6). Since the Good Shepherd knows and loves his own, and they love and obey him alone, there must be 'one flock' (10: 14–16).

This love that sits at the root of Christian community and animates its life is not something that can be verbalized only; else it ceases to be *agape*, love. For *agape* gives and gives to the uttermost (3: 16; 15: 13; 1 John 4: 10). Love is a form of obedience (13: 34; 14: 15, 21–4; 15: 10, 17). And its rewards will be 'consecration in the truth', 'unity in the Father and the Son', and a vision of the Son's radiant glory (17: 20–6).

There is a hope implied in such statements, for John cannot hide from the attentive reader the schism that lay behind the prayers of the Christ for the unity of his people. The same is true of other New Testament passages that have Christian unity as a central topic.[1]

It must also be said that the Johannine promise that the spirit–paraclete will rest for ever in the Church is in part at least one that professes a hope and offers a faith. For it is not to be believed that the spirituality of the churches, either among the leadership or the membership at large, was constantly at the fever heat of ecstasy, or was steadily patient, humble, God-dependent, trustful, loving. In the Old Israel it was well known that the spirit of God came intermittently; that certain persons were favoured far beyond others; and that men once inspired did not remain in the state of godliness this implied. New Testament evidence likewise tells us that Christians in the 'Israel after the spirit' (1 Cor. 10: 18 by implication; cf. 'the church of God', 1 Cor. 10: 32) had their critical times of dis-union, of heresy, cowardice and loss of faith. Heb. 12: 12–17 makes this point explicitly concerning one area of the Church.

It is therefore with a good deal of caution that John 14: 16 f. should be referred to the concrete situation of the Johannine Church. This applies indeed to the whole endeavour of this chapter. It must not be assumed that we have lost sight of the 'otherworldly' side of the paraclete idea. For it is true always for John that the spirit is power *from above, from heaven*, hence from God himself or from Jesus Christ who is no longer here on earth but is exalted far above all things. What we have tried

---

[1] Acts 2: 44; 4: 31–7; 9: 31; 1 Cor. 12; Eph. 4; Heb. 10: 24; Jas. 2: 15 f.; 1 Pet. 1: 8, 22; 2: 4 f., 9 f.; 3: 8; Jude 20, etc.

to do is to grasp behind the dramatic futures of John 14–16 the facts of Church life in John's day: 'the spirit–paraclete will dwell...will teach...will bear witness' means that Christians had acted in all these ways to embody the life of the Church, a communion of the Friends of Jesus.

Was it not only because the promises had been marvellously, if partially, fulfilled that John took the trouble to record his version of 'the eternal life that was with the Father and was revealed to us' (1 John 1: 2)?

CHAPTER 10

AN EVALUATION OF
JOHANNINE SPIRITUALITY

In this concluding chapter some comments must be made about the quality of the spirituality we have discovered in the Fourth Gospel.

(1) There are some extremely dangerous elements in it:

(a) An inspired leader, an evangelist, a teacher, a prophet or the like, might easily be tempted to think that he was in fact an incarnation of the spirit–paraclete. This is what one may designate the 'Montanist error'. Instead of humble gratitude to the God and Father of Jesus Christ, instead of a wise and balanced assessment of one's own spiritual powers, it is all too easy to substitute an arrogant know-all attitude.

It is this kind of assertiveness that is to be seen in the pretensions of the opponents of St Paul at Corinth, who could 'perform the signs of a true apostle' (2 Cor. 12: 12) and who claimed that Christ was speaking in them (cf. 2 Cor. 13: 3). Perhaps Diotrephes 'who likes to put himself first' was such a man (3 John 9). Dangers of a similar sort may lie behind 1 Tim. 4: 1–5.

(b) The Johannine Jesus, by definition, is such a figure; for we have noted over and over again how clearly he is a plenipotentiary superbly equipped with divine powers. The inevitable result is that he strikes the reader as being inhuman. He goes as it is ordained that he should go. He argues so mysteriously about the Father and his own status that our sympathy goes to the perplexed interlocutors. This may be all very well on a stage, but it does little to recommend the prophet from Nazareth. 'How long will you keep us in suspense?' the baffled people cry, 'if you are the Christ, tell us plainly' (10: 24). He has foreknowledge. He lays down his life, and takes it again: as though this was not the most astonishing thing! 'Which of you convicts me of sin?' (8: 46) is balanced by 'If I had not come and spoken to them, they would not have sin...If I had not done

among them the works which no one else did, they would not
have sin...when the paraclete comes, he will convict the world
of sin...' (15: 22, 24; 16: 8). Lazarus falls ill, but it is 'not unto
death' (11: 4); after two more days Jesus gets ready to go,
because 'our friend Lazarus has fallen asleep', that is, he *is* dead.
No wonder the disciples are bewildered (11: 11–15). When he
arrives in Bethany, first Martha and then Mary tell him, 'Lord,
if you had been here, he would not have died'. True, but the
whole point (known to Jesus from the beginning) is that the
man must die in order that he may be resurrected to the glory
of God (11: 4, 40, 42). So 'a man' whose father and mother we
know stands beside the grave of another man who has been
dead four days and shouts, 'Lazarus, come out'; and Lazarus
did come out, 'his hands and feet bound with bandages, and
his face wrapped with a cloth'. Jesus spoke, 'Unbind him, and
let him go': as if he were not really a man at all. For this is not
natural language.

This, no doubt, is why Käsemann thinks that John is not
anti-docetic.

This is why Hugh Montefiore writes:

Let me first say that I would agree that the Christ of the Fourth
Gospel is arrogant; but I do not believe that the Christ of the Fourth
Gospel speaks the words of Jesus of Nazareth. The life and teaching
of Jesus have passed through the crucible of its author's mind, and
the worsening relationship of Christians and Jews at the time when
it was written has left its mark upon the monologues of Jesus, and
especially on his dialogues with the Jews.[1]

It will not do to brush this off as if it were unfair to the
Evangelist; and it will not do to blame some source he has used
for the story of Lazarus. Whatever the source, John has employed it and woven it into the structure of his book.

Nevertheless I find it hard to charge John with docetic
heresy: all the trappings of divinity and predestination do not
rob the Johannine Jesus altogether of his humanness. He was
a man who had friends and enemies, who could sit down in the
noontime heat tired, who carried a cross and endured shame.
John refuses to be satisfied with a non-historical Saviour.
I believe he is intellectually anti-docetic because he is an

---

[1] *Awkward Questions on Christian Love* (1964), pp. 63 f.

'orthodox catholic' in his central faith.[1] Yet he is on the edge of heresy because his Christ is '*the Logos* made flesh' rather than 'a man in whom the spirit of God is' (like Daniel).

(c) On the basis of Johannine teaching, in the third place, the Church was liable to consider itself not as a fallible society of redeemed sinners but as a spirit-filled community which possessed the truth, knew the way, and already enjoyed life eternal (5: 24; 1 John 3: 14). Such a Church is one which will be in danger of claiming to be 'in itself' or 'as such' a sinless society, an infallible body or one that has access to infallible truth. In other words, the catholicism of John (for this is a legitimate description) could lead to the kind of Catholicism that has sometimes appeared in history and is a perversion of the spirit-led communion. It could also lead to perverse forms of Bible-dominated churches which claim to have infallible knowledge mediated to inspired exegetes by the spirit–paraclete.

(2)   John is marked by an unusual economy of statement, and this produces some serious limitations.

This economy applies to the theological ideas: e.g. the *Logos*, who is prophet, shepherd, true vine, saviour, king and son; the heavenly *Father*, bound in mysterious communion to the Son; the *spirit* or the *spirit–paraclete*, which is the power of God in the life and teaching of Jesus, and the power of God and of Christ in the life and doctrine of the Church; the *company of disciples*, the 'twice-born' who have been emancipated by Jesus for the service of divine truth; '*life*' that is eternal, and is nourished by 'water' and 'bread', the sacraments of Christ's redeeming Manhood; and finally, the *dualism* that compels a spiritual choice between the Light and the Darkness, God or the Devil, a judgment now—with the opportunity to migrate beyond it into life—or the Last Judgment, when there may be only a resurrection of death (5: 29 by implication).

The author's intention was, however, deliberately restricted, so that we need not consult his book for the names of the Twelve nor for any character sketch; there is not one exorcism in it, and none of the parables familiar from the Synoptics. There is very little movement from 13: 30 to 18: 1, even if our hypothesis

[1] Cf. F. Mussner, *The Historical Jesus in the Gospel of John* (1967).

about that section be acceptable. 'Jesus did many other signs...but they are not written in this book' (20: 30).

The Fourth Gospel is a dramatic evangelical and pastoral treatise rather than a history.

(3)   The writer tends to exaggeration.

The Christ will draw all men to be his possession, a sentence that is formally inconsistent with 5: 29.

John's ambivalence is marked in respect of the 'world' and he is by no means clear about its salvation (3: 17; 4: 42; 17: 21). What possible optimism could he have cherished that hatred, persecution, excommunication from the synagogues, and judicial death sentences would one day give way to consent, belief and brotherhood and peace?

How far had John thought through what is involved in the doctrine that even the Pilates of this world derive their power and authority from God?

The theory has a long lineage in Jewish history, and it is consistent with faith in divine providence. But will the Pilates ever learn, the Domitians, the Julians, the Ivans and the Hitlers? Will the priests of the establishment like Caiaphas ever be holy? Is there ground for hope that the historical existence of 'La Terre des Hommes' will be purified and become holy unto the Lord?

(4)   The Johannine concentration on the world and man in relation to God is typical of the canonical New Testament. If one may so put it, the documents are all sheerly '*religious*'.

There is nothing in the New Testament, for instance, that can correspond to the Old Testament understanding of human craftsmanship like that of Bezaleel, 'to devise artistic designs, to work in gold, silver and bronze, in cutting stones for setting and in carving wood, for work in every craft'; or that of his colleague Oholiab, the craftsman of the Ark and its furnishings, as something that derived from God's gift to them of his own spirit (Exod. 31: 1–11). There is no thought that men should look for such divine blessing in the *cattleman*, Jabal, the *musician*, Jubal, and the *ironmaster*, Tubal-cain (Gen. 4: 20–2).

It is as if the social conditions of the ancient world were wholly irrelevant to the religious drama being played out by

Jesus; as if nothing needed to be done about the poor (John 12: 8) or the money in the box that the traitor Judas used to carry (John 13: 29).

From the perspective of what is sometimes called the 'third world' of our contemporary age all this must seem very odd. The *life* which men were invited to enjoy through coming to belief in Jesus was 'eternal life', a kind of heavenly existence unlike the human condition amid the flux and terror, the power politics and materialism of the everyday world we all know. Hence a cynic might well ask what John 4: 14 has to offer to the populations that still lack an adequate water supply even for life 'in the flesh'; or how John 6: 57 (ὁ τρώγων με) reads in modern Bihar or any of the famine spots of Asia.

(5) What redeems this 'religious' message is that it has not lapsed into the apocalyptic pessimism which is all too common, and that it is based on a profound appreciation of what true Christlike love means.

It is strange how seldom love comes to the fore in the first main part of the Fourth Gospel (3: 16; 11: 3; cf. 5: 20). Instead, there are some repellent aspects there: the brusque surprise of 3: 10; the accusing finger in 4: 48; and the lack of compassion in 4: 50; 5: 6; 6: 6; 9: 3; 11: 4. But the atmosphere suddenly changes at 13: 1, 'he loved his own to the end'.

The disciples are bidden to love one another in the way that Jesus had loved them (13: 34 f.). Jesus' care is seen in his pioneering a road and providing an eternal home for them (14: 2–4), his repeated assurances that their prayers will be heard (14: 14; 15: 16; 16: 24), his promise to be for ever with them (14: 18–21, 23 f.), his gift of peace, a very different kind of peace from anything to be had from the world (14: 27; 16: 33; cf. 20: 19, 26), and finally his certainty that the spirit of truth acting as a paraclete will compensate for his physical absence (14: 16 f., 26, etc.). So there will be sunshine after rain and joy after sorrow; they will be comforted (16: 20–4).

Many readers find that the most moving example of the Christ's love for the disciples is in the royal prayer of intercession, the prayer in which (as C. H. Dodd taught us) the Son 'ascends' to the Father. For the Son himself must say the Lord's Prayer, 'deliver them from the Devil', and consecrate himself for their sake. Nothing short of a perfect love-communion of Father, Son and disciples will avail for the perilous adventures that lie before the men whom God gave to the Son but whom he must leave. 'I have made thy Name known to them and I will go on making it known, so that the love with which thou hast loved me may be in them and that I myself may be in them' (17: 26).

To the cynic and the critic, then, John might make answer by saying that in any age love put into effect in the spirit of the Master who washed the feet of Judas and Peter is the kind of love to feed the minds and exhilarate the hearts of men and women in all generations, in all nations, in all the arts and crafts and commerce of hand and brain. For it is a love to make the stars move and to make men saints. The supreme legacy of this Jesus whom John served as witness is his own '*spirit*' released to be a '*paraclete*' that will teach, console and inspire those who are still prepared to believe in God.

APPPENDIX I

THE LITERARY STRUCTURE OF JOHN

I

The Gospel of John is a highly integrated document, one that needs to be read backward (so to speak) as well as forward. Hence it should not be surprising that his attempt to discover the contextual range of the spirit–paraclete sayings compels the investigator to press behind 13: 1 which marks the opening scene of acts and words in the Supper Room in Jerusalem on the betrayal night. It soon becomes clear that one must have a very clear grasp of the book's structure from first to last. Certain divisions suggest themselves quite naturally at first sight:[1]

(a) 1: 1–18, the poetic introduction announcing the incarnation of the Logos in Jesus.

(b) 1: 19–12: 50, the public ministry in Judaea, Galilee and Samaria. Dodd has called this 'The Book of Signs'.

(c) 13: 1–17: 26, the Farewell Discourses and the prayer of intercession.

(d) 18: 1–20: 31, the last days of Jesus and the story of his Resurrection.

(e) 21: 1–25, apparently an appendix, describing a Galilean Resurrection appearance and the story of Jesus' commission to Peter and his statement about the Beloved Disciple.

Throughout the first twelve chapters, in the narrative of signs, debates and monologues, two controversial matters keep recurring: *By what authority* does Jesus act and teach? and, Can *a satisfactory witness* be produced in favour of Jesus' claims? (cf. Mark 11: 27–33). This whole section has the form of a great contest or assize. From one point of view, God's Word has come in judgment to the world; from another, the Jews have put Jesus on trial for his life and it is foredoomed that he will die.[2] Yet it is also manifest that for Jesus death did not mean disaster,

[1] The Commentaries all have analyses to offer. One article that is of special interest is H. Van den Bussche, 'La structure de Jean I–XII', in *L'Évangile de Jean* (Coll. Bib. Lovan., 1958), pp. 61–109.

[2] 2: 4, 22; 5: 18; 6: 51, 64, 71; 7: 8, 19, 30; 8: 20, 59; 10: 31; 11: 47–53, 57; 12: 7, 33.

155

because it was ordained for his exaltation: 'I have power to lay down my life and I have power to take it again; this charge I have received from my Father' (10: 18). The proper climax therefore is the cry of Thomas, 'My Lord and my God!' (20: 28).

It is customary to mark a decisive transition at 13: 1 in accord with what seems to be a natural break, but I wish to propose instead that this transition should be marked at 11: 55.

There are time indications at 11: 55; 12: 1, 12, 20 and 13: 1 which belong together and should not be separated:

11: 55, now the passover of the Jews was at hand...

12: 1, six days before the passover...

12: 12, the next day a great crowd that had come for the feast...

12: 20, now among those who went up to worship at the feast...

13: 1, now before the feast of the passover...

That is to say, from 11: 55 the scene is set in Jerusalem for what we may call an 'eschatological passover' and a new exodus (cf. Luke 9: 31).

The Fourth Gospel may be analysed, therefore, as follows:

I	The Prologue	1: 1–18
II	The Conflicts of Jesus with the Jews	1: 19–11: 54
III	The Secret Ministry	11: 55–17: 26
IV	The Accomplishment of a Mission	18: 1–20: 31
V	An appendix	21: 1–25

Of course it must not be thought that these divisions are hard and fast separations, or that the Evangelist worked with such a scheme in his mind! All that we can expect is that this analysis may truly correspond to a purpose that was present to John's mind; and that purpose is probably to be sought in 20: 30 f.:

Now Jesus indeed performed many other Signs also in the presence of his disciples, but they are not written up in this book. Those (that have been described) have been written up so that you may come to believe that Jesus is the Messiah, the Son of God, and that by so believing you may enjoy life in his Name.[1]

[1] Reading the aorist subjunctive with W and most authorities; the text of Vaticanus, S, Θ, and others, ἵνα πιστεύητε, might refer to existing

Chs. 1–20 owe something of their literary unity to the constant reference of the author to human response to Jesus, often by the use of a formula, 'many believed on his Name': see 1: 12, 50; 2: 11, 22, 23 (formula); 4: 39–42 (formula in 41), 53; 5: 44–7; (6: 14, 29 f. are variants on the theme); 6: 69; 7: 5, 31 (formula), 48; 8: 30 (formula); 9: 35–8; (10: 37 f., a variant); 10: 42 (formula); 11: 26 f., 45 (formula); 12: 11 (formula), 37, 44; 14: 1, 11; 16: 9; 17: 8, 20; 20: 8, 25, 27, 29.

It has been suggested that the story of Lazarus (11: 1–45) was a unit in itself and that it may not belong to the original structure; this is possible. But it founders on the obvious fact that this Gospel was intended (certainly as we have it) to place the arrest and trials of Jesus after the Lazarus stories (cf. 12: 2, 9). John had no intention of proceeding from 10: 42 to the account of the Triumphal Entry. In his retelling of the Gospel the miracle of Lazarus is the final reason why 'many of the Jews came to believe in Jesus' and it provokes the conspiracy to destroy him (11: 47–53).

II

I suggest that 11: 55–12: 50 forms a bridge between the ministry of signs and controversies and the ministry that consisted in private teaching of disciples.

(*a*) 11: 55–7 is a dramatic introduction, 'where is this Jesus? will he come to the feast? If he does, what will he say and do, and what will the authorities do?'

Jesus is deliberately pictured as a figure that raises questions and is mysterious. This agrees with earlier hints in 5: 44–7; 6: 19 f., 25, 41, 52, 60; 7: 11 f., 15, 26*b*, 28, 35 f., 40 ff., to say nothing of the prologue; and it recurs in 12: 36*b*, 44–50; 14: 7–11; 16: 29 f.; 18: 4–8, 33; and 19: 8.

(*b*) In 12: 1–19 the stories of the Anointing and the Entry are tied together for John's own purposes (contrast Mark 11: 1–11; 14: 3–11). Mary, Martha and Lazarus were central characters in 11: 1–54.

(*c*) 12: 20–50 should not be interfered with, e.g. by moving 44–50 to a place between 36*a* and 36*b*.

believers ('that you may go on believing'). The tenses are however ambiguous. On the whole, it seems right to ascribe to John a genuine missionary concern.

For one thing, 36*b* in our judgment belongs with the preceding, as the parallels in 8: 59 and 10: 39 suggest (cf. too 8: 20, 30).

For another, the sudden reappearance of Jesus at 44 is thoroughly Johannine and in keeping with the mysterious quality already mentioned: his coming and going involves heaven and earth (1: 17, 29, 33, 51 set the tone, and see 8: 59; 10: 39); and he moves in sovereign freedom (6: 15, 24 f.; 7: 8–10, 14, 37).

Hence rearrangement would ruin a skilful effect that seems to be due to the genius of John and not to the clumsy work of an editor. Jesus will next come on stage at an evening meal in the home of a friend in Jerusalem. No matter where one wishes to mark the end of the public ministry (10: 40–2, 11: 54, 12: 36, or 12: 50), no account is given of how Jesus came to this home. Similarly, although it is said (18: 2) that Jesus often went to the garden across the Kidron valley, there is no record in the entire Gospel of John of any similar visit. And at 13: 2 the supper is already in process and we are left to guess at what happened in the interim. John does not write as an historian but, as Dr R. H. Strachan used to say, as a dramatist.

Some examples may be given of the way in which earlier passages are recalled and later ones anticipated in 11: 55 ff.

(i) 12: 23, 'The hour has come for the Son of Man to be glorified', recalls 1: 51; 2: 4; 7: 6, 30; 8: 28, and points toward 13: 1, 31; 17: 1, 5 (cf. 12: 27).

(ii) The main thrust of 12: 25 f. (losing and keeping life) is forward to 13: 16, 20; 14: 3, 23; 15: 15, 18–21; 16: 27, and 17: 14, 22–4; but we are reminded of 7: 34 and 8: 21 f.

(iii) The distress referred to in 12: 27 presumably is due in part at least to the imminence of the betrayal (6: 64, 71; cf. 13: 18, 21, 30; 18: 2, 5).

(iv) 'For a little longer' has a close parallel in 7: 33 and it recurs in 13: 33; 14: 19; 16: 16–19. But the imperative, 'walk while you have the light', is entirely and fittingly a reference back only, to 8: 12; 11: 9 f., and other light/darkness passages.

The closing words of this verse, 12: 35, 'he does not know whither he is bound', have parallels in 3: 8 and 8: 14, and later at 14: 4 f.

(v) In 12: 37–43 we note the reference to '*signs*', which does not require documentation; '*his glory*', 1: 14; 2: 11; 5: 41, 44; 17: 5, 22, 24; ἀποσυνάγωγος (only in John): cf. 9: 22 and 16: 2.

(vi) Finally, in 12: 44–50:

'*Belief and light*' are linked only to what precedes in 3: 21, 8: 12 and 9: 5. '*Judgment at the last day*' recalls 6: 39 f. and 11: 24, and perhaps anticipates 16: 11. The words, 'he that sees me sees him that sent me', whilst they may suggest 1: 18 and 8: 19, must await development in 14: 7 ff. But the remaining themes are once more of the 'bridge' type.

'To *guard* or *keep the words of Jesus*' is familiar from 3: 34; 5: 47; 6: 63, 68; 8: 20, 47, 51 f. and 10: 21, with some variations in both verbs and nouns in true Johannine style. In the next division further variation takes place (14: 10, 15, 21, 23 f.; 15: 7, 10, 20; 17: 6, 8).

Judgment is a major topic at 3: 17–21 and 8: 16 but again at 16: 8, 11 (cf. 12: 31).

That Jesus does *not* speak *on his own authority* but by the *commandment of the Father* is a dominant assertion throughout the Gospel: earlier at 3: 34; 5: 30; 7: 16–18; 8: 26, 28, 42 and 10: 18; later at 14: 10, 24, 31; 15: 10.

The relation of the divine commandment to eternal life is found both in 5: 26; 6: 40 and 17: 2; 20: 31.

III

If it be admitted that 11: 55–12: 50 forms a causeway between the book of signs and the narrative of the last days of Jesus, how can we justify taking this section with what follows it rather than with what precedes?

Raymond E. Brown argues against our position:

It is quite clear that the end of ch. xii and the beginning of xiii specifically mark a break in the narrative. In xii. 37–43 there is a summary description and analysis of Jesus' public ministry and its effect on the people; xii. 44–50 are the last words of Jesus directed to the people in general. In xiii. 1–3 there is a shift in emphasis, marked by the statement, 'It was the Passover feast, and Jesus was aware that the hour had come for him to pass from this world to the Father.' All Jesus' words in chs. xiii–xvii are directed to 'his own' (xiii. 1)...[1]

[1] *John I–XII*, p. cxxxviii.

On this we make the following comments:

13: 1 reads, 'Now *before* the feast of Passover...' It is a variant of 11: 55. So far as the time factor is concerned, there certainly is no shift in emphasis. Brown is inaccurate.

The royal prayer of intercession in 17 is addressed to the heavenly Father. It may be implied that the disciples overheard it: but it is clearly not directed to them.

The private character of the discourses in the Supper Room should neither obscure similar material in the record of the public ministry, nor fail to remind us that Jesus' written words in John were intended to catch the ears of later Gospel readers and listeners (cf. 17: 20; 20: 29). There is private teaching at 1: 43–51; 3: 1 ff.; 6: 60–71; 8: 31–59; and 11: 4–16.

Is it quite definite that the great cry of 12: 44–50 was addressed to the general public? Jesus left the public at 12: 36 *b*, and the present form of the chapter surely means that all the material from verse 37 to verse 50 belongs elsewhere. Is this a cry of Jesus on the stage of the written book of John's Gospel, a cry to the world that watches in John's time and in our own?

Consequently we are not persuaded that John's division should be placed at 12: 50 as being the end of the public ministry. The time is Passover; the place is Jerusalem; the action is (1) what Jesus did a week before the Feast; (2) how he entered the capital city as a King; (3) what he did and said in the Supper Room, how Judas went out, and with what words Jesus comforted the others, and how at the end he ascended to the Father in prayer; (4) how he was arrested, tried, crucified and raised from the dead. The entire pericope 11: 55–20: 31 has its own dramatic unity, and the action in it moves with inexorable speed. It is often forgotten that the speeches and the prayer occupied a very short period of time.

IV

There is one other section within this book of the Secret Ministry that cannot be passed over without mention: *the Footwashing* (13: 1–30).

M.-E. Boismard thinks that we have here a primitive moralizing story (verses 1, 2, 4, 5, 12–15, 17–19), and a secondary pair of additions: (*a*) verses 6–11 are a Johannine

supplement, to make more explicit the sacramental meanin;
the footwashing; (b) 21–30 are an insertion by Luke, who t
how 'Satan entered into Judas' and, as usual, introduces ;
'the Beloved Disciple'.[1]

It is not necessary to discuss this theory here. In the text
have rejected the view that Lucan editorial activity can be s(
in the case of the spirit–paraclete sayings. In the chapter bef
us, it seems important that the disciples should receive a fo
of *purification* if they were to assume the work of Jesus in
power of his spirit, and this required not only the water but a
the communication of Jesus' *word* (15: 1 ff.). Judas did not h(
the final words. Moreover, it was vital that this band of m
should learn lessons about *loyalty* and *humility*, if they were to
worthy. The former is related to Judas, but to Peter as w
(13: 38). The latter is focused on the behaviour of Jesus hi
self. So by act and word Jesus seeks to qualify his men for th
commission (20: 21–3).

Hence 13: 1–30 may be retained as a genuine part of t
Fourth Gospel, quite in accordance with its primary them
and its typical technique. 13: 21 recalls 12: 27 and leads
14: 1, 27. Jesus is at once distressed and at ease, troubled a;
serene in the Father's communion. For Jesus still must endu
the shame and the agony of death; and he is not to be dismiss(
as a docetic Logos incapable of emotion altogether. 13: 23,
τῷ κόλπῳ, reminds us of εἰς τὸν κόλπον in 1: 18. Note too t
typical Johannine variation to the synonym στῆθος in vs. 2
In 13: 25–7, 30 there are four examples of οὖν, one of the mc
characteristic touches of Johannine style. 'Judas had the mon(
box' (13: 29) recalls 12: 6. Finally, the dramatic symbolism
'and it was night' in 13: 30 is fully Johannine.

What follows immediately is the scene in the Supper Roo
and then we hear the first of the Farewell Speeches.

The spirit–paraclete sayings thus belong, not merely wi
everything that is said hitherto in John about the spirit of Goc
but especially with this portion of the Gospel that is centred ;
Jerusalem at Passover time, the little book of 'The Secr(
Ministry'.

[1] *R.B.* LXX, 1 (Jan. 1964), 5–24.

LITERARY ANALYSIS OF JOHN 13–17

I. IS REARRANGEMENT NECESSARY?

The narrative of the Footwashing comes to a dramatic dénouement with the departure of Judas into the night (13: 1–30), and at once Jesus begins to speak, 'Now is the Son of Man glorified, and in him God is glorified...' Peter, Thomas and Philip in turn participate in conversation with Jesus, who baffles the disciples with what at a later point (16: 25) he calls 'riddles'. First, 'where I am going, you cannot come'; next, if they had really known their Teacher, they would have known the Father. Hence his primary themes in 13: 31–14: 31 are consolation ('Let not your hearts be troubled'), and the inspiration of his revelation ('he that has seen me has seen the Father; pray to the Father, and you will do still greater works'). Moreover, he assures them, 'I will not leave you orphaned' (14: 18). They will have both the communion of his Father and himself, and the abiding presence of the spirit of truth as a paraclete. All this he has told them in advance...so that they may cling to their faith (14: 29).

Judas had gone out, a man into whom Satan, the ruler of this world, had entered (13: 27). But now, says Jesus at the apparent close of his comforting address, 'the ruler of this world is coming...Rise, let us go hence' (14: 30 f.). We are meant to understand (*a*) that Satan is about to launch his final attack on the divine Logos, and (*b*) as one should expect from the connexion between the evil spirit and human agents, that Judas is on his way to a rendezvous where he will betray the Son of Man with a kiss (18: 2 ff., but the Fourth Gospel omits reference to the kiss of Judas).

As we have remarked in the text, it is a very old problem that faces the reader as well as the scholar in the sequence from 'let us go hence' in 14: 31 to the monologues that come next (15: 1–17: 26). Many efforts have been made to make better

sense out of John's material on the assumption that it is presently out of order.[1]

Rudolf Bultmann, for example, proposed a neat solution by the following rearrangement:[2] 13: 1–30, 31a; 17: 1–26; 13: 31b–35; 15: 1–27; 16: 1–33; 13: 36–14: 31; 18: 1 ff. One advantage of this is that 'Now is the Son of Man glorified' (13: 31b) is preceded by the petition for this act in 17: 1–5.

But this is to take the 'now' in a pedantic and non-Johannine sense. For at 2: 11 it is stated that Jesus had revealed his glory in Cana. At 11: 4 it is asserted that his beloved friend Lazarus must die in order to be raised, for his resurrection will be the means of the glorification of Jesus, the Son of God; and 11: 42 seems to indicate that the Son receives his glory when men come to believe that God the Father had sent him, i.e. as his Logos and as a Saviour. In 12: 23 Jesus cries, 'The hour has come for the Son of Man to be glorified', and yet 13: 31 says, 'No; not then...Now!' It is not to be taken literally that Jesus was to be glorified at the moment of 12: 23, any more than 12: 31 is to be understood as saying that the Judgment has actually arrived and the Devil will be driven out that very instant. The 'hour' of Jesus is most probably the time of his passion on the cross; but in another sense it is the entire ministry of the incarnate life. Similarly, his glory was there in him when he became flesh. It was, so to say, *incognito*, but John the Baptist penetrated the disguise because of the descent of the spirit like a dove (1: 29–36).

It would take us too far afield to consider how in John signs of the glory are given but only partially understood. These signs are never 'naked revelations', for their meaning requires faith in the beholder; and yet faith is possible only to the elect whom the Father 'draws' to Christ (5: 22 f.; 6: 44; 8: 14–19, 28, 47, etc.).

Hence we need not try to produce absolute consistency in the order of John's Gospel. He intends to be convoluted. He means to repeat his themes and to build up to a climax. Our sober

---

[1] Various schemes are outlined in W. F. Howard and C. K. Barrett, *The Fourth Gospel in Recent Criticism and Interpretation.*

[2] Bultmann's theory is dealt with in massive detail in D. M. Smith, *The Composition and Order of the Fourth Gospel*; he prints the Greek text, but without a single accent or breathing.

ordering is not necessarily in keeping with his profoundly spiritual and dramatic perception. In any case, the prayer of 17 fits as well where it is as it would after 13: 31 a.

Another advantage of the changes suggested by Bultmann is that 13: 36, 'Simon Peter said to him, "Lord, where are you going?"' is no longer contradicted by 16: 5, 'But now I am going to him who sent me; yet none of you asks me, "Where are you going?"'

Here too the assumption is that Jesus should say a thing once and once only, or that no loose ends be allowed to his dialogues and monologues. 17: 11, 'And now I am no more in the world...and *I am coming to thee*', precedes 16: 5 even in Bultmann's plan: if the disciples had heard this, why should any of them ask Jesus where he is going? and why should Jesus complain that no one had asked him?

It is a serious defect of the proposed rearrangement that the spirit–paraclete references would start with the witness theme of 15: 26 f. and then proceed to consolation, judgment, prediction and the Son's glorifying in 16: 7–15. Only after all that would we have the promise of 14: 16, 'I will pray the Father, and he will give you as another paraclete...' and the message of 14: 26 ('he will teach you everything'). This makes nonsense of the sequence.

Even on the present arrangement of the text it is problematic how ch. 17 is to be interpreted. Are we meant to see the man Jesus alone on stage, in private, intimate prayer to the Father? Is this a Johannine substitute for the Marcan prayer in Gethsemane? Note, for example, Mark 14: 33, 'Jesus began to be greatly distressed and troubled': cf. John 11: 38; 12: 27; 13: 21. Mark 14: 35, 41, 'the hour has come', a familiar expression in John and Mark 14: 38, 'pray that you may not enter into temptation', recall not only the Lord's Prayer but the following in John: 14: 30; 15: 18; 17: 14 f., for this *peirasmos* is an assault by the Devil and it produces 'tribulation' (cf. John 16: 33 and 15: 18–16: 4a). The Marcan scene comes to its climax at 14: 42, ἐγείρεσθε, ἄγωμεν, the exact words of John 14: 31, where ἐντεῦθεν is added.

This interrelationship is hard to explain. There is no textual authority for interfering with the final words in John 14: 31, removing them perhaps as a harmonizing gloss taken from

Mark or a Passion tradition very similar to Mark's account. It may well be that these words were fixed in the narrative of the Passion as John had received it. If then he was accustomed to associate 'rise, let us be going' with a Gethsemane story (as related at the celebration of the Eucharist?), his removal of them to another position was deliberate. The prayer put into the mouth of Jesus in John 17 too is not a Gethsemane prayer and it is in spectacular contrast to a passage like Heb. 5: 7, 'in the days of his flesh Jesus offered up prayers and petitions, with loud shouting and tears, to him that was able to save him from death, and he was heard for his piety'.

The incarnate Logos in John does not shout in agony, and great drops of blood do not fall from his anguished brow. In the garden Jesus takes the initiative to surrender himself and to protect his disciples, like the good shepherd he is (18: 1-11). He *will* drink the cup his Father has provided (18: 11, another Gethsemane reminiscence?).

It is unnecessary to review any other rearrangement schemes, since our analysis of Johannine technique discloses a subtle and dramatic mind that is not easily classified and is resistant to modern editing. Thus the well-known proposal of C. H. Dodd to interpret the final words of 14: 31 as a great battle cry, 'Up, let us be at them!' or the like, although it is attractive from a dramatic angle, founders on the meaning of the Greek as it is evident in the Marcan parallel.

None of the suggested alterations in the Johannine order within chs. 13-17 satisfies one, and for that reason it is permissible to make an attempt to understand the speeches as they stand but without insisting on temporal movement after the words of 14: 31 have been uttered.

II. THE DISCOURSES

As indicated in the text (above, pp. 70-4), we wish to analyse 13-17 into three speeches and a prayer:
(A) 13: 31-14: 31: a dialogue that becomes a monologue.
(B) 15: 1-16: 4a: a monologue.
(C) 16: 4b-33: almost all monologue (not 16: 17, 29).

A. 13: 31–14: 31. *First Statement of Christ's Last Message.*

(i) 13: 31–8. Jesus is about to go away, and his disciples cannot follow him any longer in the old way. Not even Peter can follow, in the sense that he can 'keep the faith', for when his braggadocio is tested he will fail.

Yet the disciples will never be able to plead ignorance of their duty in the time of their life that lies ahead: for Jesus, their Teacher and Lord, gives them a single specific new commandment that will replace all other rules and regulations if properly understood and obeyed: 'Love each other!' Jesus' own example is to be ever before them: 'Love as I have loved you.'

(ii) 14: 1–7. It is almost inconceivable what a grand canyon of separation the departure of Jesus could come to seem to the forlorn disciples in the time of his absence, in the hour of his death. For they have not yet entered, as Jesus has, into the amazing significance of the Passion as the sacrifice of the Lamb of God and the atonement of the world. Their hearts will be troubled, can be nothing else than distressed.

So he must comfort them. God will always be God, Father, holy and immortal. Jesus is going to prepare in that Father's 'house' a place for his beloved.

(iii) 14: 8–11. Philip, acting as a foil to Jesus, begs that this 'Father' be shown to them (cf. *Gospel of Thomas*, logion 91). The answer is that a true vision of Jesus is a vision of the Father. Not that the Father and the Son are identical. The Son is a theophany in his own person.

(iv) 14: 12–24. Further promises of Jesus about prayer, the spirit of truth, and his own 'return'.

Mutual love is always the commandment. Obedience is always requisite in disciples.

(v) 14: 25–31. Final promises of the Christ, first concerning the spirit–paraclete, then concerning his peace, a peace that is offered on the frontier of death, the greeting (*shalom*) of the uniquely godly and obedient man, the peace of a Victor that can and must console and strengthen the faithful.

Verse 25 contains what we have described as the typical formula of these chapters: 'I have told you these things, while still with you; but the paraclete whom the Father will send in my name will teach you everything...'

Similarly, verse 29 is formulaic: 'And now I have told you before it takes place, so that when it does take place you may believe': but what? that Jesus is going to the Father? or that the disciples are surely going to see Jesus again? or that the spirit of truth will come as another paraclete? Perhaps all these elements are meant to be included.

B. 15: 1–16: 4a. *A Second Version of Jesus' Final Message.*

We take 16: 1–4a with what precedes on the grounds that 15: 18–25 require them for completion, and that a fresh start is made with 16: 4b, 'I am about to leave you'.

The formula appears in 15: 11; 16: 1, 4a.

(i) 15: 1–11. The allegory of the True Vine may be regarded as a word that was prompted by the proximity of the Temple, where the great Vine that is the symbol of Israel was portrayed above the entrance to the Holy of Holies.

Disciples will find security and fertilization in a spiritual sense only through union with Jesus, the obedient Son of the Father. They are the 'branches' of the Vine, and they are in danger of ruthless pruning with consequent burning if they prove to be useless. The proof of discipleship is like the proof of Sonship: obedience, and especially successful witness to the Word (later in verse 15).

Two remarkable promises are made, *about prayer* (verse 7) and *about joy* (verse 11).

(ii) 15: 12–17. Here the elect disciples are given a new name, the 'friends' of Jesus, the recipients of his heavenly disclosures and the inevitable representatives who must soon go forth to repeat the Word. As Jesus would lay down his life for them, they must be ready to die for their friends; for love is ever prepared to make the last sacrifice.

The promise about *prayer* is repeated, and once again the *commandment* is given to the Companions of Honour, 'Love one another'.

Much of this material is already familiar, but enough of it is new for the speech to be marked as no mere alternative to 13: 31 ff.

(iii) 15: 18–16: 4a. This is equally true of the last section of this second statement, for there is considerable emphasis on the details of tribulation that wait for the faithful: the hatred of the world, persecution, a mixed reception to the Word. The future for the disciple could be patterned only on the past of the Master in a sinful world.

Since the Master was to stand before Pilate as a witness to the truth (18: 37), the disciples would bear witness also; and to aid them in this function the spirit of truth would come. This theme is one of the dominant notes of the whole Gospel: 1: 7, 19 ff.; 5: 32 ff.; 8: 13 ff.; 9: 24–34; 12: 46–50.

The closing imperative of this statement is 'remember'. The Church well knew that it had the duty of remembrance, for its message of the Saviour's appearance as a man, Jesus of Nazareth, made this essential. A myth cannot be remembered in the same way. If the discourses in John's narrative of the Secret Ministry spring from eucharistic practice, this function would belong naturally to it. The longer text of Luke 22: 19–20 and the tradition in Paul (1 Cor. 11: 24 f.) both ascribe to Jesus himself at the Last Supper the words, 'Do this in remembrance of me'.

C.   16: 4*b*–33. *A Third Statement of Jesus' Last Message.*

In this address the formula is found in verses 25, 33.

One of the most notable features is the repetition of so many themes that were already present in 13: 31–14: 31; indeed it could be argued that this is a duplicate version of the first statement. Yet, as we have indicated in the text, there are also differences, not least in respect to the forensic function of the spirit–paraclete.

(i) 16: 4*b*–15. Here Jesus says with solemn intensity that his departure is not unrelieved sorrow. Consolation is certain, in fact it is to the advantage of the disciples that Jesus should return to the Father. This does not mean that they will be better off without him! John speaks through Jesus to remind the Church that the spirit–paraclete comes as Comforter as the direct effect of the Crucifixion and Resurrection of Jesus. All the promises in this paragraph concern this gift of the spirit. 16: 12 f. recall 14: 25 f.; 16: 14 f. will be echoed in 17: 10.

(ii) 16: 16–24. Some relief from the monologue form comes at this point, when the disciples discuss among themselves what Jesus means by 'soon you will not see me, then in a little while you *will* see me'. He tells them again, by way of analogy with a woman in childbirth, that they will be desolated in sorrow but just as dramatically they will be consoled and come to a new and more wonderful joy. The prophecy is surely about the resurrection appearances. (Cf. 14: 3, 18, 21, 23.)

The promises *about joy* (15: 11) and *prayer* (14: 13; 15: 16) are reiterated; presumably these were of supreme importance to the Evangelist.

(iii) 16: 25–8. The revealing of the Father is mooted once again, but rather differently from what is said in 14: 6–14.

'You have loved me and have believed' (verse 27) unites what must never be disjoined in Johannine theology. Compare 2: 11; 6: 69; 13: 13; 14: 15. When the Christ (as the great High Priest or as the true King of Israel?) prays for his own, it is because they are his beloved who believe in his mission (17: 7).

16: 28 states afresh the mystery of the Son's *coming and going* (cf. 3: 2, 31–6; 5: 43; 6: 14, 38, 50f., 62; 7: 27–9, 33–6, 41f., 52; 8: 14, 21–5, 42; 9: 39; 14: 18, 23; 18: 37; 19: 9). In this too we must see a master clue to the unity of the Fourth Gospel.

(iv) 16: 29–33. The opening dialogue cleverly and neatly brings everything down to earth again. For the disciples profess to understand all that Jesus has said: 'Now you are talking plainly!' It is as if at last, after all the tentative visions of Christ's glory and all the repeated assertions of their belief, Jesus can say, 'So now you believe!' And then the crash of cold water falls on their simple-mindedness, 'The hour is coming, it is already here: you will be scattered and you will abandon me!' Peter's discomfiture (13: 38) will be repeated elevenfold. What a contrast to Jesus' promise in 14: 18, 'I will not abandon you!'

But Jesus is not completely forsaken; there will be no cry of dereliction at John's Calvary: 'for the Father is with me' (vs. 32; cf. 3: 2, 35; 8: 18; 10: 30; 17: 11, 21f.). Jesus cannot fail; he must be glorified, and so he can make always the most astounding promises: 'in me you can enjoy peace'; 'be of good cheer, I have overcome the world!'

His hour had come. The Father (well he knew it) had committed all things into his hands. He had come from God and he was going to God (13: 3). 'We have seen his glory, the glory as of an only-begotten from a father' (1: 14).

III. THE ROYAL PRAYER

17: 1–26. Jesus' Last Will and Testament expressed in Prayer.

The blazing confidence of 16: 29–33 is like the loud shout of 12: 44–50, and it must be allowed to die away into the silence, while the stage remains empty and in the dark, until once again the curtain is lifted and Jesus is disclosed kneeling in prayer before God the Holy Father.

(i) 1–8. The hour has come (still another tolling of this bell) not because the traitor is at hand (that too), but chiefly because the Son has accomplished his Father's will, revealed the Father's Name and handed on his Father's words. The man who kneels is not merely another prophet, then, a second Moses: he is the unique expression of God in a human life, the incarnate Logos.

Every phrase in this paragraph recalls passage after passage throughout the Gospel, but it is needless to document them in detail.

The task of Jesus was to ingather the elect of God (11: 52) and eventually, not before the Resurrection and not without the mission of the spirit of truth as another paraclete working in and through the apostolic community, there will be a single family, a *yaḥadh* or 'union' (συναγάγη εἰς ἕν, 11: 52; cf. 12: 32, 'I will claim and take possession of all men'). Here in 17: 6 'the men whom thou gavest me' is a definition of more than the faithful Eleven; it is the definition of the catholic Church.

Jesus has magnified the Father and opened to believers the gates of knowledge and of life eternal (cf. 1 John 5: 7 ff.; 1QS 2: 2 f., with Wernberg-Møller's notes).

In one sense the petition of verse 1, 'glorify thy Son', is justified, in another it was quite unnecessary. Yet still it would take the action of God to open the eyes of men to see the glory of the Son in the humanity of the Nazarene.

An entire Gospel is contained in verses 1–8.

(ii) 9–19. This prayer for the disciples demonstrates that they need above all *joy* (cf. 15: 11; 16: 20, 22); a state of peace and satisfaction amidst the tribulations and changes of life. They need also *protection* from the Devil, *unity* and *consecration* (with the power of the spirit that implied).

17: 13 seems to be a variant of the formula already referred to as one of the binding elements of chs. 13–17.

(iii) 20–4. Now there is a prayer for the disciples of the Disciples and for all believers: that they may come to spiritual unity and at length see the glory *and share the glory* of the Son.

The world has not reached this knowledge, and nothing really justifies the conclusion that verse 23 optimistically looks forward to the world's conversion. The parallel with 16: 8–11 is clear, but there is no allusion here either to the judgment or to the coming of the spirit–paraclete.

(iv) 25–6. In repetitious, fully Johannine style the prayer comes to an end with a statement of Christ's claims: he has revealed the Father *and he will go on making known* the Father's Name, presumably through his chosen witnesses and through this written record of his acts and words, but again, strangely, without reference to the ministry of the spirit–paraclete.

In a moment more Jesus has left the quiet of the Room, and before long he is out *in the night, where he will act as a paraclete for his men*: 'here I am; let these men go' (18: 8). In a little while, they too will learn to act as paracletes in the Name of Jesus for the children of God.

SELECT BIBLIOGRAPHY

Barrett, C. K. *The Holy Spirit and the Gospel Tradition*. London, 1947.
The Gospel according to St John. London, 1955.

Betz, O. *Der Paraklet*. Leiden, 1963.

Black, M. *The Scrolls and Christian Origins*. London, 1961.

Borgen, P. *Bread from Heaven*. Leiden, 1965.

Braun, F.-M. *Jean le Théologien*. Paris, 1959, 1964.

Brown, R. E. *The Gospel according to John, I–XII*. New York, 1966.

Bultmann, R. *Das Evangelium des Johannes*[17]. Göttingen, 1962.

Chevallier, M.-A. *L'Esprit et le Messie*. Paris, 1958.
Esprit de Dieu, paroles d'homme. Neuchâtel, 1966.

Davies, W. D. and D. Daube, eds. *The Background of the New Testament and its Eschatology*. Cambridge, 1956.

Dodd, C. H. *The Interpretation of the Fourth Gospel*. Cambridge, 1953.
Historical Tradition in the Fourth Gospel. Cambridge, 1963.

Farmer, W. R., C. F. D. Moule and R. R. Niebuhr, eds. *Christian History and Interpretation: Studies presented to John Knox*. Cambridge, 1967.

Haenchen, E. 'Aus der Literatur zum Johannesevangelium 1929–1956', *Theologische Rundschau* (Neue Folge), Tübingen, 1955, 295 ff.

Hahn, F. *Das Verständnis der Mission im neuen Testament*. Neukirchen-Vluyn, 1963. (E.T.) *Mission in the New Testament*. London, 1965.

Hare, D. R. A. *The Theme of Jewish Persecution of Christians in the Gospel according to St Matthew*. Cambridge, 1967.

Hill, D. *Greek Words and Hebrew Meanings*. Cambridge, 1966.

Howard, W. F. *The Fourth Gospel in Recent Criticism and Interpretation*, revised by C. K. Barrett. London, 1955.

Johannson, N. *Parakletoi*. Lund, 1940.

Käsemann, E. *Jesu letzter Wille nach Johannes 17*. Tübingen, 1966.

Lys, D. «RÛACH». *Le Souffle dans l'Ancien Testament*. Paris, 1962.

Martyn, J. L. *History and Theology in the Fourth Gospel*. New York, 1968.

Meeks, W. A. *The Prophet-King: Moses Traditions and the Johannine Christology*. Leiden, 1967.

Mowinckel, S. 'Die Vorstellung des Spätjudentums vom heiligen Geist als Fürsprecher und der johanneische Paraklet', *Zeitschrift für die neutestamentliche Wissenschaft und die Kunde der älteren Kirche*, XXXII, Berlin, 1933, 97–130.

Mussner, F. ZΩH. *Die Anschauung vom 'Leben' im vierten Evangelium unter Berücksichtigung der Johannesbriefe*. München, 1952.

'Die Johanneischen Parakletsprüche und die apostolische Tradition', *Biblische Zeitschrift* (Neue Folge), v, Heft 1 (Jan. 1961), 56–70.

Perrin, N. *Rediscovering the Teaching of Jesus*. London and New York, 1967.

Ricca, P. *Die Eschatologie des vierten Evangeliums*. Zürich, 1966.

Ringgren, H. *Word and Wisdom: Studies in the Hypostatization of Divine Qualities and Functions in the Ancient Near East*. Lund, 1947.

Ruckstuhl, E. *Die literarische Einheit des Johannesevangeliums*. Freiburg, 1951.

Russell, D. S. *The Method and Message of Jewish Apocalyptic*. London, 1964.

Schweizer, E. *Ego Eimi*. Göttingen, 1939.

The Spirit of God. London, 1960.

Neotestamentica. Zürich, 1963.

Scott, E. F. *The Fourth Gospel: Its Purpose and Theology*. London, 1906.

The Spirit in the New Testament. London, 1923.

Smith, D. M. *The Composition and Order of the Fourth Gospel*. New Haven, 1965.

Strack, H. L. and P. Billerbeck, *Kommentar zum Neuen Testament aus Talmud und Midrasch*. München, 1922–8.

Swete, H. B. *The Holy Spirit in the New Testament*. Cambridge, 1909.

Wilson, R. McL. *The Gnostic Problem*. London, 1958.

Gnosis and the New Testament. Oxford, 1968.

Yates, J. E. *The Spirit and the Kingdom*. London, 1963.

INDEX OF PASSAGES CITED

INDEX OF AUTHORS

INDEX OF SUBJECTS